College

and

Character

edited by

Nevitt Sanford

Joseph Axelrod

LA
228
.C59
1979

Copyright © 1979 by Montaigne Inc.
2728 Durant Avenue, Berkeley, California 94704

LIBRARY OF CONGRESS
CATALOG CARD NO.:   79-84481

Nevitt Sanford, Joseph Axelrod, editors
College and Character.

Berkeley, CA : Montaigne Inc.

7903   790215
International Standard Book Number
ISBN 0-917430-01-8

Table
of Contents

List of Contributors

Nevitt Sanford

Sanford is founder and President of the Wright Institute, Berkeley, California. He has served as Director of the Institute for the Study of Human Problems, Stanford University, Associate Director of the Institute of Personality Assessment and Research at Berkeley, Coordinator of the Mary Conover Mellon Foundation at Vassar College, and Professor of Psychology, University of California, Berkeley.

Joseph Axelrod

Axelrod was a faculty member a Chicago City College and at the University of Chicago. He served as Dean of Humanities and Fine Arts, California State University, Dominguez Hills, and Dean of Undergraduate Studies, San Francisco State University. He is currently Professor of Comparative Literature, San Francisco State University.

Joseph Adelson

A graduate student of Nevitt Sanford's at the University of California, Berkeley, in the late 1940's, Adelson taught at Michigan State University and at Bennington College before joining the psychology faculty at the University of Michigan, Ann Arbor. He was a member of the staff of the Survey Research Center and Coordinator of Graduate Training in Clinical Psychology. At present he's Professor of Psychology and Director of the Psychological Clinic.

Christian Bay

After arriving in the United States from Norway, Bay taught at Michigan State University, the University of California, Berkeley, Stanford University, and the University of Alberta. He is now a member of the Department of Political Economy, University of Toronto, Toronto, Canada.

David Beardslee

Beardslee taught at Wesleyan University before moving to Oakland University. There he continued to teach and served as department chairperson, and as Director of the Computer Center before moving to his present post. He is now Director of Institutional Research, Oakland University, Rochester, Michigan.

Carl Bereiter

Bereiter is a Professor in the Department of Applied Psychology, Ontario Institute for Studies in Education, and in the Department of Educational Theory, University of Toronto, Toronto, Canada. Bereiter was awarded a Guggenheim Fellowship, and was Fellow at the Center for Advanced Study in the Behavioral Sciences.

Donald Brown

Brown served as a research associate on the Mellon Studies at Vassar College while teaching at Bryn Mawr. Since 1964 he has been on the faculty at the University of Michigan and a researcher at the Center for Research on Teaching and Learning, University of Michigan, Ann Arbor.

Joshua Fishman

Fishman served as a faculty member at City College of New York, the

University of Pennsylvania, and Yeshiva University, where he was Professor of Psychology and Sociology and Dean of the Graduate School of Education. He is now Distinguished University Research Professor in the Social Sciences and Vice President for Academic Affairs, Yeshiva University, New York.

Mervin Freedman

Currently Professor of Psychology at San Francisco State University and Dean of the School of Social-Clinical Psychology, Wright Institute, Berkeley, Freedman had earlier served as Assistant Dean of Undergraduate Education at Stanford University, Chairperson, Department of Psychology, San Francisco State University, and Coordinator of the Mellon Foundation for the Advancement of Education, Vassar College.

Paul Heist

After serving as a faculty member at Carthage College, the University of Minnesota, and Oregon State University, Heist came to the University of California, Berkeley to direct research and teach in the area of higher education. He is now Professor of Higher Education in the School of Education and also Research Psychologist at the Center for Research and Development in Higher Education, University of California, Berkeley.

Christopher Jencks

Jencks has held a variety of posts: an editor of the New Republic, *a fellow at the Institute for Policy Studies, a faculty member at the Harvard Graduate School of Education, a Guggenheim Fellow, and a visiting professor at the University of California, Santa Barbara. He is now Professor in the department of Sociology, Harvard University.*

Joseph Katz

Katz directed the Student Development Study at Stanford University and served as Director of the William James Center of the Wright Institute, Berkeley. He is now Professor of Human Development and Director of Research for Human Development and Educational Policy at the State University of New York at Stony Brook.

Robert Knapp (Deceased)

Knapp became well known in the early 1950's following his publication (with Joseph Greenbaum) of Origins of American Scientists. *Born and educated in Oregon, he served as area operations officer (OSS) during World War II, and then took his Ph.D. at Harvard. From 1946 on he taught psychology at Wesleyan University, Middletown, Conn., with time off for two one year sojourns in Berkeley.*

T. R. McConnell

McConnell was a member of the faculty at Cornell College, the University of Minnesota, and the University of California, Berkeley, where he is now Professor Emeritus of Higher Education. McConnell has served as a Dean at both Cornell College and at the University of Minnesota, and as Chancellor, University of Buffalo, New York.

W. J. McKeachie

McKeachie became a member of the University of Michigan faculty in 1946. He is now Professor of Psychology and Director of the Center for Research in Teaching and Learning, University of Michigan, Ann Arbor.

Theodore M. Newcomb

Newcomb served on the faculty at LeHigh University, Case Western Reserve University, and Bennington College. He is currently Professor of Sociology and Psychology and Associate Director of the Residential College at the University of Michigan, Ann Arbor.

Donald D. O'Dowd

O'Dowd taught at Wesleyan University and at Oakland University, where he also held administrative posts in Student Affairs and Academic Affairs. He is now Professor of Psychology and President of Oakland University, Rochester, Michigan.

Frank Pinner

Pinner studied with Peter Odegaard and David Krech at Berkeley in the early 1950's, writing his Ph.D. dissertation on nationalism. His interest in political psychology has persisted over the years. He has taught for more than 20 years at Michigan State University where he is currently Professor of Political Science.

David Riesman

Riesman was a member of Lyndon Johnson's White House Task Force on Education and also served on the Carnegie Commission on Higher Education. He is now an Advisory Member of the Carnegie Council on Policy Studies in Higher Education. Riesman is currently Henry Ford II Professor of the Social Sciences, and a member of the Department of Sociology, Harvard University.

George Stern (Deceased)

After spending most of the World War II years in the USAAF, Stern took his Ph.D. at the University of Chicago, where he remained as a teacher of psychology and as a staff member in the Offices of the Examiner. After 1959, he was Professor of Psychology and Executive Officer at the Psychological Research Center, Syracuse University, Syracuse, New York.

Harold Taylor

Taylor taught philosophy at the University of Wisconsin and was President of Sarah Lawrence College. He is currently Distinguished Professor of the Social Sciences, City University of New York, and Director of the Center for International Service at the College of Staten Island, City University of New York.

Harold Webster

Webster has taught and done research at several institutions, including University of Kentucky, Vassar College, University of California, Berkeley, and the National Institute of Education, India. He is presently Professor of Psychology at Brooklyn College of the City University of New York.

Preface

This volume of essays is addressed to everyone interested in the intellectual analysis of what goes on in our institutions of higher learning: to professors who are teaching in them, to trustees and administrators who run them, to students whose lives are influenced by them, and to everyone else who is active in a world that is enormously dependent on them.

The book will of course have special meaning to those who are directly involved in the educational process taking place on and off college campuses, namely, to students and to everyone who works with and for students. It seems clear that the educational process becomes more effective only as students become more aware of themselves as learners and only as others involved in this process come to know more about the students they are working with—their personality structures, the differences between them, and their successive stages of development.

As colleges and universities become more and more bureaucratized, with more decisions made by committees and less individual power in high places, all the people who are part of the that world must, if they are to maintain their humanity, be able to predict, or at least explain, what happens. If they do not understand the machinery they are working in, they are destined to become cogs within it.

As colleges and universities become more and more bureaucratized, with more decisions made by committees and less individual power in high places, all the people who are part of that world must, if they are to maintain their humanity, be able to predict, or at least explain, what happens. If they do not understand the machinery they are working in, they are destined to become cogs within it.

The reader will notice our emphasis on increased understanding and on knowledge-based action. We want to stress here the intellectual character of this book. Many administrators and most faculty members and students—even those who were forced to think hard about higher education during the disruptions of the Sixties—still discuss problems in higher education as though this field had no discipline, no shared terms or organized knowledge. What is worse, their discussions often reveal that they do not even believe such knowledge is required. They are like a group of adults chosen at random and asked to discuss the upbringing of children on the basis of limited experience and deeply-held opinions. For example, when such faculty members and students who now hold membership on key committees at many colleges discuss curricular change at their institutions, decisions are all too often made without benefit of any theory or research data on the basis of which the effects of the proposed change might be predicted or evaluated.

In the current atmosphere, with pressures on faculty and students toward the "quality control" that was often missing in some of the exciting innovations of the last decade, it is more important than ever that decision-makers speak from a basis of reliable data and a sound theoretical framework. It is just such knowledge and such a framework that we attempt to supply through the essays in this volume. The purpose of the book is to apply modern social and personality theory to an analysis of the structures and processes of American undergraduate education, and to organize some crucial empirical information within the same theoretical framework, in a form that will be useful to everyone now involved with the American college.

The present volume has had a curious history. One must go back to at least the year 1962, for at that time an 1100-page volume of essays called *The American College* was published. The thirty authors whose work appeared there had been developing theories and collecting data that displayed the complexity and diversity of the American college and how that institution changes under the impact of certain forces in American society. For the first time in the history of American higher education research, there could be found in a single collection of essays an exhaustive analysis by distinguished humanists and behavioral scientists of what was really happening to the American college during the college years.

Appearing in 1962, *The American College* reflected the new era in higher education that had already begun and the analyses presented there focused on many problems that were not to become visible to most people in our country until much later in the decade.

But since *The American College* was essentially directed to a professional audience, some of the reviewers, while highly praising its scholarship, called for a briefer version that would make the essential ideas of the book available to a wider audience. In 1964, the first edition of *College and Character* appeared. It contained abridgments of almost all of the essays that had appeared in *The American College* together with a new concluding chapter.

When the first edition of *College and Character* was published, student unrest was already visible but the explosions that were to be heard for the better part of the next ten years had not yet occurred. Yet, during the remaining years of the Sixties, both *College and Character* and *The American College* played a role in educational change on many campuses, for each book was found by educational reformers to be a rich source of suggestions.

While many of the reforms of the Sixties have by now been eroded, certain innovations—for example, new governance processes, a different student-university relationship (most visible in the legal realm), unionization of faculty members, new programs and whole institutions that identify themselves as "non-traditional"— have become part and parcel of the academic world. However, the trends that most influence the *vast* majority of undergraduates in this country today can more accurately be described as reactions against the reform of the Sixties—for example, tighter degree designs and new "core" requirements, liberal arts frameworks that are integrated with principles of "careerism," strategies for increasing "quality control," "accountability," and other conditions that often discourage education risk-taking and impede experimentation. On almost every traditional campus in this country, a blue-ribbon committee is busily at work, charged with designing a new long-range academic plan. Change is in the air; and yet everyone seems to be afraid of it.

These conditions have led a number of experts in higher education, (appalled at the recent appearance of so many "trendy" and quite mindless books in our field) to suggest that it might be time for decision-makers in undergraduate education to have available to them an updated edition of *College and Character*. After further discussions, the editors became persuaded that such a volume is quite sorely needed just at this time.

Some of the original essays have been completely rewritten for this new edition and many omitted altogether, while a few others have undergone extensive revision. A few of the original essays needed very little change, for it turned out that they describe today's world as accurately and as perceptively as they did the world of the early Sixties. And several essays in the volume are brand new.

In addition, the editors have added headnotes to precede each group of essays in order to help the reader see the scope and texture of the whole design. For though this is a collection of essays written by a widely diverse group of humanists and scientists, there is a single basic framework that pervades it; and what emerges for the conscientious reader, we hope, will be a single whole far larger than the sum of its parts.

Berkeley, California   NEVITT SANFORD
San Francisco, California   JOSEPH AXELROD
                    September 1978

I

The College in Society

The essays of Part One draw a picture of the American college as a social institution. They emphasize both the great differences that exist among colleges and the complexities that lie within colleges, and they show the extent to which these differences and complexities depend upon forces in our larger society. This relationship with the larger society is one of the reasons why systematic reform in higher education is so difficult to carry out: everything is part of a single, gigantic supersystem; elements intertwine so greatly that a fundamental change in one of them affects them all. But the essays of Part One make clear that reform in higher education is possible and that educators—if they have knowledge and apply intelligence—can influence the direction of change.

In Chapter 1, "Higher Education as a Social Problem," Nevitt Sanford not only states the issues that are basic to the entire volume, but also—let it be confessed—evokes attitudes toward them. Sanford's essay shows how our colleges and universities are embedded in the very soil of our society and why fundamental change can come about only when there is a shift of emphasis in the society's system of values or a change in its social processes.

Still, Sanford believes that it is possible for colleges to bring about their own reforms. But they will not be able to accomplish this task, he emphasizes, without the knowledge and techniques that are being developed in the social and behavioral sciences. Only behavioral theory and research, he says, can improve our understanding of educational processes, and only through the application of this theory can we, at the same time, improve the theory itself and the techniques for applying it. This is one way, Sanford says, in which we can build what he calls "a science of higher education."

In Chapter 2, "Toward a Social Theory of Intellectual Development," Christian Bay focuses attention upon the goal of maximum intellectual development, namely, rationality, and asks how various factors in the college community and its larger environment favor or hamper the attainment of this goal. His essay is basically an argument for (in Bay's own term) "the liberation of the intellect," and he asks that we look at the college's role in this crucial process. But for Bay, the development of rationality is not an educative process that emphasizes mental training alone. The intellect is not part of an individual; it is an aspect of the whole person, and it is inseparable from the rest of the personality. Chapter 2 will be important for those readers who mistakenly believe that if they accept the educational philosophy of personal development they must become anti-intellectual.

In Chapter 3, "The State University in Conflict with Its Publics," Frank Pinner observes that the newer state university, as it develops—improving its faculty and becoming more like the older and more prestigious universities of the nation—becomes increasingly alienated from its local "publics." These are the people of its town or city and the surrounding countryside, its alumni and other benefactors, and even its students and most of its older faculty members.

The university's conflicts with its publics are reflected also in divisions within its own ranks, particularly in differences of opinion about the university's mission. Does the university exist to render a "service" that it owes to its supporting taxpayers—a service to be given largely on the clients' own terms? Or does a university, if it is worth its salt, never give the public what it wants but only what it needs? Pinner's view tends toward the second of these alternatives. Like Bay, he feel that what the American college needs is to have its power of rationality and its levels of cultural attainment raised.

David Riesman and Christopher Jencks, in Chapter 4, "The Viability of the American College," compare colleges with each other and with other kinds of institutions, going on to compare the educational process itself with other kinds of processes. Once a college has been founded and set upon its course, it becomes interested in surviving. To maintain its "viability" in a world in which interest groups change in their purposes and power, the college must be prepared to redefine its goals, to introduce activities that serve other interest groups besides the founding one, to find ways of resisting or adapting to pressures from its political and social environments, to evolve in directions set by the more prestigious institutions. In this light we can see that change in a college is usually made in response to pressures from the outside.

One could easily get the impression from Riesman and Jencks's analysis that a college is like a rudderless ship set upon a sea of impersonal social forces. The reason for this impression is that we are offered here an analysis in dynamic terms, a study in the interplay of forces. Such an analysis is bound to dwell more upon the relatively unpalatable than upon that which calls for congratulation. But the purpose of these authors must not be misunderstood: precisely by calling attention to the irrational, the dysfunctional and the "antidevelopmental," we can raise the level of rationality in human affairs.

Behind the essays of Part One there stands a fundamental belief about reform in higher education. In the views of these authors, colleges are not playthings of forces over which no one has any control. Where educators have accurate knowledge of conditions and are free to use their intelligence, they are able to influence the course of events.

1

Higher Education as a Social Problem

Nevitt Sanford

The trouble with students, the saying goes, is that they turn into alumni. Indeed, a close look at the college-educated people in the United States is enough to dispel any notion that our institutions of higher learning are doing a good job of liberal education.

A professor in one of our great state universities arrived almost at the end of his career with the feeling that things had not gone too badly. Then he had occasion to work closely over a period of time with the organized alumni of his institution. He quickly came to the conclusion that these products of his and his colleagues' labors had no respect for learning, understood nothing of the conditions necessary to it, and were quite willing to sacrifice fundamental freedoms of the mind to the interests of expediency. Nothing happened later to rescue this retiring member of the faculty from his disillusionment.

But the failures and shortcomings of the colleges seem to be not at all discouraging to the general public or the large segment of it that supports the colleges—in spite of the highly negative public image of college students in the 1960s. It is remarkable that a culture which places relatively little value on learning or the intellectual life and has little understanding of, or sympathy for, what professors are trying to do nevertheless regards college—the experience of college for young people—as one of the greater goods, virtually as one of the necessities of life.

Increasing numbers of high school graduates are now delaying their entrance to college, and many are considering lifestyles for themselves in which formal education beyond high school will play no role. But for the great mass of our middle-class high school students, "going to college" is still a future event second in importance and glamor only to securing a job or getting married and having children. If they fail to make the grade, or if they leave college to get married after a year or so, they are easy targets for an insurance salesman armed with a policy that will make it easy "for the children to go to college." The situation is much the same with the parents of these young people, particularly if the parents have, or aspire to, lower-middle-class status or above. They are willing to make painful sacrifices to pay the necessary fees, and parental anxiety about acceptance is often greater than that of the young people more immediately involved.

It is clear that, in the eyes of the general public, college offers important benefits quite apart from those described in the college catalogues. For one thing, it seems that increasing demands for college are a concomitant of our increasing affluence and our chronic state of overproduction. Since there is little need for young people in the world of production, a practical choice is to keep them in school for as long as possible, and college is the next step after high school. In an employers' market, it is a simple matter to list "college degree" among the requirements for a job and thus create the widespread conviction that "you have to go to college in order to get anywhere these days." College, of course, has long been a major channel through which one went up in the world economically. Studies recently publicized in the news media suggest that college graduates may no longer have the advantage they once had in obtaining high-paying jobs, but it is still clear from the data that a college graduate is at an economic advantage.

The social benefits of college seem to be regarded as highly as the economic ones—and to be inseparably interrelated with them. For the great middle class, college has become a social necessity, while for members of the lower classes it is a prime means for social advancement.

Since colleges serve so many fundamental needs and desires of the people, they are subjected to little *enlightened* public criticism. The recent and continuing public discussion of desirable changes in education, occasioned by the sputniks of the 1950s and the dissatisfactions expressed by students in the 1960s, has left the colleges unscathed. There have been few changes in recent years that can be seen as improvements or reforms. Rather, the question has been phrased in a way that asks for a different kind of answer: How can colleges remain as they are in the face of social change? Faculty members and administrators have their own way of putting it: "How can we maintain quality?" And few ask the natural question "What quality?" or suggest that the problem is how to come closer to the realization of the goals they announce to students and their parents. The suggestions for reform that have found most favor with faculty members and administrators ask for changes that will allow bachelor's degree programs for on-campus students to remain more or less the same—then to create more community colleges for "less-able" young people and external degree programs for older "re-entry" students interested in second careers or in enriching their lives.

The official position of the colleges seems to be: "We must maintain quality by getting money to ensure that increases in personnel and resources keep pace with any increases in enrollment, by raising the standards for admission. And of course, we must reform the high schools." The structure and functioning of public high schools have been the objects of much scrutiny and discussion, and the questions raised have included not only cost factors but genuine educational issues as well. Why have the colleges been largely exempt from this kind of examination? Why has criticism been limited to questions of budgets and dollar expenditures? Why have the educational reforms of the 1960s already been all but eroded?

For one thing, it seems that the great majority of our articulate citizens value the nonacademic benefits their children derive from college and do not really want to see things changed. They can criticize the local high school because it may not be doing enough to get their sons and daughters into a good college. To get them into that college and, to a somewhat lesser degree, to keep them there is often an end in itself.

Again, and perhaps more important, enlightened citizens have often been the victims of considerable bamboozlement. They do not know what goes on in the colleges, and they have no ready means for finding out. Nor are there means for evaluating the effects of a college program. A well-to-do citizen may be an influential critic of our foreign policy, of the conduct of the federal judiciary, or of the local city planning commission, but when it comes to policy and practice in higher education he is silent. He likes to know what he is talking about; and besides, his real problem is how to find a good college for his daughter. He picks up some gossip and vague impressions from his friends, speculates wildly about how some imagined features of this or that college will bring out the various potentialities of his daughter, and supports her in her several applications. While he is in the position of having to wait upon the college's pleasure, he cannot bite the hand that might feed him. If he has to deal with a rejection of her application, his case is worse; he does not want to be a sorehead, and even if this were his inclination he would be silenced by the notion, effectively implanted by the college, that it is all his fault, anyway—for not supplying her with the right genes or with the right solution to her Oedipus complex.

The chances are, however, that the serious-minded daughter of this influential citizen will be admitted to a college which through careful public relations has been able to put across the notion that it is highly intellectual, but which is in fact just like all of the others and is still living on a reputation established 30 years ago. Having doubted that she is worthy of such a college, the daughter reports to her amazement that everybody is so friendly and helpful.

At first she finds the courses "interesting." But by the time she discovers that a set of academic prerequisites and distribution requirements do not add up to a stimulating intellectual life, she has found attachments and benefits which, though different from those she looked forward to, are nonetheless real. Her reports home continue to be favorable—which is a great joy to her father, who by now has invested so heavily in this venture that any other kind of report would be hard to take. So he recommends this college to his friends and goes along with the idea that the colleges in general are doing a good job.

Institutions Embedded in the Culture

It must be said, however, that if the general public has little interest in improving the colleges, many of the colleges themselves seem to have but little more. To understand the attitudes of the colleges it is necessary to consider that they are, in an improtant sense, corporate enterprises. Much of their activity must be devoted to surviving, expanding and maintaining a strong position relative to other institutions. To a very considerable extent, this statement holds true for state institutions as well as private ones. Our colleges and universities are actually very sensitive to the desires and needs of their constituents, and they are prepared to stay within certain limits set by them. It is difficult for the ordinary private college or the smaller state institution to rise above the level of value and taste that prevails in its immediate community. It often has to come to terms with the demands of large donors or the state legislature.

For nationally known institutions the situation is different and more complicated. They are in competition for the status of a leading intellectual center, and they attempt to further their cause by recruiting on a nationwide basis the brightest students and the most distinguished faculty members. The two go together. A distinguished faculty member is one who publishes, and typically he is more interested in research than in teaching, prefers graduate to undergraduate teaching, and has little patience with students who are not already devoted to scholarship. The constituents of these institutions go along with these arrangements—up to a point. However little they may value the intellectual life, the college of their choice must be a "good" one by educational standards in order for their sons and daughters to obtain the important "unintellectual" benefits to be had there.

The excitement about "getting into college" today is greatest among people who are disposed by reason of background and financial solvency to think of the more distinguished places. But there is a limit to how far constituents will go in supporting a leading intellectual center. Obviously, our leading private colleges could not exist if they went too far in the direction of excluding the sons and daughters of people who can afford the fees and support drives for funds and who feel with some justice that such institutions belong to them. These institutions are thus under some pressure to prevent their standards from going too high too rapidly.

The colleges' main strategy is to silence their unhappy constituents. This task is not too difficult, particularly if these institutions stick together, present a united front to the public, and discourage public discussion of their inner workings. They tend to do these things instinctively. If the alumni or the trustees suggest that "the intellect isn't everything," they may be reminded that our institutions of higher learning do not exist to promote athletics or the acquistion of social skills, that not everybody is ready to benefit from going to college, and that in a time of national crisis all good citizens should support the maximum development and utilization of our "human resources." The constituents do not know or cannot phrase the counter-arguments, and there are few who will speak for them. The plain fact is that our leading colleges do not do nearly enough for their large majorities of uncommitted, or vocationally oriented, or unintellectual students. These students may not be the brightest in the world, but they are bright enough for most good purposes. Alumni and friends of these colleges have every right to ask that something be done for these young people besides preparing them for the scholarly or other professions. They have this right so long as they grant the same to people who cannot afford private colleges.

This discussion is intended to underline the point that the American college, and American institutions of higher learning generally, are embedded in our culture and in our society. They are expressive of persistent trends, and persistent conflicts, in the American value system, and they have a diversity of important functions in society. This means that fundamental or widespread change in the colleges can come about only when there is a shift of emphasis in our general system of values or when there is a change in our general social processes.

Basis for Reform: The "Science" of Higher Education

Who, then, is to reform the colleges? And how is such reform to come about?

The notion that these institutions exist within a "surround" of cultural social forces and necessarily reflect the prevalent trends is, from the point of view of social science, the beginning of wisdom. But it is not wisdom itself. There is another side to the picture. The colleges are not playthings of forces over which no one has any control. What saves them from this status is the element of rationality in our social processes; where we have knowledge of conditions and are free to use our intelligence we are able, within limits, to influence the course of events. Our colleges and universities have the functions of supplying this knowledge and developing this intelligence. It would be a very sad state of affairs indeed if these institutions were completely overpowered by the forces they were designed to understand and to modify.

Fortunately, this condition has not yet been reached. Counterforces to the trends that have been described can readily be observed, and we may expect these counterforces to increase in strength as the need for them grows more apparent. Things may well get better, after they have got worse.

Our professors and intellectuals are not entirely without support, and not without sanction, in their efforts to supply the necessary criticism of our society and to raise the level of our culture. They are permitted these functions by our society—the same society that would use the colleges for keeping the youth out of trouble, showing them a good time, and offering them social advantages. This society not only arranges for the satisfaction of diverse low-order wants and needs, but it also pays its respects to ideals which have their roots in Western Civilization and in some American traditions. It expects the colleges and universities to look after these ideals, whatever else it may demand of these institutions and however many obstacles it may put in their way.

Linus in the comic strip "Peanuts" is, as every serious-minded undergraduate knows, addicted to his blanket, an unfailing source of comfort and gratification. But he wants to break himself of this habit, so he gives the blanket to Charlie Brown with the request that he hold on to it no matter what he—Linus—says or does. Then Linus immediately says that he has changed his mind and that he must have the blanket back. Charlie says, dumbly, "Okay, here," and Linus screams, "You're weaker than I am." Our society suffers from addiction to practicality, power, success, social adjustment, excitement, and the gratificiations of popular culture, but in a sense it has asked of our colleges and universities, "Get us out of this, no matter how much we may protest from time to time."

The mandates of these institutions come from the people, but they come from the people's better selves, and they were given at times when the people were thinking well or had found spokesmen who could express their higher aspirations. The colleges sometimes seem to forget this and yield to impulsive demands for the return of the blanket; or they may try to quiet the clamor arising out of desire and fear by undertaking to return the blanket for a little while, or by offering a piece of it. Faced with a need to exist as corporate enterprises, they often have to calculate how much they can give of what their constituents *want*—and still give them something of what they *ought* to want, or *do* want when fear and impulse are relatively quiet.

The crisis in higher education is chronic. The great problem today is essentially the same as it has been for a long time. It is how to do better the things that the colleges were intended to do; how to realize more fully, despite pressures from without and divided councils within, the aim of developing the potentialities of each student.

Our colleges have the task of influencing the youth of the country in directions set by the higher ideals of our culture. Although the public often has two minds about this aim, and contrives to put various difficulties in the way of its execution, the colleges still have a fighting chance to realize their objectives. For four years they have in their hands young persons who are or can be—for part of their day, at least—relatively isolated from the rest of society, and who are still open to influence by instruction and example.

If the colleges should achieve moderate success—that is, if a substantial proportion of their students instead of a handful were influenced in the desired way—the level of our culture would be raised. And if our culture and our society are to be changed at all by the deliberate application of intelligence and foresight, no agency has a better chance of initiating change than our institutions of higher learning.

The burden of carrying out educational policies rests mainly on college faculties, and as professionals they have a right to a major voice in the determination and reform of these policies. There is no denying, however, that when there is a movement toward reform in a college it is the collective faculty who usually seem to be dragging their feet. There have been few fundamental innovations in higher education during the past 50 years; and by no means all of these have been initiated by college or university faculties. College presidents, students, trustees, foundations, large donors, influential citizens, and even state legislatures have from time to time sought progressive change only to find themselves effectively blocked by faculties. The same, of course, holds for individuals or groups within the faculty who would like to undertake new departures.

What are the reasons for this state of affairs? For one thing, the typical faculty member is by training, by inclination and by the requirements of his position, a specialist in an academic subject. He is devoted to the advancement of his specialty by research and by teaching, and it is as a specialist that he expects to make his career. It is thus his natural inclination to see the problems of liberal education in a limited perspective.

The college administration or the governing board—or the social scientist—may view the college from a distance as it were, attempting to gauge what progress is being made toward certain broad objectives; but the teacher typically is focused on narrower, more immediate and more personal goals. Because each teacher is a special advocate, the liberal college faculty *as a body* is not competent to make the judgments and evaluations required to design a curriculum in liberal education. One may be led to this conclusion either by observing faculty meetings (which are often futile rituals and sometimes mob scenes) or by examining existing curricula (which are best understood as uneasy compromises or treaties intended to be broken). With the sharp increase in democratic decision making that occurred in the 1960s, it is now no longer possible for educational reforms to be fashioned by the trustees or by the president; the faculty must be centrally involved, and on many campuses students also participate to some extent in decision making. One of the main theses of this book is that when we know enough about higher education and have enough conviction about its purposes, faculties will do what they know they ought to do.

But that time has not yet arrived. Faculty bodies still constitute a major barrier to reform. Unfortunately, most college and university faculties have organized themselves in such a way as to make deliberate and concerted change of any kind exceedingly difficult. This situation has it logic and its history. Although, traditionally, faculties have had the professional status necessary to free inquiry and instruction, they have always had to stand ready to defend themselves against unintellectual or anti-intellectual forces in the larger community. The struggles of American colleges and universities to withstand the demands of business, religious or governmental groups are perennial. Even within the last decade faculties of some of our large state universities have by heroic efforts barely averted the loss of their professional status. Many attacks on academic freedom are being made today in the name of a new concept—actually an old concept but newly applied to the work being done by college professors—called "accountability." Small wonder that the defensive stance of faculties has not been altogether relaxed!

To resist pressures from outside, as well as to further their most immediate interests, faculties have fostered an ingroup spirit, built up traditions of faculty prerogatives and installed the machinery of campus democracy. These are the very things that now make change very difficult, even when the impulse to change arises largely from within the faculty itself. Measures contrived for one purpose tend to be put into service for other purposes as well, until they become autonomous. Interests become vested in different parts of the machinery itself, so that the machinery persists even after the connection with its original prupose has been lost.

Faculties sometimes go so far in protecting their professional status, or in using their professional status to satisfy their desires for security and the advancement of their own interests, that they neglect the legitimate needs and aspirations of the society that supports higher learning. Faculty-governed European universities, for example, have become extremely conservative institutions; it has sometimes required acts of parliament to bring about changes in the curriculum.

One of the main barriers to reform in the colleges, however, is the lack of a scientific basis for educational practice. College teaching is constantly in the awkward position of having promised more than it can deliver. The public is told that the college experience will "liberate the mind," "build the capacity to make value judgments," and "inculcate the attitudes and values of democracy," but little evidence is offered on the degree to which these changes are accomplished. There are rival claims for different policies and programs, but the public, and indeed the faculties themselves, have little basis for a reasonable choice among them. The reason, of course, is the lack of knowledge about what kinds of educational policies or practices have what effects with what kinds of students. More fundamental than this is the lack of a generally accepted theory of individual human development in accordance with which colleges may state hypotheses pertaining to the relations of ends and means.

But a new "science of higher education" is coming into existence, and a body of fact and theory—a discipline of sorts, in which individuals can become specialists—is beginning to take shape. What needs to be further developed is the profession of higher education, a profession that has its own sanctions, its own ethics and its own "know-how" as well as its scientific basis.

2

Toward a Social Theory of Intellectual Development

Christian Bay

Striving or effort of any kind presupposes some kind of problem or difficulty. This is a fundamental principle of individual development as well as of social and cultural history. Growth and maturation in the child can occur only when mere repetition no longer serves well. Children's accustomed responses may become inadequate either because changes in their developing physiology bring changes in the nature of their drives or because their parents or peers come to expect more mature behavior as they grow older; both things keep happening, of course, in the life of every child. To the extent that children can cope with these problems and frustrations, they not only grow but mature; whenever they overwhelm them, neurotic developments ensue.

Every child faces "social" problems of at least two kinds: how to be accepted by or win approval of parents or peers, and how to understand why they behave as they do, and thus anticipate their future reactions. The former problem is resolved by palatable opinions and behavior; the latter by the development of beliefs that are realistic and that improve the child's capacity to understand and predict. For adults, too, to hold and express a given opinion may serve primarily the purpose of facilitating their immediate social acceptance or the purpose of cognitive enlightenment of their universe. Some opinions, however, may serve a third kind of purpose: they are self-defensive; they allow the individual a psychological escape from remainders of problems and past events with which he could not cope and which now persist unconsciously as sources of much anxiety.

Discovery of the motivational basis of an opinion makes it possible to understand how it can be influenced. A rationality-motivated belief can be influenced by opinion leaders within the group to which the person belongs or aspires to belong; whereas a belief that serves self-defensive functions is a hardy perennial that may be subjected to change only in the course of psychoanalysis or some other sequence of profound experience. It should be added that many of our beliefs and attitudes serve more than one of these kinds of motives; this circumstance sometimes means that we are pulled in opposite directions at the same time, and we respond with conflicting impulses, indecisive acts and vague language.

In a limited sense, each type of motivation or tension is a *rational* basis for the appropriate opinion, in that the opinion does serve some immediate function for the personality. However, if a time perspective is added, the question of rationality comes into a different light. Self-defensive opinions may for the moment help keep anxieties in check, but they are self-defeating in the long run in that they also keep the individual from seeing and grappling with the sources of the anxiety. Conforming opinions make for temporary external adjustment but keep the individual from gaining a broader understanding of oneself and society, understanding that could help one anticipate one's own future needs and society's changing requirements. Only what has been called rationality-motivated opinions indicate a type of response to problems that is constructive in terms of the individual's long-range needs; to say nothing of the fortunes of the society in which one has a stake as a citizen. The term "rational," consequently, will henceforth be used with reference to task-oriented efforts, and never to self-oriented or self-defense-oriented efforts.

Relatively simple traditional societies may require very little rational effort on the part of their members. Complex modern societies, on the other hand, require a great deal of rational intelligence of many of their members, and this is the ultimate reason for the existence of colleges and universities. It does not follow, unfortunately, that the colleges actually deliver the intellectual power they are assigned to produce. In fact, most of them fall far short of producing even a moderate proportion of graduates who have been educated to utilize their own minds effectively for meaningful purposes of their own choice. This has remained a basic fact in higher education in spite of all of the "developments" that have taken place on American campuses in the three decades since the end of World War II.

This discussion, however, will focus on the present and the future rather than on the past; it proceeds on the assumption that the university will continue, increasingly, to open its gates to all persons who can and who want to become educated, regardless of whether or not they can pay for what they get. "America needs all its brain power" is one familiar rationale for this policy; another rationale, however, is to be preferred: "Individuals need to grow as much as they can; this is what America is for."

The theoretical point of departure is contained in the following fundamental hypothesis: All organizations, however rational in design, tend to become transformed as they endure and become institutionalized. The dynamics of this process needs study, with particular reference to the college; and this kind of study needs some clarification of concepts. In the next section an attempt will be made to define some key concepts in the study of what may be called the erosion of rationality in the processes of higher education. Using these concepts, the third section will review, very sketchily, various factors in the college community and in the larger society that seem to militate against the development of rational, independent, intellectually bent individuals. The fourth and final section will seek to account for the fact that some students nevertheless do become well educated; it supports the view that many more students—theoretically *all*—could, with incentives possible under different social circumstances, gain a fuller use of their rational faculties.

Some Key Concepts in the Erosion of Rationality

"Intellectual development," though of course a crucial concept, will be given a somewhat open-ended definition here. The reference is to man's rational faculties, the extent to which the person becomes able to question conventional and habitual beliefs and to develop a truly autonomous individual outlook on the basic issues of life and of society. "Intellectual" will mean roughly the same as "rational" in the sense developed in the foregoing; more precisely, the reference of "intellectual" is to a rationality for the whole person and for his or her whole life span.

A person is an *intellectual*, then, to the extent that one's mind produces and uses the insight—into oneself, into others, into the nature of society—that is required for coping with and anticipating the problems of living a full life and facing death with serenity. The long-range rationality associated with "intellectual" is also a broad-gauge rationality, moreover, in the sense that the intellectual recognizes his or her stake in an enlightened society and in enlightened citizenship on one's own part. It is this propensity of the developed intellect that makes a rich and continuing supply of intellectuals not only an advantage but a necessity for a civilization if it is to survive in a complex and rapidly changing world.

The student's social surroundings should for the present purposes of analysis be viewed as a variety of *social systems*. A social system is conceived as being composed, not of individuals, but of the actions and behaviors of individuals, the principal units of which are roles and the constellations of roles. Like Chinese boxes, large social systems contain a succession of subsystems. And, what is more important, many social systems overlap, so that most individuals in a complex society belong to a variety of social systems. Sometimes overlapping systems are in harmony, but sometimes they are in conflict, and the person in the middle is torn.

Every new rational venture—for example, a new college or department or type of course—creates a new social system. The difficulty of keeping a new venture rational should be apparent from the fact that each individual who takes on a role in the new system continues at the same time to play many of one's familiar roles in other systems, of which one's habitual or deliberate kinds of behavior are component parts.

New social systems frequently are the result of deliberately planned human efforts; if so, they are *organizations* as well as social systems. By "organized" we mean simply: deliberately arranged with some purposes in mind. Generally speaking, organizations are established to solve problems—that is, to expand the rational at the expense of the institutional, merely customary components of social interaction.

However, no organization works entirely according to its rational design. Even the procedures for making decisions are invariably molded in directions that deviate from those on the organizational charts. Partly, this may be because no planners, however well informed and wise, are capable of making rules that fit all future situations. Then, too, social systems develop a momentum of their own, so far insufficiently explored by students of behavior; the merging and meshing of new institutions with old lead to unanticipated types of stresses and opportunities, which are influenced also by varying personalities of individuals in key roles at crucial moments. Partly, again, leadership groups in any social organization may be in a position to use their prerogatives of leadership to bolster their own power at the expense of other groups or potential groups within the organization. Every stable organization, to conclude, has presumably developed some informal compromise between deliberate plans with purposes in mind, unanticipated stresses and incentives, and general tendencies toward entrenchment of leadership, of privilege, and of institutional stability. This informal structure is often referred to as the "informal organization."

Most American colleges are relatively stable formal organizations, within which a variety of informal organizations or social systems operate. It is always legitimate to ask to what extent the informal institutions tend to defeat the purposes that the organization should serve. But if we want to pursue this inquiry, we need to focus on what the college experience means to students. How do they see their role as student, and how do they feel about it?

Suppose we define *role* as it is usually defined by behavioral scientists: A set of evaluative standards that are applied to an incumbent of a particular position. This definition leaves an important question unanswered. Applied to *whom*? The same role can be defined very differently by the incumbent, and by various others who are in a relationship to that individual. And no matter how much of an agreement may be established about the requirements of a given role, different incumbents may approach it with very different degrees of independence, "willingness to play the game," loyalty to the various reference groups, personal involvement in objectives, and so on. Moreover, the same person's attitude to one's role may undergo considerable changes during a given time interval, and such changes may be due primarily to factors in one's own private life or personality development, and not necessarily be responsive mainly to changes in the social environment of his role.

To connect role expectation and role definition with the whole range of motives that account for the individual's attitude to a given role, we shall introduce the term *incentive*. It refers to the prospects of satisfaction in a given role, or a given conception of that role, seen from the individual's points of view, compared to roles or role-conceptions which one sees as alternatives. Incentives are in a sense embedded in the social system, where they correspond to motives in the individual; as individuals perceive the various elements in their situation, those elements that they value or disvalue—and think or feel that they can do something about—are for them incentives.

Social, Academic, and Intellectual Student Incentives

Let us now define three types of incentives that are of significance to the role of student. There are, first, the *social incentives*, meaning the prospects of social acceptance, of being admitted to membership in desired groups, and of being respected, liked, admired, or loved by relevant persons. *Academic incentives* refer to the value the student attaches to a good academic record, in terms of conscientious fulfillment of course requirements and, above all, the achievement of good grades. This is something very different from *intellectual incentives*, which refer to the intrinsic satisfaction the student perceives in striving to broaden his understanding and sharpen his power of reflection. Combinations of two, or all three, of these types of incentives are of course frequent.

Each student who enters college is motivated by a variety of *social* incentives; the immediately obvious reference group, or group in which he aspires to be accepted, is normally that of his peers or that of a section, at least, of the student community. Because all students on each campus will have many interests in common, a social system of all students will develop, along with a *student culture* influenced by and in turn contributing to the various norms and expectations that make up the variety of student subcultures.

For the average entering student the new social role must appear a very complex one. There are, first of all, the role expectations developed by peers in the student culture; in the vast majority of the colleges these norms are primarily nonintellectual as well as nonacademic, and sometimes anti-intellectual though rarely anti-academic. One reason for this nonintellectualism may be that students with social skills almost inevitably acquire more influence in the shaping of peer-group culture than do those with intellectual skills, who by and large participate less persistently in social activities or at any rate tend to strive less for student leadership (at least when it comes to purely social leadership or leadership in organizations without independence and political influence). Furthermore, those who become social leaders will tend to be recruited in part from those with a self-assurance and relative lack of concern for academic achievement associated with a relatively wealthy upper-middle-class family background, and in part from the star athletes.

In many colleges the system of student clubs and other organizations, including the fraternities and sororities, serves to magnify even further the dominating influence of the less intellectually bent students in the continuous development of the student culture; very frequently these socially adept nonintellectuals dominate student governments as well, and with the university administration's blessings, more often than not. From a public relations point of view, these are the best students: never radical or even militantly liberal; outwardly submissive to authority and as obedient to the deans as they are to their own fathers. And they find the conventional limits to academic freedom fully in order; their interest is not in questioning any fundamental assumptions, either in politics or in other fields of inquiry. They are in college to achieve credits and formal qualifications, and also to have a good time.

Yet *some* academic incentives are likely to confront even the otherwise carefree good-time Charlie; and in the better universities they may well be the overriding incentives for the majority of students. Every college can make their students work hard by toughening academic requirements, and this is, of course, the way up in the status hierarchy of colleges and universities.

It may be allowed that efforts to do well in courses will benefit most students more, with respect to their intellectual development, than efforts merely to be liked by their peers. Yet the hunt for grades need not be very much of an improvement over the hunt for peer-group popularity. Neither the social nor the academic status seeker is primarily concerned with developing rational powers; both shun bold reflections and cling to what seems safe and sound.

If academic incentives in this narrow sense tend to overshadow intellectual incentives for most students, this is largely because the system of teaching so frequently is tuned to the desires of the academic strivers rather than to those of the intellectuals in the class. This is so for many reasons. One is that academically oriented instructions are easier to communicate to students, who usually want to know specifically what is expected of them in each course; it is hard to be specific about how to meditate and become wiser. Another is that the proliferation of courses and the fragmentation of the student's time, and the process by which he is given a daily spoonfeeding of reading assignments and lectures, all militate against deep reflection. Still another circumstance is the fact that the professor's energies are fragmented, too; it is easier to throw the narrowly academic course requirements at one's students than it is to try to develop a frame of mind for embarking on a joint intellectual adventure. Also, the teacher has to give grades, and it is far simpler to assess narrowly academic achievement than to evaluate intellectual effort or reflective achievement.

A further circumstance that strengthens the academic at the expense of the intellectual incentives is the tendency for many teachers in uninspiring environments to lose whatever intellectual interests they may once have had, so that for them, too, the classroom experience may tend to become primary social experience with students, regulated only by the essential academic duties of teaching performance that are stipulated in the college employment contract. The problem of "dead-wooditis" is not limited to second-rate colleges, of course. And among the younger teachers, less susceptible to this disease, the desire for financial security through academic tenure may well forestall the development of a strong interest in teaching. In spite of lip service paid to the importance of the teaching function in the better colleges and universities, these teachers are given to understand that their prospects for promotion depend almost entirely on the quantity or quality of their research and publications. Most young professors are in effect told not to devote their energies to the teaching task—at least not at the expense of time and effort invested in research. By the time tenure is granted, the instructor is too much a part of the established order to take a renewed interest in students and to improve his teaching. Moreover, the race to publish tends to be a lifelong one, with both future salary raises and academic prestige, and sometimes one's self-esteem, dependent on—as one college faculty employment form is alleged to have phrased the question—one's "current rate of publication."

Another circumstance of pervasive significance is that the horizons of most schools of education appear to have been limited by the far greater ease with which research can be done on academic rather than on intellectual achievement. The literature on prediction of college achievement has invariably focused on narrowly academic achievement; so has the vast literature on experiments in teaching techniques and classroom arrangements. The reason so much of this literature is so uninspiring is because often what is studied is not particularly important. We study grades because they offer a convenient measure, even though the crucial task of the educator, most of us would agree, is to help develop the students, rather than equip them with masses of facts and the kinds of skills that are rewarded with grades in the majority of college courses.

One of the crucial needs, if academic incentives are to allow more room for intellectual ones in the role perspective of the average college student, is a greater inventiveness in the study of educational processes. It is obviously easier to count A's and B's to the exclusion of more meaningful inquiries. It is difficult but not impossible to develop a variety of indices for such variables as reflectiveness, intellectual curiosity, depth of intention in interpersonal and political attitudes, universalism of moral judgment, psychological insight, and so on—qualities which in an intellectual college community would be promoted in preference to agility in memorizing.

There is yet another and possibly even more pervasive source of pressures that work against allowing intellectual incentives much scope in the educational experience in most colleges. It is the nature of the larger society of which the college is a small part, and in particular the tenuous relationship in this society between intellectual quality and social mobility. To what extent and in what ways may *intellectual* effort seem *useful* for the long-range career purposes of most students? To a very limited extent, probably. For students aspiring to become, eventually, members of the academic world, intellectual incentives may often prevail. But in most fields there are few if any incentives for average students to exert their minds for any purposes other than mastering the isolated fragments of human knowledge to which they are exposed. Their minds become tailored to the anticipated needs of the type of job to which they aspire, not to the needs of one's own person and to the fuller individuality that one might have developed.

A relatively low esteem for the intellect and for intellectual excellence prevails in contemporary American society; although "ability" in all jobs is admired, a display of articulate reflectiveness is widely considered "high brow" or something peculiar to a special breed of impractical people who are not to be imitated. The somewhat derisive term "egghead," which was so common two decades ago, told more than volumes of analysis could about the orientation of the contemporary mass culture toward the more reflective and sophisticated minds. And that basic anti-intellectual attitude on the part of "the common man" in America has, if anything, increased in recent years.

From the vantage point of many students who hope for future success in our kind of society, to develop skill in "selling their personalities" may appear far more important than to develop any personalities worth selling, or indeed worth having, in terms of their own long-range personal needs. A manipulative congeniality may appear more useful to students than a contemplative genius. Students with this attitude toward learning, whether they are conscious of the attitude or not, may acquire no more profit from college than verbal glibness and the shallow smugness of half-learning: by a trained incapacity for serious reflection, they may become genuine bores and be doomed to bored lives.

It would be beyond the scope of this chapter to pursue an inquiry into the long-range prospects for anti-intellectualism in American society. It seems clear enough that political changes *could* seriously affect the quality of American higher education for better or for worse. Let us instead ask: Given the present political and economic system, what can be done most effectively to improve the American college? The principal answer, perhaps, is to be found in the small college stressing intellectual values that creates its own ethos within the larger college. The intellectual university community cannot be built all at once, much less the intellectual society. Ideas must become truly important to a few professors and students before they can excite most members of a college community; and a good beginning is made if small groups are created within the large college in which a vigorous exchange of intellectual stimuli is pursued.

The point that must be emphasized is that piecemeal innovations *are* possible within the present system of higher education, innovations which conceivably can lead to wider changes of educational processes even in the absence of any previous improvement of the intellectual climate of the larger social system. In the absence of such innovations, or of significant changes in the larger system, the turnout of truly educated minds from the colleges will remain distressingly low. I see this as a tragic waste of potential talents and undeveloped wisdom, indeed, as a great brain robbery.

The Enduring Intellect

For all that has been said about social circumstances inside and outside the college, which at the present time appear to forestall intellectual learning and development, the fact remains that some students nevertheless do develop into full-grown intellectuals. How does this come about? There is in human beings a basic tendency toward health, both mental and physical. The human being has somewhere deep down a will to recuperate; the organism is not indifferent to the alternatives of illness or health. Educators need a similar assumption: embedded in every man and woman is a will to grow, mentally as well as physically; the personality is not indifferent to the alternatives of unfolding or blocking the rational faculties. The intellect is like a fragile plant. It requires the right kind of surroundings and nourishment, of soil and air and water; within the confining limits set by the surrounding social circumstances, the intellect will grow to whatever stature each individual is capable of achieving.

The social limits to intellectual growth appear from the individual's perspective primarily as anxieties; in addition, there is the kind of limit that is imposed by keeping information or knowledge or stimulation away from the individual. Since the colleges in the Western democracies give students physical access to almost all varieties of books, the failure of most students to take advantage of this opportunity to broaden their rationality must be explained largely in terms of the limits set by their various kinds of anxiety.

Some anxieties are deeply rooted and subconscious; they drive the individual to acquire and hold on to beliefs and attitudes that serve self-defensive needs. These anxieties usually revolve around fundamentals such as guilt and shame and doubts about one's own worth as a human being, and they frequently emanate from feelings of rejection by one's parents during infancy or early childhood. Other anxieties are preconscious or conscious and revolve around one's social relationships; some take the shape of worries about being accepted in the appropriate peer groups or by the appropriate reference groups, whereas others are concerned with the unknown future and are manifested as worries about adequate performance or rewards in future social roles.

All varieties of personal and social anxiety presumably have one thing in common: while they may or may not stimulate mental effort, they invariably forestall a fully rational, task-oriented approach to human and social problems. Our anxieties keep our gaze focused on the ground or in a straight line ahead of us most of the time so that we fail to study the wider horizons, even though the wider vision might have eased our walk and certainly would have helped us decide more independently where to go. Like rats in the psychologist's maze, most of us are driven through our social labyrinths by our needs and anxieties; physically we walk erect but mentally we are too unsure of ourselves and our steps to stand upright and gain an overview of society and a perspective on life.

Higher education exists, it may be assumed, to give us this opportunity, both for our sake as individuals and for society's sake, on the assumption that a fuller view of reality produces a more responsible and a wiser, more foresightful citizenry. Students will take advantage of this opportunity to the extent that they can; but the social odds against any spectacular unfolding of the fragile intellect are large, given the present type of college community and our present social order.

Genuine curiosity belongs to the child and to the child in adults. In most lives the capacity to be curious keeps declining; every time a young person is induced to accept an answer for self-defensive reasons or on the ground that a belief is socially expected, the capacity to be curious is curtailed. On the other hand, every time a person is permitted to make an intellectual discovery, to see a new connection, or make sense of a new idea, for example, one's curiosity is nourished and expanded. This is how it happens that intellectual development tends to become either stymied at an early age or self-generating in a lifelong process. It becomes blocked in college or earlier if students remain prisoners of their immediate or anticipatory social anxieties; a person who has no intellectual curiosity at 20 is unlikely to develop it later, though there are, of course, exceptions to this rule.

The intellect becomes liberated in college or earlier to the extent that students have been helped to achieve a fair degree of mastery of their personal and social anxieties and have developed the courage to define for themselves what kind of lives *they* want to live. The chances are that they will want, if they are in a real sense able to choose for themselves, lives of long-term humanitarian solidarity with their fellow human beings, in preference to psychologically lonelier lives in quest of more narrowly self-centered, short-term goals.

3

The
State
University
in Conflict
with Its Publics

Frank Pinner

Many institutions of higher education have drastically modified their missions—and their public images—during the past quarter-century. The largest group of such institutions are the newer state universities—the institutions that in 1950 or 1960 (or even in 1970) were still designated as "state colleges." The histories of these newer American colleges and universities resemble those of religious denominations. In their early, sectarian state they appeal to special clienteles, often local or regional in character, recruited from narrow social layers and largely agreed on fundamentals. As they proceed toward churchly universality, however, they shed some of their old clienteles and aspire to new ones; they seek to enlarge their geographical domains by erasing their bound-

aries; and the undisputed verities of the past give way to a multiplic-
ity of aims and convictions. Perhaps this is the growth pattern of all
successful institutions in a highly mobile society.

"Dissensual" Knowledge and the University's Publics

Those who teach in these large new universities of America have
experienced, during recent years, the strains and stresses of such
transformations. These have arisen not merely from the growth in
staffs and enrollments, the addition of teaching programs in areas
previously neglected or deliberately omitted, and the development
of physical facilities, but they also reflect many changes in policy.

There is, for instance, the steady and insistent effort to stimulate
"research,"which administrators and professors alike regard as the
open sesame to the world of universal scholarship. Many of the
newer institutions, seemingly ashamed of their former
provincialism and bent on escaping its remnants, have eagerly
embraced programs that would bring the faculty into closer contact
with national and international affairs. Government-sponsored or
foundation-sponsored programs of technical assistance to the less
developed nations, for example, were typically conducted by the
"developing" large universities rather than those with older and
more cosmopolitan traditions.

Some observers of the university scene have viewed such involvement with national policy as nothing more than a shift from
local provincialism to that of the nation-state. At the very least,
however, the province itself has become immensely larger. And the
enlargement of the university's geographical reference does imply
some broadening of its intellectual scope.

But this very urge toward universalism has made for ambiguities
and tensions. Although it reaches toward far-flung horizons, the
newly emerged university cannot and dares not forsake its familiar
surroundings of town and countryside.It is bound to these by its
own alumni and other benefactors, by its older faculty, by the
origins and the expectations of its students, and by those of the
surrounding community. In playing to two rather disparate
publics—the local public of its immediate surroundings and the
cosmopolitan audience of the republic of letters—it risks raising
suspicions in both.

The alienation of the university from one or both of these publics tends to become a particularly acute problem for state universities. More than other institutions of higher learning, they depend on the good will of local people. Since public funds are the most important sources of their income, they must find ways to stimulate the generosity of the lawmakers. They must not merely maintain good relations with legislators; they must also nurse, within the state, their own social constituencies, groups of people who believe in the benefits of higher education and who are capable of exerting pressure toward its expansion.

Administrators of state universities, in appealing to the legislature and to supporters in town and country, tend to make two points: their university performs services important to the people of the state, and their university is among the "greatest" or "most distinguished" in the country. The two arguments do not necessarily reflect congruent sets of facts; what is conceived to be "service" to the state is not likely to be closely related to the criteria of "distinction" in the academic world.

Thus the state legislator or the small-town businessman may feel that the main services of a university are undergraduate training and consultancy for public and private bodies; but the current mood of the larger academic community bestows "distinction" on schools with large programs of graduate—not necessarily undergraduate—instruction, and of "basic"—not immediately utilitarian—research.

The separation of the state university from its local publics has not occurred in spite of the improvement of its faculty, but because of it. Where once there was a community, there are now two or more separate groups. Where once there was implicit understanding of common purposes, there are now many purposes. Moreover, administrators are caught between their loyalty to the older members of the faculty and their esteem for the new professors they have fought so hard to win. Unable to take sides, they must—for they are human—rationalize their situation. They must make themselves the bearers of myths which might restore to the university the unity of a tribal society.

One of these myths is the consoling belief that knowledge can be pursued in many ways, and that each new set of facts is a building block destined to find its place in the structure of truth. This belief is consoling because it so conveniently relieves its holders of the most arduous task facing academic administrators: to define criteria for encouraging some academic endeavors while discouraging others. Because this belief yields no guidelines for policy, it is a myth. The dilemmas of our state universities bring into sharp relief some basic problems in the growth and management of human knowledge. As teachers and researchers, we must become articulate about our grounds for preferring certain kinds of knowledge to others, for only thus can we expect university administrators to act with appropriate discrimination in allocating resources.

What criteria, then, can be proposed? Which knowledge is it most urgent to pursue, to teach, to explore? Surely the university must give preference to the knowledge that is least likely to be sponsored and supported by any other institution of society, the knowledge that only anxieties and fears prevent human beings from pursuing, the knowledge that is most needed *because* of these widespread apprehensions. This is "dissensual" knowledge.

The term "consensual" may be applied to all those disciplines about which the public at large tends to have no reservation, either about the competence of the scholars and the truth of their findings or about the values which inform their work. Correspondingly, the term "dissensual" may be applied to all disciplines whose values or procedures are widely questioned among the public, either explicitly or implicitly.

Few people in the community will express doubts about the research and findings of a chemist, nor will they ever question his motives and wonder about the values underlying his work. But the findings and teachings of philosophers and economists do not elicit similarly general confidence. The public tends to wonder about the worth of these scholars' work; it tends to look for hidden motives and it easily discounts their teachings and even their data, either by directly opposing or by conveniently forgetting and ignoring them.

This has nothing to do with the public's understanding of these disciplines. The man in the street knows no more about chemistry and the life work of chemists than he knows about economics and its practitioners. His reactions are not based on direct experience, but on the status the consensual disciplines have achieved in the community.

The logical deductions of a philosopher are just as secure, and the empirical findings of a sociologist often just as convincing, as are the theories and findings of scholars in the consensual disciplines. It could be argued that disciplines in which aesthetic judgments play a role—for example, music—are perhaps on less secure ground since these are "matters of taste." This is likely not so, even though it is difficult to sustain an argument against such a statement. Surely, however, standards of beauty are as ascertainable as standards of truth in scientific endeavors. In either case, the exact formulation of such standards of beauty testifies to the direction of our interests more than to the feasibility of either task.

There was a time, not very far in the past, when the medical doctor was looked upon with as much suspicion as is the psychotherapist today; and the findings of the early chemist (or alchemist) were held up to as much ridicule as those of the social scientist today. Even in the recent past, advances in agriculture were made the butt of ridicule by farmers who saw agronomic innovations as a challenge to their accustomed way of life.

To be sure, the disciplines which are now consensual have undergone a great expansion in knowledge and have gained greatly in precision. But much of this gain was made because the public came to perceive the utility of these disciplines and was willing to support them with money and status. Growth of knowledge and growth of public acceptance are closely interrelated, and neither of the two can for long proceed without the other.

Much of the expansion of the newer state universities has taken place in the dissensual disciplines. The liberal arts, the social sciences and education have seen great increases in the strength of their faculties and in student enrollments. Nor is this all. The frame of mind of the men who have recently joined these faculties tends to favor those areas of inquiry which are still largely dissensual. Also they are less likely than were their predecessors to compromise with community sentiment. They hold values and are led to findings which typically are not shared by the community.

Economists know, for instance, that productivity is not necessarily a function of competition and that, indeed, productivity in our country increased at an accelerated rate at the very time when insecurity in business and jobs was greatly reduced. No matter how well founded such findings of the economists might be, they do not really reach the public. Rather, at every public meeting of businessmen, orators will sing the praises of business and job competition as the surest stimulants to productivity. Unaware of the questionable nature of such beliefs, the public expects the university professor to confirm them, rather than challenge them.

The implications are clear: the weaker the faculty, the less its concern for the inviolability of thought, the more likely it will be to make concessions to the conventional wisdom and to say what the community wishes to hear. Bring to the university people with better training, more deeply committed to their disciplines, more enamored of the truth as they have come to know it, and a breach is bound to arise between the proponent of objective knowledge and the public committed to the conventional wisdom.

The Main Bases of Conflict

The resistance of the public to the proponent of unconvential beliefs is automatic. It can be active or passive, and both types appear among students. Active resistance takes the form of conscious rejection; the less acceptable teachings are discounted as being impractical or old-fashioned, or heretical. Passive resistance takes the form of systematic but unconscious misunderstanding, or selective perception, and gross distortion of the teacher's message.

Active resistance—when the teacher encourages its overt expression—is easier to deal with than passive, because it exists on the conscious level, can be expressed, and is therefore a possible topic for debate. But whether such resistance is expressed or not very much depends on the teacher's classroom style. In the great majority of instances, student resistance remains unexpressed, either because its expression is penalized or because the resistance is passive—that is, inarticulate, unrealized, amorphous. Passive resistance is most likely to sever all possible community ties between the teacher and students, for it makes communication impossible. Similar observations can be made, no doubt, about the relations between the able teacher of a dissensual discipline and the larger outside public of the university, but they are not so apparent and not so easily detected.

Resistance to unaccustomed knowledge and doctrine is generally not surprising, but when it occurs in universities as frequently and consistently as it nowadays does, there is reason to be perturbed.

Many students do not expect to learn in the profound and the only meaningful sense of the word *learning*. They do not expect that their understandings of the world will change, that their beliefs will be altered, that old interests will be replaced by new ones, that on the day of graduation they will be—as human beings—quite different from the freshmen who entered the university four years ago. They attend the university not as the truly religious person attends worship, for the sake of an experience which will transform him; but rather as does the average Sunday churchgoer, for the sake of social conformity and from habit.

The gap does not arise from the differences in intellectual preparation and maturity which are ordinarily expected between students and teachers. All important ideas can be taught on many levels of complexity; and there are people of great profundity in their fields of knowledge genuinely excited by the task of teaching highly sophisticated ideas in a manner which will make them accessible to students with minimal preparation. The gap arises, rather, from a difference in foci of interest. The good academician focuses on changes in the structure of knowledge, and he does so in both of his capacities, as a scholar and as a teacher. But most students and most members of the wider publics are interested only in accretion.

Students nowadays are the products of a mobile society; their very presence in the universities attests to this. Yet as a rule they appear to be intellectually and emotionally more rigid than are students in less mobile societies. Oddly, the presence of barriers in the mind reflects the relative absence of barriers in society. Where education is still regarded as the privilege of gentlemen, students of plebian lineage show a grasping and combative eagerness to acquire knowledge, refinement of taste, and new interpretations of human experience. To them, education is a step in the fight for social equality, and they enter it with a will to change. Such attitudes are still common in many of the students who come from minority backgrounds. But middle-class students exhibit no such eagerness. They happily take it for granted, as does the society generally, that there are no social hurdles to learning. The majority of students, in entering the university, cannot feel that they are overcoming ancient restrictions and embarking on a new way of life. For them, education spells advancement rather than change, improvement rather than transition. The fixedness of their points of view is thus a counterpart to the equalitarian ethos.

Yet such attitudes are ill adapted. Great transformations are under way in our society, and there are no signs of respite. It is imperative that students, once they leave the campus, be flexible enough in mind and personality to cope with unexpected and perhaps still inconceivable problems. A few simple precepts, such as those contained in conventional wisdom, can scarcely be of any help to the engineers of a still-clouded future, however broadly or narrowly the term "engineer" might be construed.

There are thus two seemingly incompatible conditions of education: a changing world which calls for a leadership of insight and originality; and students who, in view of the relative ease with which they can cross social boundaries, are under no compulsion to play new roles and to cast off old habits of mind and heart.

In an effort to cope with this difficulty many universities have programs in "general studies" designed to give the student the background that was lacking at his arrival on campus. In addition to specially designed courses, there are appearances on almost every campus of great artists, lecturers and foreign films. These efforts have usually fallen far short of expectations, and not for lack of good will or hard work. Teachers and researchers have not been able to detect any difference between students who have been exposed to the courses in various specialties that "count" as general studies courses and those who have not. Even if the teaching in such courses were dismally poor—which is by no means the rule—this would hardly explain such minimal results. As for out-of-class activities, the number of students who attend concerts, theatrical performances and discussion meetings is disturbingly small. Again, even if these performances were consistently mediocre—which by no means they are—this would not explain such perennial truancy. Only one conclusion is possible: students, in general, have no use for these things. It must be accepted as a hard social fact that much of human thought and culture is, in the form in which it is presented to students, unrelated to their experience and, hence, unintelligible.

Professors have their own share in the academic tragi-comedy of misunderstandings. Like their students, American professors are the creatures of a fluid social milieu. Since status is achieved rather than conferred, professors feel forever impelled to prove to themselves and to others that they deserve the trust and responsibility placed upon them.

Such proof is difficult, for professors are producers of intangibles, and thus status anxiety is their most frequent occupational disease. Nor can they find comfort in aristocratic pride. Most of them do not issue from nobility of rank or wealth, nor even from a patriciate of letters. They come from every social layer in every region of the United States and of the world.

Thus, professors are both similar to students and different from them. Like students, most professors are recent arrivals, and they came to the university because the hurdles were not too high. Professors are, perhaps, of more diverse and more mingled expectations than are students. But the main difference is this: professors have experienced change within themselves, and students have not. Professors are not too sure of their position in the world; students are not too sure of theirs. The students' status striving has the determined push of careerism; the professors' status anxiety is a gnawing worry lest they fail to live up to the expectations which they themselves and others attach to their position.

Such feelings do not make for good teaching or learning. A snobbish professor alienates the student because his tone and manner constantly imply the unattainability of knowledge and good taste. His earthy colleague, on the other hand, by exhibiting an excess of common sense, affirms that there is not very much to be learned or communicated. The student, sharing the American public's ambiguous attitudes toward men and women of letters, and sensing moreover his professor's disquiet, vacillates between formal subservience and excessive informality. This does not help the professor, who becomes even more defensive; and it does not help communication, which becomes even less articulate.

Toward the Academic Community

Education means openness to change. It means that the professor helps the student shed the conventional wisdom and enables him to make rational choices by the use of information, insight and sensitivity. It means, first of all, that the professor generates the willingness to change. The professor communicates excitement about the worlds of knowledge and of the arts, so that students will want to expose themselves to unaccustomed experiences. To the extent that they do, they will gain the respect of the faculty, and they will learn to appreciate their teachers. Thus, education is the same thing as the creation of the academic community.

For the teacher, education is forever an act of self-revelation. The good teacher does not simply attempt to fill minds with information as one fills barrels of wine; it is not a physical process. Rather, he exhibits himself as a demonstration case, showing his students how at least one member of his profession tackles a problem, how he feels about it, how he judges his own work, how he doubts and battles about its social value and the truth of his findings, how he may often be tempted to cheat himself and others by saying more than can be responsibly asserted. Science, the humanities, and the arts are human and fallible activities and must be understood as such.

For the student, too, education is self-revelation. He must be able to expose himself to the teacher and to other students so he may be helped better to realize his own potential. All discussion that is not to some extent self-revelation is, in fact, anti-intellectual. The student of mathematics and science has not learned anything about his discipline unless he is able to exhibit the process whereby he arrives at a solution. The most elaborate repertoire of formulae and operating rules will never add up to the first beginnings of mathematics or science.

In the dissensual disciplines, self-revelation is even more important; almost invariably questions of value are mingled with questions of theory and fact, and if the student does not learn to be articulate about his values, if he takes them for granted, he has not begun to penetrate into his field of study. Self-revelation is the surest path to self-awareness; and without self-awareness, change is impossible and education is an empty ritual.

The academic community must be an assembly of men and women humble enough and yet secure enough to exhibit to one another their doubts, their weaknesses and at times their wretchedness. This is the price of knowledge and of truth. Set teachers up on a pedestal and ascribe to them all the conventional virtues, and you will reduce their scope to that of dog trainers. Limit the students' range of experience by imposing disciplines other than those emerging from the search for truth and understanding, and you will make them into parrots. But foster understanding and the free but organized search for new forms of thinking and living, and you will be educating people.

4

The Viability of the American College

David Riesman

Chrisopher S. Jencks

Whole libraries have been filled with books on higher education in America, and much can be learned from some of them. Many have been historical studies either of a single institution or of an educational tradition. Others have been quantitative appraisals of logistic problems in contemporary higher education. The effort here is somewhat different: it is to compare colleges not only with each other, but by a series of analogies to relate what happens in college to other aspects of our national life. Such an effort risks the dangers and invites the stimulation of analogies and metaphors that may sometimes appear far-fetched.

Colleges, looked at in terms of a theory of the labor force, might be described primarily as *personnel offices*, feeding properly certified employees into business and the professions. Some colleges supplement these general efforts by direct tie-ins between their teacher-training division and local schools, their engineering division and local industry, or their business division and local commerce. All colleges inevitably participate in the informal network through which graduates of each college tend to recruit fellow alumni, or perhaps more correctly alumni of their own in-group on campus. Such enclaves may help explain why alumni of Ivy League schools have incomes considerably higher than graduates of other colleges—or even the fact that half the trustees of major philanthropic foundations hold degrees from these same schools.

But why, it may be asked, should business and the professions depend on colleges for employees, and why should scholars oblige by supplying them? During the nineteenth century, American higher education was not so heavily age-graded as it has become since, and college was not seen as a necessary prerequisite to the study of law or medicine. As the country has become richer and the professions stronger, however, the latter have been able to postpone choosing their apprentices, compelling the colleges to provide a litmus for measuring both intellectual and social aptitudes. This is quite compatible with the argument that the apprentice can be more readily turned into a respectable and reponsible citizen, as well as a more discerning student of his specialty, if he has had the extra four years of college education.

But beyond such more-or-less rational considerations the American college exists as a vast public works project, which gives promising adolescents work to do while keeping them out of the job market—and also keeps hundreds of thousands of faculty members off the streets. Of course, such a comparison seems to ignore the great numbers of undergraduates who are actually in vocational programs, such as engineering, education, business administration or nursing. Many students, however, in these apparently preprofessional programs are not actually committed to a career, but are still shopping around.

It is difficult to say to what extent college, along with the rest of the educational system, trains students not only to seek work of their own devising, but also to respond in a disciplined attitude toward work *not* of their own devising, and to what extent colleges help inculcate a distaste for work precisely because of its frequently imposed and alienated quality. Certainly, quite apart from the technical skills acquired in college, the colleges do provide the locale for inculcating social and personal skills on which employers put increasing emphasis; the more so since they themselves are increasingly college trained. For this purpose the curriculum is important only insofar as it spills over from the classroom to the dining hall, from the library to student government headquarters, from the teacher-student relationship to the administrator-student and student-student relationship.

One major influence of most occupations on the attitudes of the worker is to encourage him to meet certain people, and prevent his meeting others. The same thing is true of a college. In this perspective it may be helpful to view the college as a human relocation project that removes a student from parents, community and employment to submerge him in the student culture of his adolescent peers. In the same manner a college nationalizes the student, taking him out of his ethnic, religious, geographic and social parishes and exposing him to a more cosmopolitan world where the imagination is less restricted by preconception and ignorance.

College as an Initiation Rite

College is an initiation rite for separating the middle from the lower class, and for changing the semi-amorphous adolescent into a semi-identified adult. All studies of taste and opinion suggest that one of the great cultural cleavages in our society is between those who have been to college—even if they have not completed degree programs—and those who have not. To go to college is to join what commencement orators call "the fellowship of educated men and women," and what other observers more skeptically dub "the diploma elite." In part, this transformation is a matter of faith.

By standing as the watchdogs of the middle and upper-middle classes, the colleges have greatly circumscribed the range of behavior common among the national elite. Furthermore, precisely because college is now the gatekeeper to the middle class, as well as a decisive influence on its styles of life, every minority group of any standing in America has an interest in putting pressure on colleges to accept more of its own members and to introduce courses and programs to suit its own particular needs. Nevertheless, as American nationalism, the national economy, and the mass media reflect an increasingly uniform color, colleges tend to copy one another to make sure that their programs remain acceptable as certificates of respectability.

Occupational Interest Groups. In the Colonial Period some of the zeal that went into the founding and maintenance of the first American colleges came from the fear of educated immigrants that their children, born in less urbane surroundings than their European parents, might revert to barbarism. This fear evoked an effort to perpetuate the educated classes, which is most areas meant both the ministry and the class of gentlemen.

This pattern of mixing occupational and social training still persists. Hundreds of colleges have been founded to provide some community with theologically orthodox leadership that could not be conveniently recruited from colleges elsewhere. As the theological and geographical schisms that generated the new colleges faded, they could no longer count on recruits and patronage from those who once thought their ideological specialization important; and so most such schools have expanded, sometimes to train men of several faiths, but more often to train laymen. Such expansion has produced alumni of less religious commitment, who have in turn opened their college to new cadres of unbelievers or indifferents. Equally important is the fact that religious sects have tended to upgrade themselves socially, in part through these very colleges. As a result, a pulpit that at first needed only a smattering of Biblical passion eventually demands a man with a liberal education who can converse with the now-educated parishioners. Once the facilities for such liberal education are provided, they can seldom be supported solely by future preachers.

In the last century the need for ministers has inspired fewer new colleges than has the need for teachers. During the late nineteenth century, state normal schools spread across the country to provide teachers for the ever-increasing primary school population. As the demand of secondary teachers caught up with the demand for elementary teachers, normal schools became teachers colleges, with liberal arts divisions. Conversely, liberal arts colleges added education units in order to cash in on the single biggest source of potential college students.

With this distinction of purpose abolished, the former teachers college began to feel that it was distinguished from other liberal arts colleges only by low prestige and low standards, that it had to move therefore with all possible speed to emulate the liberal arts college program. Once the liberal arts curriculum was established, the teachers college became suitable for the education of students headed for other careers, so that even in its clientele it came to resemble the liberal arts college.

In arts and sciences there are perhaps three dozen universities that turn out the vast majority of doctorates. Yet none of these universities has seriously considered abolishing the BA degree or eliminating undergraduates. Some have merely neglected the undergraduate, some (for example, Columbia and Chicago) have set up semi-autonomous undergraduate divisions, and some (for example, Harvard) have merged graduate and undergraduate instruction as much as possible.

Some of the presently leading institutions have grown from the demand, which began to be felt more than a century ago, for trained engineers, agriculturalists, veterinarians, and technicians of every sort. Congress was moved in 1862 to pass the Morrill Act providing for the training of such men and women in what were often called Colleges of Agriculture and Mechanical Arts. In relatively new states these land-grant colleges often attracted an increasingly wide cross section of students now envisioned by their founders. This magnetism was enhanced in such states as Minnesota, Wisconsin, and Nebraska, which combined the technical college with the state university. The same rapid growth did not occur in some states like Massachusetts which had a tradition of private education and were long unable to see what legitimate functions a public institution might serve beyond those specified by Congress.

Because of the widespread influence of the Morrill Act, most of the nation's schools of agriculture and engineering came under the aegis of a comprehensive college or university that lent the facilities and prestige of the liberal arts to technical programs. And now, over a century later, on many campuses, it is the technical programs that lend prestige—and facilities—to the liberal arts. During the last century, efforts at vocational training were increasingly permeated by the liberal arts, thereby elevating the vocations to more dignified positions; and there has been a seemingly endless cycle of new occupations whose practitioners want colleges oriented in their direction. One area of rapid growth, for example, has been business education, sometimes under the auspices of local magnates who want recruits, but more often sponsored by colleges which want to attract and retain local students to whom the liberal arts seem irrelevant and difficult.

It is true that in the many selective colleges students avoid business careers altogether. Nevertheless, the majority of middle-class college graduates consider business quite respectable—an attitude that is strengthened as business executives are exposed to, and even influenced by, such academic values as breadth of view, skepticism and the ability to master complex chains of information.

The spread of the degree hierarchy has encouraged students in many occupations requiring even less technical expertise than business to seek a certificate which will set them off from mere high school graduates. For many, this distinction has come from the two-year AA degree awarded by the community colleges. But although these institutions were often founded to provide such terminal vocational programs, they have rarely been content to tie themselves to middle-level occupations. Today the majority of students who enter community colleges do not start in vocational programs but in transfer programs that will, if completed, allow them to spend only two years away from home for the BA, instead of the usual four years.

The community college has grown so fast in recent years that it is now proper to speak of the community college "movement." Many of the nation's community colleges are still supervised by local boards of education. Some still use the buildings of the local high schools, and some still recruit their faculties largely from secondary school teachers. Thus, the community college in many localities has become, in its academic temper and its conciliation of local powers and felt needs, a near automatic, upward extension of high school to the thirteenth and fourteenth grades—an easy option for students who are not yet prepared to make the final decision about college or whose families cannot afford the sacrifices that going away to college might entail.

Some community colleges have been tempted to attract gifted students by expanding their programs, and almost all two-year colleges awarding the AA degree have a strong component of courses in liberal studies designed to serve the goals of general education. The development of liberal studies courses at the community college—and also at the four-year technical colleges—has been partly justified by vocational arguments. The liberal arts, for example, are supposed to teach engineers to communicate verbally with one another, thereby making them better engineers. An important consequence of liberalizing the engineer is to help make his occupation a possible career for those middle-class and upper-middle-class students whose parents have been to college and who are therefore likely to regard a little culture as a *sine qua non* of any collegiate program. Such students have traditionally taken a liberal arts degree and then gone into law or medicine or business. But as the number of students from college-educated families grows, and as the prestige of the business world falls in the better colleges, new professions must be found to supplement law and medicine as high-status pursuits. By coming to terms with culture, engineering and applied science, architecture and various forms of civil service have attempted to fill this role, hoping to combine the economic rewards of business with the intellectual appeal of science, as medicine (and law, in another sense) have long done.

One difficulty is that, as community colleges and technical colleges add liberal arts programs, the combination, although undoubtedly producing better employees and citizens, may keep out some of the traditional socially mobile recruits who believe they have no time for "cultural bull." The leaders who are at the top in business, however, insist that they prefer recruits who are at least minimally trained in the liberal arts. They do so partly because this has become a fashion, but also because they realize that the scientific revolution has outdated technical skills almost as fast as it has required them. Many employers have discovered that their technicians must be rapidly replaced by younger people who know more recent developments. Older employees must therefore be given administrative positions that require the ability to organize one's fellows instead of the material environment. Hence, the liberal arts.

At the same time, on the lower levels of businesses that put specific job descriptions in the hands of campus recruiters, the demand often remains for the graduate who has been rather narrowly trained in a single technical skill. If and when these often gauche technicians are ultimately promoted to managerial posts, many businesses find they have to retrain them, and even then they often discover that employees with a purely engineering background cope badly with administrative problems whose intricacies seem to defy purely rationalistic analysis.

Thus, although in a sense the decline of the liberal arts can be proclaimed—for the majority of undergraduate "major" programs are now career-oriented—it must be understood that these preprofessional programs conceal much study that has only indirect relevance to the students' future work. In fact, if the academic training of influential Americans in 1900 and 1979 were examined, it would probably be discovered that today's elite spends far more time studying at least nominally liberal subjects. To be sure, many more would also have had vocational training, but it seems paradoxical to assume, as many humanists do, that liberal subjects are worse off when students study engineering than when they leave school after the eighth grade or after high school. It is true enough, however, that few American institutions can claim academic purity. That colleges must serve many masters offends those who want institutions to serve a single clear-cut purpose and who perhaps correctly fear that what they most deeply care about cannot survive in pluralistic competition.

Religious Interests.   Although the direct influence of Protestant and Catholic religious bodies over the religious schools has weakened considerably in the last two decades, there are still, today, many church-related colleges scattered across the country. The Catholics arrived late in the college-founding business, but they have now nearly caught up with the Protestants. Although the Catholics are theologically more uniform than the Protestants, competition and jealousy among their various Orders have resembled the rivalry among Protestant sects and have contributed in the same way to the multiplication of the Church's colleges. Contrary to popular opinion, there has been no comprehensive plan for Catholic education in America, and many colleges have no better reason for existence than, let us say, the desire of Franciscan Fathers not to let the Jesuits capture all of the talented youngsters, or perhaps the conviction of the Dominican Sisters that the local Sacred Heart College is snobbish or intellectually radical.

The ties of the major Protestant denominations to their colleges have become increasingly attenuated, and subventions from the churches, although still of great importance especially in the small institutions of the south, seem less and less able to assure solvency. No less important, the merger of Americans into a kind of ecumenical Protestantism, impatient of sectarian distinctions, has lessened the monopolistic position of any given Methodist, Presbyterian, Baptist, or other college over a particular flock. Such monopolies survive only in the more other-worldly sects, such as the Adventists. The more worldly religious colleges increasingly compete for the same students and endowments as nonsectarian institutions. Often they can be distinguished from the latter only by a scheduled chapel service during the school day (at which attendance is optional), a few ministers on the Board of Trustees, and a tenuous connection with a mission college in the Middle East or Africa.

Whatever the osmotic pressure of the Congregational tradition at Oberlin, the Episcopalian at Denyon, the Quaker at Swarthmore or Bryn Mawr, for all practical purposes these and similar colleges live today in the secular world of the private institutions, seeking good students and faculty from everywhere, people with every shade of belief and unbelief.

Comparable forces have been at work on Catholic education; most of the Catholic colleges *have* become secularized, but not in the same way as so many of the Protestant-founded ones have done. Catholic higher education (like Catholicism generally) copes with secularization by incorporating parts of it. Thus, the architecture of Catholic colleges, where they are not the converted mansions of the once-rich, is generally meant to be imposing rather than ascetic—even though it is about as tasteless and imitative as American collegiate architecture generally. What is striking here as elsewhere is the historical ability of Catholicism to expand and to hold within its orbits such conflicting departures and desires. Changes in Catholic higher education during the last decade have been rapid and changes in patterns of governance have been fundamental; yet the long-run future remains opaque. With the possible exception of the Mormons, who have brought to higher education the same enormous communal zeal as to other activities in the state of Utah, no religiously oriented culture has so far managed to grapple with modern industrial society in the United States in a way that is satisfactory to the most sensitive and talented. The campuses where religious interests seem most intensely intellectual (as distinquished from devotional) are often the secular ones where Tillich and Niebuhr, Berdayev and Barth and Buber, Bernanos and Father Darcy, are read and discussed.

While there are some residually traditional Catholic campuses where the very presence of Churchly religion may somewhat minimize the search for personal insight, there are many others where that search individually or in more or less Pentacostal groups, resembles that of the religious concerns of more liberal Protestants and Catholics today in the society at large. Many lukewarm Protestants, like many lukewarm Jews, discover in secular colleges that their sect is a remarkable historical and intellectual achievement that can provide a frame of orientation, if not devotion.

Geographic Interest Groups. Geographic and religious interests have sometimes worked together in generating new colleges. Thus, when the Connecticut ministers founded Yale, religion was only the symptom of a broader difference and jealousy between Massachusetts and Connecticut. Likewise, when the Amherst divines revolted against Unitarianism a century later, they may have succeeded less because of their theological orthodoxy than because they represented the underprivileged western half of Massachusetts against the dominant Bostonians.

In general, however, the provinces are becoming more cosmopolitan, and so are their colleges. In many Midwestern colleges the cadre of self-conscious intellectuals among students, usually said to come from "New York," is growing in both numbers and influence. We have developed a national market for college recruiting. From all directions students are solicited who would once automatically have attended either the nearest denominational institution, their parents' school, or the state university. And, as this process robs the local institutions of their presumptive customers, they in turn are forced to expand their orbits of recruiting to a regional if not national scale. Just as many local brands of food have given way to the chain-store brands, so students everywhere are gradually becoming conscious of the fact that they might apply equally to Cornell, MIT, Harvard, Michigan, Stanford, Oberlin, or Haverford.

Feminine Interest Groups.   Although Oberlin admitted women in 1837, three years after its founding, and although the University of Iowa and Cornell also did so quite early, throughout the nineteenth century women's higher education continued to be regarded by many in both sexes as debilitating to mind and body. Today, women are the most numerous minority seeking higher education.

Only in the intellectually laggard institutions has the notion that women are the "opposite" sex led to an effort to create an equally opposite form of education. In some of the Southern women's colleges this has meant an emphasis on social skills and gracious living, and in some of the Catholic women's colleges a similiar emphasis on "learning to live together" is sometimes still evident. Until the recent advent of the women's liberation movement, the only kind of program that could have been conceived as "women's studies" was the major in home economics, which, indeed, could (and often did) become highly scientized and difficult—a kind of "women's engineering" program.

More recent developments, under the influence of "affirmative action" programs which have been set up to end discrimination against women and members of ethnic minority groups, have included the burgeoning of "women's studies" programs. But here, too, as in the case of Catholic higher education, the long-run future remains opaque.

Professionalism in College.   The interest groups described help shape higher education in America. Few groups have been happy with the compromises they have had to make for the survival of a college, and still fewer have been pleased to discover that, having labored together, they bring forth progeny with a life of their own. Once a college is established, those nominally in charge become more interested in the college's survival than in the welfare and contentment of the interest groups that fathered it. Metaphorically, a college gradually comes to have more respect for its peer group of other colleges than for the public that stands *in loco parentis*. The academic profession itself gradually becomes the dominant though never the sole voice in the operation of the college.

In theory this professionalization is wholly praiseworthy, for if academicians are truly professional educators, they presumably are able to serve the interests of competing interest groups better than these groups serve themselves. The difficulty, however, is that there is no such profession of higher education. The only aspect of college life that has been professionalized is research; professional scholars are often only trained as educators while they are on the job and do not consider this their principal function. They are economists or literary historians or biologists first, and teachers only second.

To be sure, there are professionally committed teachers dedicated to producing the right kind of alumni rather than to the equally important but difficult task to "pushing back the frontiers of knowledge." But there are no graduate schools that offer an academic equivalent to the clinical years in medical schol. There are no professional standards governing classroom activities comparable to the standards governing research work. There is no effort at evaluation of teachers by outsiders comparable to the evaluation of research. There are hardly any graduate schools that make a serious effort to induct graduate students into teaching, in contrast to throwing them as underpaid auxiliaries into large introductory classes to sink or swim, haze or be hazed.

And of course, if the teaching situation is amateurish (if not worse), the overall operation of colleges is frequently chaotic and improvised without being truly creative. Despite efforts here and there to give some minimum of training to college administrators after their selection, the management of higher education is only now, especially in unified state systems, beginning to be professionalized. This reflects partly the envy and resentment that college faculty members, along with other Americans, share against "bureaucrats." Such disdain, unfortunately, has not prevented bureaucracy in the pejorative sense, but it has played its part in preventing professionalism.

The colleges themselves, in their relations to their customers and each other, behave like small businesses before the entry of union pressures. On a national scale, there are hardly any policies for getting the right teachers and students to the right college, and then to the right classrooms. A few private and public commissions have made notable efforts to look ahead at the prospects for higher education, but—except for the widely publicized reports of the Carnegie Commission—most faculty members are unaware of their findings. In the past ten years, a number of colleges have *planned* their future programs, though only a handful have done so on the basis of rigorous and continuous self-study.

The College as a Subculture

A college is not only an institution but also a subculture through which students pass for a few years and to which faculty and administrators are likely to dedicate their adult lives. To the extent that a college is a subculture with its own idiosyncratic customs and concerns, an anthropologist can study it in much the same way that he studies a primitive tribe or a modern community.

Of course no college is immune to outside influences, for students have parents, and many undergraduates are also married or have set up housekeeping without the formality of marriage. Furthermore, most students have had jobs, and all have future occupations. Even among the faculty, aspirations and friendships often extend beyond academia, if only because no American is immune to messages from the mass media which are frequently at odds with the ideas and attitudes that the college culture purveys.

Political Environment.   Any sizeable educational institution can be seen as a vast relocation project that upsets normal ecological expectations, disrupting typical patterns of taxation, land use, housing and local business. These competitive strains and disruptions have been one source of the frequent political attacks on the colleges, combining ideological differences with economic complaints. The latter, it should be added, are usually without realistic basis.

The leadership in a small town will often join together against the liberals and other deviants at the college and in alliance with those faculty members who, through Rotary or sports or ideological ties, have become integrated into the business-minded community of Main Street. On the other hand, the sort of small-town hegemony Veblen satarized is rare today, and open Philistinism and open Veblenism are vanishing phenomena. The environment of a college is, in a sense, a series of front organizations lying between the inner core of discipline-oriented faculty members and the outer rings of community-oriented alumni (and employers of alumni). The trustees face both ways. In the wealthier private institutions, where to be a trustee is both an honor and a considerable responsibility, the president and higher administration have an opportunity to educate the trustees as they are co-opted, and to use them as the first line of defense against outside attack as well as against insolvency.

Like any other organization faced with multiple constituencies, the colleges have set up public relations departments in an effort to control or at least moderate the image they present to their public. Naturally enough, these departments also serve to remind faculty members of the tigers—or the customers—at their gates. Public relations activities both create and stem from the increasing awareness of all university personnel (including students) that they may be watched and that a "foolish" speech or donation may bring repercussions. During the years since the student revolts of the 1960s, public relations activities have had as one of their main purposes the reversal of the anti-law-and-order image that the American university gained a decade ago.

Inevitably, the president of a university, like the president of a nation or a corporation, becomes the chief public relations officer of the enterprise—an activity that, combined with fund-raising, takes him increasingly away from the more discipline-oriented phases of his work, just as it has taken the presidents of other corporations away from their industries into negotiations with Congress and other publics. As a result, the president, deans and other ancillary nonteaching personnel often become scapegoats for faculty resentment and feelings of deprivation and insecurity.

In the graduate schools and elite colleges the faculty can look to its own outside publics for protection. The professional organizations of the various academic disciplines, the agencies that accredit colleges, and the general intellectual public all offer some support. But in some of the weaker and less prestigious institutions the academic freedom arm of the American Association of University Professors is less able to help than it should be. In church-related colleges, the relevant Protestant ministry may be either a bulwark or a fifth column, depending on the denomination, the issue and the history of previous incidents.

Social Environment.   The place of environment in studying a college, however, extends beyond geography and politics. In the broadest sense, what proves important is the range of publics from which the college recruits its faculty and student members. This depends on the impressions of the college that are current in various academic circles, among adolescents and young adults, and in the public mind generally. The brand-name imagery of a college, like that of a car, is a complex thing, and little research has been done in this area.

As competitive free enterprises, individual colleges have not been willing or able to do much in the way of explaining themselves. Their catalogues are seldom designed to help the high school student distinguish one institution from another, or tell what any of them is like. A few colleges have attempted to put useful information into the hands of applicants by such devices as supplying the high schools with scores of entering freshmen on entrance examinations. But the majority of colleges have feared that this, or any other form of honesty, would be misunderstood or misused by the applicants.

Most colleges resist consumer research not because they do not want people to know what they are like now, but because they fear that their shortcomings, if generally recognized, will become fixed in the public mind, and hence be irremediable. Most secular colleges want to change faster than the natural evolution of their constituency allows. All colleges seek the freedom to acquire new clientele even when, like Reed, their applicants are mostly the traditionally "right" ones for the college, or when, like a few of the most sought-after institutions, their admissions officers sometimes feel they could pick as well by lot as by free choice among the many highly qualified applicants. Graduates of evolving colleges often discover that their sons cannot gain admission and that "their" fraternities are now inhabited by liberals and semi-intellectuals— and that some of these new members are Jews or blacks who, by the newer liberal-intellectual college standard, may be the elite rather than the dregs.

Yet, although college officials are anxious for as much leeway as possible in picking their freshmen, they have shown very little consistency or planning as to the actual formulae used for selection. These formulae represent a compromise among pressure from alumni, faculty, parents, high schools and affirmative-action officials on campus and in federal agencies; the formulae rarely reflect any fairly empirical determination of what combination of students will best produce mutual development and learning.

The foregoing, however, are problems of surfeit, based on the success of the brand name and the attraction of students whom most colleges would be glad to have. The majority of institutions have no image whatever, other than the local coloration provided by one of the interest groups described earlier. Many institutions, especially but not exclusively the newer ones, are seen by both high school and college students as essentially similar—just plain "college." Students choose these imageless institutions because they are convenient or because they offer some half-desired occupational training, or for other unformulated reasons.

Even in the selective colleges, however, there is always a small group of intellectually well-equipped students who select themselves out after having been selected in. Frequently they want to travel or work a year, and then, confidence restored or illusions about "life" dispelled, they reenter and graduate. Certain public colleges use their freshmen year as the real basis for selection; thus, in certain state universities less than half of those who begin the year finish it. Some of these dropouts certainly find other colleges that will allow them to earn a BA. Others probably transfer to a community college and settle for the AA. Still others may join the ranks of the academically fed-up, raw material for the forces of anti-intellectualism and political reaction or social "privatism." Whether such people resent a college more if they flunk out or drop out voluntarily than if they are refused admission is not known, and their overall impact on the social environment is equally difficult to appraise. Furthermore, if the behavior of many alumni is any index, there are numerous degree holders who feel as bitter about their college as one would expect the rejects and dropouts to feel.

Some Evolutionary Approaches

The mere fact that colleges themselves believe in evolution and play follow-the-leader makes an evolutionary perspective relevant. In a culture so "linear," metrical, and evaluative as that in the United States, it is understandable that academic institutions should seek to rank themselves along some scale, just as developing countries now tend to do.

Economic Hierarchies. Like tribes that depend on hunting and gathering, there are hundreds of colleges and universities that are struggling to survive without adequate means of support, scrounging for private gifts or public appropriations while staving off creditors with promises, gaining subsidies from an ill-paid faculty who, in a period of job scarcity in the academic world, are unable to find jobs elsewhere. At the other extreme, the prestigious institutions have undergone what might be called the academic revolution, which introduces them to the affluent world of foundations, expense accounts, teaching assistants, private faculty offices, secretaries, and other luxury items. Even these, however, must make annual struggles to balance the income from tuition, taxes and philanthropy against the outgo for buildings, professors and the ever-rising costs for the myriad services that support the educational process.

Among public institutions, taxes are the most important source of revenue. These institutions also seek support for research from government agencies and foundations, but only a few, such as Berkeley, Minnesota and Michigan, have produced alumni who are generous with buildings, professorships and the like. Among the accredited private colleges, tax money may play a minor role, whereas tuition and philanthropy provide the main support. In practice, of course, the difference is less than it appears, for legislatures in many ways resemble recalcitrant philanthropists, and public institutions must cajole the reluctant lawmaker with the same coyness that private colleges exhibit in courting their alumni.

A crucial difference between public and private institutions is that the public institution knows a few hundred people it must court, whereas the private institution has thousands of potential benefactors and only a few dozen actual ones. In the legislature, on the other hand, every vote counts for one, despite the tendency of crucial men, and the lobbyists around them, to make or break the annual budget.

In general, colleges are divided into the "haves" and the "have nots." The "haves" attract able applicants and make them feel that attending college will in large measure be responsible for their future success. As a result, their alumni are likely to be both successful and nostalgic, and to be generous with Alma Mater, either as donors or legislators. Moreover, such alumni tend to gravitate to positions where they can ask mutual favors of one another on behalf of educational or other philanthropic goals. In this, as in all respects, the majority of "have not" colleges are caught like the "have not" countries in self-perpetuating poverty. Unable to attract gifted students or high-calibre teachers in large numbers, they can seldom produce alumni or research that would bring solvency. Instead, they breed an atmosphere of mediocrity in which the talented minority feel alienated from their college. Nevertheless, since self-made men in America are often not ashamed of the fact, one or two graduates who do succeed in the world may come to the rescue of their Alma Mater, putting it, along with themselves, on the map.

Organizational Hierarchies. In college as in other societies, however, the evolutionary scale is more than a matter of economics. It is also a matter of social organization. There are perhaps a dozen huge graduate universities, primarily concerned with research and the training of researchers, which play the same role in the academic world that the metropolises play in the American nation. These universities shape and are shaped by the various academic disciplines, just as the metropolises shape and are shaped by various industries. Both universities and metropolises look largely to one another rather than to the provinces for examples of what can be done next. It is even tempting to make specific analogies between the private monoliths (Chicago, Columbia, Cornell, Harvard, Pennsylvania, and Stanford) and the older centers of commerce, or to compare the public superstates (Berkeley, Indiana, Michigan, Minnesota, Illinois, Texas, UCLA, Wisconsin) to newer industrial complexes. These institutions produce the most influential PhDs and most of the research, and they have most of the surplus money that can be directed into experimentation and luxury.

Similar in name only to these national research universities, the regional universities, both public and private, produce many MAs and an increasing but still small number of PhDs. They are really indistinguishable from perhaps 200 or more "complex colleges" that have a whole variety of preprofessional undergraduate programs to supplement their liberal arts divisions. Many of these institutions also have substantial numbers of graduate students—mostly terminal MAs. Often, however, they will let go from the teaching staff an MA who is a good teacher in favor of a PhD who is an indifferent or vindictive one, because the doctorate looks better in the catalogue if not in the classroom.

Furthermore, since the more ambitious institutions want not only PhD holders but also professors who will become widely known beyond their classrooms, there has developed a kind of arms race, in which one or two showpiece departments are built up to do nationally known work, subsidized where possible by foundation or government money. Such symbols often conceal the lack of supporting resources, or infrastructure, that might be used to solve the problems of the students or the local community instead of the problems scheduled by the national disciplines.

By the same token, the faculty acquired for this showpiece purpose comes from outside the community and remains loyal to the discipline rather than to the institution. Their readiness to pack up and move on to a better department may stimulate improvement of their present institution, or it may merely give them a temporarily privileged status at the expense of less mobile faculty. The conflicts that ensue between itinerants and home-guarders bear some resemblance to the struggles in many middle-sized cities between the itinerant executives brought in by national corporations and the traditional local elite.

To attract scholars and enter the big league, an institution needs not only research money but also graduate students. Imported scholars want graduate students as research assistants and apprentice-colleagues. These graduate students are often used to grade, test and instruct the undergraduates face-to-face, thus saving the professor's time and protecting him from having to confront often stultifying indifference to his academic interests.

By working for nominal wages these teaching assistants also help to subsidize their professors; they provide one of the means whereby the college can keep a balanced budget while paying decent wages and giving relatively light teaching loads to the top-rung scholars. By acquiring its own graduate students, furthermore, a university may eventually save itself money in another way, for these students will come to regard the school as "their" university and may not follow the pattern, set by professors trained elsewhere, of leaving whenever a better salary or department is offered.

The majority of American colleges are still too far from the world of scholarship to worry about such problems—just as the majority of towns are still too far from being wholly industrialized to worry about city planning. They are provincial and often unspecialized, with teachers handling aspects of their discipline (or even related disciplines) with which they do not feel completely at ease, and with students usually taking a fairly limited repertoire of general courses plus some preprofessional training. Very often, these colleges will resemble one-industry towns, relying on a single well-known program (in teacher training, for example) to carry the college both economically and otherwise. When such resources vanish, as sometimes happens in both colleges and towns, the college may fail unless enterprising leadership can quickly generate alternative sources of students, funds and respect.

Subcultural Pressures. There are some important differences between the institution-oriented and the discipline-oriented faculty member. If the professor is an alumnus of the college where he teaches, he may feel a special loyalty to it. This may engender parochialism, but it may also produce a concern for the problems of his institution, instead of merely his department.

The administration is also likely to play a critical role in evolving the college toward university status and thus toward the destruction of administrative initiative at the hands of a powerful and contemptuous group of scholars. Despite this situation, college presidents are familiar with the social and economic advantages of the next upward stage of evolution and, unlike many of the faculty, are committed to their particular institution. Even when the president or dean hopes to move to a bigger college, he knows that his best maneuver is to make his present institution as prosperous as possible and thus get a reputation as a builder.

In many situations, the administration has little room for maneuver when faced by faculty organized into departments, highly tenured, and in an increasing number of institutions, protected by collective bargaining contracts which remove the power from both administrators and senior faculty and locate it in negotiations between the hired gun of the union and the hired gun of the institution or the state system of which it is a part. Looking for leeway in such situations, administrators have sometimes made use of students as a counterfoil vis-a-vis entrenched faculty, although it has been difficult to persuade students that the administration is their ally, rather than to look on "management" with a contempt characteristic of many professors. Shrewd administrators can thus play students off against faculty, although students who can "vote" with their feet and with their span of attention, often have the last word.

The students also determine the rate of evolution toward university status—or the next step upward in the hierarchy—by forming various subcultures which produce different kinds of alumni and different public images. Up until the last decade, very little effort had been made to map these subcultures or to channel students into the ones that seem most likely to encourage growth and productivity, as opposed to failure and departure. A few colleges have elaborate and self-revealing admissions forms that make possible highly individuated initial guidance of students, assigning them to advisors and roommates in a genuine effort to create optimal matchings. Others ask entering students in a very off-hand way to say what "types" they will and will not accept as roommates. Still others assign roommates and freshman advisors on a random basis, despite the often crucial nature of these decisions for the individual's career in college. In freshman orientation week, such places ask neophytes to "buy" a variety of courses, sports and extracurricular activities—a procedure often more like a country fair than a serious introduction to an intellectual or even social community.

In the larger institutions, such decisions as whether to take athletics seriously, whether to join this or that student organization, and what field to major in are made on the basis of the networks of the peer culture. Few large colleges have done much to bridge the gaps, caused by age and occupation, that prevent faculty members from doing a great deal to understand, let alone influence, the choices college students make. A few colleges have tried to make their advising systems more effective by mixing resident graduate students with freshmen. Most colleges have also sought to provide students with ancillary psychiatric guidance and to make advice from this quarter seem unthreatening and "normal." Although these efforts reflect sympathetic concern for the casualties attracted to or created by higher education, the psychiatric services can also become a center for obtaining a fuller understanding of basic dissatisfaction with the overall pattern of college life—dislike for impersonality, suspicion of alienated learning and so on. Not all the evolution that occurs in the collegiate world needs to be blind.

But evolution can, so to speak, be overdirected, and at some colleges with extensive personnel services, students may be well advised to avoid the guidance department. In an effort to help students make only right choices of department or occupation, it is possible simply to confirm existing tendencies both in the students and in the institutions to which they are sent. Yet it is only by allowing students to make apparently wrong choices that a college can encourage them to change, becoming something they are not, instead of confirming themselves as they are.

Only a few advisers have the gift of helping students discover their potential rather than their visible abilities, encouraging them to try things at which they now look inept but may do well. Yet many students who have chosen a college for the wrong reasons profit immensely from their blunders, and many whom any judicious adviser would have told not to study physics, or not to enter the law, have been so changed by the experiences of entering these fields that they become immensely successful. As a result, they may even have helped change what law is, and what physics is, and hence recruitment to these fields in the future. Yet some of the enormous suffering that is the uncreative price of occasional anarchy might be alleviated if choices were less irrevocable.

There is much unnecessary suffering and misdirection of effort that colleges, like all other human institutions, can bring about. However, there are many students who are able to ride their college to their own destination relatively unaffected by such of its purposes that were not theirs. There are students in every college who pursue their interests because they are talented enough and tough or pliable enough to do so. By the same token, whatever the deficiencies of higher education as an organized system, these scarcely excuse students' lack of ingenuity and their readiness to assume that their own actions could not possibly make any difference. Given the chaos and confusion of purposes, the cross pressures from customers, the mixed motives of faculty members and administrators, the very idea that American colleges and universities form a "system" needs to be clarified. American higher education has been analyzed by recent observers as a complex system. But this is not because there is a plan behind it; there are only osmotic pressures that bear unevenly throughout the landscape, and models that are imitated at different levels of excellence and ambition.

These are some of the gaps separating the ideals of higher education from the institutional practices, but the ideals have their own weight and an individual dedicated to them can exert enormous leverage if he wishes. He can still more easily resist current pressures by creating a niche or enclave for himself. Periods of reformation in higher education can always succeed periods of acquiescence.

II
Students as Consumers of Higher Education

Many goods and services in America are bought by consumers on the basis of an image that is often far from reality. In the case of the American college, the image presented to the potential consumer is largely mythological. Descriptions in college "literature" sent to prospective students do little to reveal—indeed, they actually hide—the many differences between one institution and another. For students and their parents, to find the right school is, even under the best of circumstances, a difficult task; under present conditions, a good choice is often simply a matter of good luck. The four chapters of Part Two comment on different facets of the frequently poor "fit" between the characteristics of the students and the educational programs of the colleges.

In Chapter 5, "The Diverse College Student Population," T. R. McConnell, Paul Heist, and Joseph Axelrod document the impressive diversity of American college students. There are striking differences among institutions with respect to the students they attract, and there is a wide range of difference among entering students at each institution with respect to various educationally significant characteristics.

McConnell, Heist, and Axelrod emphasize the relevance of characteristics present in the entering freshman to performance in college and to achievement of educational goals. Their findings underline a basic problem in American higher education: more attention must be devoted to discovering ways to make a better "fit" between student and college.

Joshua Fishman, in Chapter 6, "Student Selection and Guidance," follows the same line of reasoning and is impelled by the same motive— improving the quality of education offered by each college for its consumers. Fishman criticizes conventional selection practices and proposes a different approach based on new theoretical foundations. He calls for a moratorium on prediction of the usual sort by admissions officers and suggests, in its stead, studies of how college environments might be arranged so that academic predictions based on individual potential and achievement can come true.

One of the major goals of college programs is to prepare the student for the world of work. The last two essays of Part Two deal with several aspects of this function of the American college and its success—or lack of it—in meeting this need in the consumers of its product.

One would suppose that when students choose their fields of concentration, they would do so mainly on the basis of careful investigation and a considered judgment concerning how their studies might prepare them for the work they propose to do in the future. One would also suppose that their colleges would encourage and help with such investigation. But this is not the way things work out. In Chapter 7, "Fields of Study and People in Them," Carl Bereiter and Mervin B. Freedman show that motives for choosing majors are often irrational or superficial, if not entirely irrelevant.

In their investigation, Bereiter and Freedman discovered that a given scholarly "field" embraces various areas of subject matter and intellectual disciplines and that the field consequently offers a variety of roles that an individual may assume. Such different aspects of a field may have varying appeals for the individual: they may be perceived differently, evoke different attitudes, have different functions in the development of the individual personality. Experience in a discipline may thus change the individual—and in time, perhaps, the disciplines themselves may begin to undergo change.

This last observation raises a fundamental question of policy. Should a scholarly or professional discipline recruit mainly people who are likely to be well-adjusted? Or does it also need people who are likely to be less happy with the present state of the field to press for changes?

When a department recruits a student into its discipline, what responsibility does it have to present to the student—as part of his studies and not as a departmental public relations effort—an accurate picture of the occupations to which the specialization leads? In Chapter 8, "The Career Has Its Shadow," David C. Beardslee and Donald D. O'Dowd show that students have much the same stereotypes in their notions about occupations as do other educated people in our society, and little happens in college to alter this way of thinking among students. Moreover, the findings of their investigation show that most students, in their thinking about vocations, are much less concerned with the work they will do than about the "lifestyle" they will be living. Beardslee and O'Dowd describe in some detail the images that students have of the lifestyles of people in different occupations.

It is clear from the last two essays in Part Two that the young person's chances of making a happy choice of vocation—happy for him and for society—can be greatly increased by giving him fuller information about the realities of the alternatives and also by reducing the insecurity and emotional stress that tend to dominate his thinking. This process needs to take place systematically, not by chance. Lower-division programs in four-year institutions, as well as the programs of community colleges, must discover how to perform this task better than it is currently being done.

5

The Diverse College Student Population

T. R. McConnell

Paul Heist

Joseph Axelrod

The greatly increased interest during recent decades in the expanding variety of college students and their total development may be traced to the growth of the behavioral sciences, particularly sociology and psychology, and the cross-fertilization of these two disciplines. Two other factors have also contributed to the interest in development per se: the expansion of student personnel programs—with emphasis on the emotional, social and cultural elements that influence academic achievement—and a broader conception of education that became widespread in the 1960s and encompassed not only academic achievement but also emotional and social development as a desirable end in itself. The influx of new students from diverse backgrounds has given impetus to searching and expanded considerations of educational values and objectives, to the differences in the educability of students who vary widely in interests, motives, dispositions and abilities, and to the possibility of attaining a better "fit" between students and institutions. The often-asked question of the late 1950s, "Who should go to college?," was changed in the 1960s to "Who should go where and for what?"

This overall shift in point of view and concerns was a long time in coming. Not until the mid-1950s was much attention given to this new concept that the characteristics of the student body represented important contributing determinants in the atmosphere of a college and its educational effectiveness. In the early 1950s, in fact, two important studies, investigating differences among colleges and universities in the production of future scientists and scholars, placed more emphasis on the influence of the college (faculty and curriculum) than on the quality and orientation of the students it attracted.[1] Later studies, however, showed that there is a relationship between the type and quality of students and the institutions in which they enroll as well as a relationship between students and their academic success and pursuits.[2] It was then that researchers began to turn to the interaction between student characteristics and the social-psychological dynamics of college environments (and/or subcultures) to examine the productivity of graduates and earlier phenomena of personal development during the college years.

In the later 1950s, the staff at the Center for Research and Development in Higher Education at the University of California, Berkeley, began to conduct extensive studies of the composition of student bodies and of the differential selectivity of particular colleges and universities and whole groups of institutions. An underlying premise in these investigations was that certain student attri-

---

[1]Knapp, R. H., and Goodrich, H. B. *Origins of American Scientists.* Chicago: University of Chicago Press, 1952; Knapp, R. H., and Greenbaum, J. J. *The Younger American Scholar.* Chicago: University of Chicago Press, 1953.

[2]Holland, J. L. "Undergraduate Origins of American Scientists." *Science,* 126, 1957, pp. 433-437; McConnell, T. R., and Heist, P. A. "Do Students Make the College?" *College and University,* 34 (4), 1959, pp. 442-452; Heist, P. A., McConnell, T. R., *et al.* "Personality and Scholarship." *Science,* 133 (3450), 1961, pp. 362-367.

butes in addition to measured ability—social and cultural background, personality characteristics, attitudes, interests and goals, for instance—are important determinants of general institutional climate, peer cultures and subcultures and the final educational "product."

Institutions and the Students Who Enroll

The findings in these studies raised four sets of provocative questions. The final answers to some of these questions are still being worked out, and the answers to some of the others will always remain conjectural.

The first set of questions was concerned with the great diversity within the student populations of most campuses. Findings in one Center study showed that the diversity within the majority of student bodies was as striking as the diversity among institutions. In over eighty-five percent of the schools in the sample, the difference between the lowest and the highest ACE scores found among entering students was as great as eighty percentile points. As a conservative estimate, it would be safe to say that the teachers in the great majority of colleges were facing classes where the intelligence quotients of the students varied by more than fifty percentile points.

Some leaders in higher education have favored the general policy that some institutions, to maintain their special qualities, should select their students from a narrow range of measured aptitude. Such attenuated distribution presumably would stimulate students from every level of ability to fulfill their potentials more completely than they would in diverse student bodies. However, only a small number of highly selective colleges are, or can afford to be, relatively homogeneous in student ability, and the matching of students and institutions within various limited ranges, even if it was desirable, would be difficult to carry out. A number of relevant questions must therefore be considered: Is it more desirable to have a narrow range of ability among students or to have enough students of high ability to stimulate each other? What is the effect on the motivation of students when those of high ability have to compete with other students equally capable, or nearly so, and a number of them just adjust to getting C's when in high school they received mostly A's? At the same time, what is the effect on the motivation of students when they find themselves mentally outclassed by most other students in their college?

A second set of questions revolves around another issue in student selection. Institutions whose student bodies have relatively low-ability mean scores generally enroll a proportion of students who score above national norms and a few students of exceptional ability. Should the exceptional students be advised to enter a more selective institution initially or should they be advised, after a semester or two, to transfer to another college? If the presence of exceptional students in a student body of below-average ability represents a mismating of students and institution, are there any means of avoiding such a poor "fit"? Is the stimulus offered by a small proportion of students with high ability—supposing that they perform reasonably well in an environment with low general demands—sufficiently valuable to the less-able students and to the faculty to justify admitting them and keeping them?

A third set of questions concerns criteria other than scholastic aptitude. If an institution chooses to be highly selective on the basis of scholastic aptitude, should it be similarly selective on other grounds, such as social and cultural backgrounds, the *kind* of intellect or cognitive style a student has (theoretical or empirical, for instance), attitudes, and values? More particularly, would students whose interests and values are mostly practical and utilitarian in nature fare well and succeed in a student body pervaded by those who are free-thinking and liberal, assuming that the scholastic aptitude scores of the practical students were adequate or more than adequate? Alternatively, would students who are intellectually and socially unconventional perform successfully at a college where the majority of students were drawn from a conservative religious denomination?

A fourth category of questions revolves around another issue: What kind of student "mix" involving a variety of backgrounds and behavioral characteristics would be most productive for students with particular *patterns* of interests, abilities, attitudes, values, emotional histories and social backgrounds (for example, the pattern or syndrome of potential creativity or the syndrome of contemplation and introspection)?

Diversity in Nonintellective Characteristics

The last two sets of questions suggest that institutions are differentially selective or attractive, not only on a criterion of academic ability, but also in the area of interests, values, attitudes, intellectual dispositions and social backgrounds. In this section attention is focused on three groups of such nonintellectual factors: vocational interests, student attitudes and opinions on social and religious matters and personal characteristics. The intent of the presentation is to introduce relevant concerns and raise appropriate questions.

Variation in the Vocational Interests of Students. The distribution of vocational interests and vocational interest patterns among individuals is conceivably a product of such influences as the interests of parents, the economic and cultural level of the home, sex and sex-role expectations, previous social and intellectual experiences and the individual personality. With such variation in the pattern of determining factors, one might well expect the scores on measures of specific interests to be distributed normally in any group drawn at random in our society. But such normal distribution would not be expected in the scores of student bodies of specific colleges or universities, and it is much less likely to occur in those of students in a particular major program. In fact, large proportions of students are found in certain curricular fields who exhibit similar and distinctive interests. The interest patterns of the majority of students in business, for example, are amazingly similar, and they are quite different from those of students in the theoretical sciences or the humanities.

The substance of the research on measured vocational interests suggests that this aspect of human behavior is a sufficiently potent differential to be regularly employed in analyzing the composition of student bodies (or subgroups on particular campuses) or in attempting to infer the variety and intensity of student motivation. Students who possess certain interests are more suited for some curricula than for others, as student personnel workers have long argued, and it is true that the particular interests of individuals give them a greater "readiness" for some institutions than for others.

Diversity in Attitudes.   How diverse are expressed attitudes at the time of entrance to college? Are such differences among the student bodies of various institutions commensurate to the differences in their interests and aptitudes? Are there identifiable subgroups representing certain attitudinal sets in the more generally diverse attitudinal climate of a large, complex institution? To what extent do those who choose various academic majors differ in attitudes and opinions?

The data collected in a variety of studies strongly support the conclusion that a national "norm" of attitudes and values seems to prevail across the gamut of colleges and universities. The diversity that is discernible among institutions and groups of institutions seems to be obscured by the great similarity of student thinking from campus to campus. It is important to observe, however, that the data typically offered by institutional research offices generally give no clues concerning the existence or size of subgroups on the campuses. The heterogeneity of religious attitudes within the student body on any one campus, or the existence of vocal minority groups, may give sufficient color to the student culture to disguise the beliefs of the majority.

In the light of the presumed or apparent diversity among the institutions, it is surprising that the differences in the orientations of the students are not greater. Even allowing for the fact that there are several fairly distinctive exceptions, it is still difficult for an observer to distinguish one student body from another, as far as the expressed attitudes and beliefs of most students are concerned. However, there is evidence to indicate that there are differences among institutions in the absence or presence of identifiable subgroups with certain sets of attitudes.

Variations in Personality Characteristics.   Most people would probably agree that attitudes, interests, aptitudes and values can legitimately be viewed as aspects of personality. The term "personality," however, is also used to describe a core pattern of orientation and a type of measured behavior that tends to influence a good deal of that individual's other behavior. For example, the authoritarian syndrome may be expected to influence in significant degree much of a person's thinking, many of that person's specific attitudes, and that person's relationships with other people. Consequently, dif-

ferences of this type may in many instances be as potent educational "determiners" as academic aptitude and previous academic
achievement.

The Center for Research and Development in Higher Education
at Berkeley engaged in a series of studies of changes in students at
precisely this deeper level. These investigations have yielded considerable evidence that higher education has failed to touch the
pervasive elements of character, personality and intellect in young
people.[3] The findings of these studies support some earlier conclusions,[4] thus casting strong doubt on the accomplishments of
American colleges in encouraging students to appraise, and perhaps to alter, their social and psychological behavior patterns. This
observation brings into focus the basic relationship between student change and institutional goals, addressed in the following
section.

Divergent Institutional Goals:
Encouraging Change or Preventing It

In every era of American higher education, including our own,
the majority of parents and the society at large have feared certain
kinds of change. In recent years, many—perhaps most—parents
have become deeply perturbed when college students have questioned accepted moral standards and challenged the values and
practices of an acquisitive society—when, for example, they de-
nounced the Vietnam war and the alliance between industry, the
military services and the universities. Many parents have expected
educational institutions to confirm, not to criticize, the values which
family and social class have inculcated; they have valued schools
and colleges more as a means of occupational training and social
mobility than as instruments for modifying beliefs or altering social
structures.

---

[3]For supporting data, see McConnell, T. R. "Do Colleges Affect Student Val-
ues?"*Change*, 9, March 1972, pp. 63-64; and Clark, B. R., Heist, P.A., McConnell,
T. R., *et al. Students and Colleges: Interaction and Change.* Berkeley: Center for
Research and Development in Higher Education, University of California, 1972.

[4]Jacob, P. E. *Changing Values in College.* New Haven: The Edward W. Hazen
Foundation, 1956.

Changes in personal characteristics arising from the interaction of students and institutions have been interpreted by Feldman and Newcomb as anchoring, accentuation or conversion effects.[5] On first thought, it might seem that a college may be considered to have influenced its students only when it has changed their characteristics. However, the protections of original orientations against change may be an important effect, and in numerous colleges this may be a deliberate institutional objective.

Accentuation seems to be the principle effect among many colleges that strive to attract and select students who, on admission, display the characteristics that the institutions desire in their graduates. These colleges neither accelerate nor retard student development, but serve as wombs in which the already-established course of development can take place.

Conversion is by far most likely to occur in settings where the student is initally out of joint with the more commonly held values of the campus. Such dissonance puts the student under strong pressure either to shift toward the dominant values of the campus or of one of its subcultures or to search for shelter where he can be insulated from prevailing points of view. Where the dissonance is too great, the individual may flee the scene by withdrawing. But the "misplaced" persons who stay and who do not retreat into a protective environment become possible candidates for conversion.

Optimal "Mix" in the Student Body Composition

It follows from the foregoing discussion that ideas and values take shape from challenge as well as support, from invalidation as well as confirmation. The very large campus, whose students stand in little danger of strangling homogeneity of student body composition, may not be able to provide the unity and the consistency of relationships and experience in groups small enough for teachers and students with common interests and values to find one another, to engage in vigorous intellectual and moral dialogue, to question, to dissent, to strike out in new directions and generate new ideas.

---

[5]Feldman, K. A., and Newcomb, T. M. *The Impact of College on Students*. San Francisco: Jossey-Bass, 1969, Chapter 3.

Organizationally, it should be possible to combine the best of the unity and consensus of the small liberal arts college with the pluralism and diversity of the large, complex institution. But even when that combination is established and maintained, there may be other problems. Suppose that the dominant social groups in a college cater to students from well-to-do families: Will a student from a lower-class home find himself so alienated that his well-being and his academic work are affected? The answer is probably not simple. One student from a lower-class background may perform poorly in the classroom, while another may compensate for social inferiority by devoting all of his energies to study or to athletics. What are the factors that are responsible for these differences in scholastic performance? Would the student who earned high grades, but who had little social experience, have been better off—in terms of full personal development—in a college where most of the students were comparable in social and cultural background, even if the institution's stimulus had been inferior?

An individual with strong authoritarian attitudes might make better grades in a college that condoned or rewarded conformity and dependency than in one that attempted to stimulate intellectual independence and rewarded unconventional intellectual behavior. But should students and colleges be so paired? One might also ask whether a student with a strong theoretical orientation should attend an engineering school where there is a decided academic emphasis of an applied and utilitarian nature. Or, another possibility: Would it be desirable for a student with the abilities, values, interests and intellectual dispositions that are fundamental to research and scholarship to attend a medical school that stresses education for these careers and that attracts many students like himself, or should he go to a school that is primarily oriented toward medical practice?

There is evidence that the climate of colleges which produce many future scientists differs from the climate of colleges which are noted for the undergraduate preparation of scholars in the humanities and the social sciences. This evidence can only lead again to a question about whether there should be a greater effort made to fit the student to the college. In a complex insitution (not necessarily large), should an effort be made to fit the student to the program or the program to the student? In attempting to solve such problems, educators would do well to view the efficacy of a particular college as the product of the fortunate conjunction of diverse factors: a stimulating curriculum, student characteristics and expectations, *and* the demands, sanctions and opportunities of the college environment and its subcultures.

6

Student Selection and Guidance

Joshua A. Fishman

Today the American secondary school and the American college frequently pursue quite separate, if not antithetical, educational principles in the selection of students. They may serve very different clienteles, different both geographically and socially. Many colleges would wish to select their freshman class from applicants all over the country (and in some cases, all over the world), with widely varying family backgrounds and cultural traditions. Those colleges that succeed in realizing their hope must pay a price, however. Applicants arrive presenting credentials for secondary schools that vary widely in scholastic content and quality. Presented with this kaleidoscope of grades, courses and curricula, American colleges rely on selection and guidance techniques that maximize descriptive impartiality but contribute little to solving the most significant problems facing administrators of admissions and guidance programs.

In spite of the wide diversity of educational experience offered at the secondary level, the most usual way of predicting college performance is to look at high school grades and scores on scholastic aptitude tests. As going to college becomes an increasingly universal American experience, more and more information has become available concerning the high schools and the communities from which college applicants come to any given college. This information permits colleges continually to refine their use of test scores and high school averages as predictors of intellectual performance in college.

This "improvement" comes about by "correcting" or weighting the high school averages and the test scores of applicants coming from particular high schools—on the basis of the college performance records of many previous applicants from the same high schools, on the basis of the records of many applicants with similar community and school characteristics, or on the basis of the records of many applicants with similar social and cultural characteristics. There is also an urge to use personality and other nonintellectual measures in addition to high school grades and aptitude-achievement test scores. So far, however, these efforts have not proved entirely successful. Why?

The Ubiquitous High School Average

To a much greater extent than is commonly realized, high school grades are influenced by relatively nonintellectual factors such as personality, adjustment and motivation. Frequently, indeed, school grades merely reveal how closely a student's personality resembles the generally preferred personality of the middle-class academic world. High school grades, like scholastic aptitude test scores, also indicate important social characteristics. As a result, the simple addition of a nonintellectual test to the selection or guidance battery does not accomplish much. The added personality test simply measures the same factors that grades measure and yields no improvement in prediction.

The same is true at college. Since college grades reveal many of the same personality and social preferences revealed by high school grades, it is scarcely surprising that high school grades should be the best predictors of college grades. What *is* surprising is that so many educators and social scientists should value grades purely for what they say about intellect.

In fact, high school grades are the summary of a life story. It is easy to forget this, but the crudity and simplicity of the index must not be allowed to mask the subtlety and complexity of real life. Through practical necessity, experimental designs must simplify nature, but the simplification must not then be permitted to substitute for reality.

An Alternative to Selection of "Safe" Students

The principle of equality of educational opportunity—and the fears and challenges its realization holds for college administrators and faculty—must not lead to an inflexible reliance on personnel selection devices to accomplish the college's ends. Even industry, which has provided the model for personnel selection, at times shows awareness that it owes something to society besides an exclusive dedication to maximizing profits—and to producing profit maximizers.

Similarly, American higher education owes something more to society than a continual pursuit of the "safest" cream that can be discovered at the secondary school level. Of course, given the great institutional and cultural diversity of America, it may be justifiable and even desirable for *some* colleges to adopt this approach exclusively. Another approach also has merit, however—one based not only on personnel selection but also on deliberately changing individuals and their educational environments. Its broadest features will be outlined here.

The Need for New Theoretical Foundations

To understand the relationship between intellectual and nonintellectual factors in student performance, and to use the latter predictively, it is necessary to identify the difference, both in behavior and environment, between high school and college. Of course there are similarities between the two settings, but these similarities, it must be remembered, are already being used to predict intellectual achievement; this is simply the same as saying that college admissions officers assess applicants at least partly on high school performance.

Now if both the individual and the environment are the same in high school and college, no new nonintellectual predictors are needed, since (as already noted) high school grades are a composite measure of *both* intellectual attainment and nonintellectual adjustment to the environment. If, however, there *are* differences, and if these can be attributed *primarily* to changes within the students themselves (for example, impulse expression, social maturity, self-questioning, complexity of outlook and so on), separate nonintellectual predictors—that is, ways of assessment that consider the student's personal development—are needed. In the same manner, if the differences between high school and college can be attributed primarily to differences in the two *environments* per se (for example, religious auspices, coeducation, rurality-urbanity, institutional size, and so on), separate predictors that take into account institutional contrast are needed. Furthermore, where *both* developmental and environmental differences, as mentioned previously, obtain, both nonintellectual predictors and institutional predictors are called for.

It should be recognized that differences in personality and environment between high school and college may not by themselves lead to an accurate prediction of success or failure in college. There may be other factors that determine how an individual will turn out. Individual changes due to protracted illnesses, deaths, or other major dislocations in the immediate family, serious financial reverses and so on, cannot be predicted. A counterpart to such random individual change may also be discovered in the institutional setting. Membership in a jazz group (or a chess group), four out of five professors in the freshman year who are "liberals" or who use the "nondirective" instructional approach, two geniuses from New York in the tough physics course—such unforeseeable phenomena may form part of the individual's college environment. All of these can be treated only via "*post*diction" (guidance and counselling) rather than via *pre*diction. Postdiction is certainly as important as prediction (many would say it is more important) for its takes the initiative in a way that mere predicition does not. It involves helping students to change, and to plan environmental change, for the purpose of attaining desirable academic outcomes.

Educators are quite far from having sufficient knowledge of either individual or institutional differences for the purpose of effective guidance. The social psychologist's greatest contribution to education may well be to persuade those concerned with predicting absolute standards of ability to forget about it. For a while at least, it would help to think less of *level* than of *kind*—kinds of students, kinds of high school environments, kinds of college environments. Too much emphasis on prediction has entailed a rigid, absolutist view of what constitutes "ability"; what should be considered instead is how different kinds of students make different kinds of uses of different kinds of college environments.

In all likelihood there will ultimately be a return to prediction; research proclivities as well as larger social pressures will push in that direction. Nevertheless, if prediction is set aside for a while in favor of some basic theory and research, it can ultimately be returned to with greater understanding and flexibility.

7

Fields of Study and the People in Them

Carl Bereiter

Mervin B. Freedman

Among the high priority goals on almost every American campus is the institution's responsibility to help its students find specialized fields of study that suit them. Thus far, higher education research has been of little help in this overall task but some data have been gathered which show differences among student groups specializing in various fields. Group for group, college students majoring in different subjects have been found to differ psychologically with respect to three main characteristics: intelligence, liberalism of attitudes and psychological adjustment. In each instance, the ordering of groups seems to follow a consistent pattern.

Difference in Mental Ability

The average intelligence scores of students, grouped by major, regularly fall into an order with the physical sciences, engineering and mathematics at the top, followed by the humanities and social sciences, and with the applied fields, agriculture, business, home economics and education at the bottom. An obvious explanation for this ordering is that it reflects the varying intellectual difficulty of the subjects as they are usually taught at the undergraduate level. Or it may reflect the *reputation* for difficulty; the order has, in fact, been found to match closely the reputations for difficulty that these fields enjoy among undergraduates. For this reason, the average scores, although they may be of practical importance, have little theoretical significance. Any department could raise the average score of its students by raising entrance requirements or requiring a stiff "portal" course that would eliminate the dullards. It is one thing, however, to keep out the less competent students; it is quite another thing to attract those of superior intelligence. If we take this principle into consideration when we assess the attractiveness of different fields, then it seems best to ignore less intelligent students who must, of necessity, be concentrated in the easier fields. When we consider only the college graduates who rank in the upper sixty percent in general intelligence—students who would rank in the upper two-thirds of any group in the student body—what is most immediately striking is the even allocation of top talent among the various major disciplines. Fields, such as business and education, that look poor in terms of mean intelligence scores or overall distribution of scores come in for about the same share of the top students as do the more academic fields.

If we lump engineering with natural science, however, as is often done, it is evident that this field does attract a large portion of the more intelligent students—over a quarter of them. Moreover, this field is seen to attract a relatively larger portion of the top intelligence group than of the lower group, whereas the reverse is true of business and education.

There is, of course nothing in data of this sort to prove that one field is intrinsically more appealing to the intellectually able than another. Such extrinsic factors as prestige and remunerativeness, as well as the intrinsic factor of difficulty, must also be considered, although the possibility that some fields are in a very general way more intellectually challenging than others should not be summarily dismissed without further investigation.

Differences in Liberalism of Attitudes

During the past forty years the attitudes of college students toward such public issues as war, communism, labor unions and religion have frequently been measured. With some consistency, students in certain fields of study have tended toward positions that are popularly regarded as liberal, whereas students in other fields have tended toward conservative positions.

More often than not, students in social science are found to be the most liberal group. With even greater consistency, students in engineering and agriculture appear among the least liberal. Literature, arts and natural science students are usually found between these extremes, with the natural science groups tending to be less liberal than the others. Students in education are difficult to pin down. Those in secondary education tend to reflect the attitudes prevalent in their prospective teaching fields, and those in elementary and physical education tend to be among the most conservative groups.

The most conservative groups are thus all in applied studies rather than purely academic fields. One factor that may help to account for this conservatism is that these fields tend to draw students from lower social-class levels than do the academic fields. Looked at in another way, the attitudes of students in the applied fields differ from those of academic majors in the same way that attitudes of the public as a whole differ from those of college students. It seems quite reasonable to suppose that students who seek higher education mainly for some special vocational preparation should tend to resemble people in the workaday world more than do academicians.

Differences in Psychological Adjustment

Familiar academic stereotypes assign quite different personalities to such figures as the art student, the engineering student, the business student and the history student. Attempts to investigate these types by mental tests have succeeded in establishing only that there exist what for the moment might be called differences in "adequacy of psychological adjustment."

The groups reporting the most fears, worries, conflicts and the like are almost always in the literary or fine arts fields, whereas applied majors—such as engineering, business, agriculture and education—regularly show the fewest of these psychological problems. In the middle are natural science and social science students, the natural science students tending to show less disturbance than those in social science.

This order—humanities, social science, natural science, applied science—presents a hierarchy of increasingly concrete, down-to-earth content. Shall we hypothesize, then, that the more "neurotic" or complex and troubled people are drawn to intangibles or, conversely, that they are repelled by the mundane? There is evidence to support such a hypothesis. There are, however, some other aspects of the sequence of major fields also worth attending to.

To take another line of reasoning, it makes sense that a psychologically disturbed person should give some weight, in any major decision he makes, to alternatives promising relief from his disturbance. It has been found, for instance, that students who elect courses in abnormal psychology tend to be more abnormal than those who elect other kinds of psychology courses.

Fields concerned with human beings and their more human problems are certainly more directly relevant to an individual's own psychological problems. But this could be more a source of further disturbance than of alleviation. It might make more sense for the neurotic person to seek refuge from his problems in a field where they would not be brought to his attention so often. We need not delve here into all the psychological dynamics that might lead to one or the other course of action, but we should note one point that bears directly on the data.

The evidence on psychological adjustment of college students is based largely on scores on the Minnesota Multiphasic Personality Inventory and a few other tests of questionnaire type. Although these tests may have some power to unearth fairly deeply hidden disturbances, there is no denying that among reasonably normal subjects, like most students, those who are conscious of their difficulties will get worse scores than those who repress them. If so, it would make sense that those people whose adjustment depends more on repression of symptoms should tend toward impersonal fields—for example, engineering —where their repressions are in less danger of being shaken.The small differences in scores between major groups might, therefore, not really reflect differences in *amount* of disturbance at all.

Another complicating factor is that unconventional people are likely to give unconventional responses to diagnostic test items and thus obtain scores indicating the presence of psychopathology. Socially withdrawn students, likewise, may well give test responses that are scored as symptoms of psychological disturbance. Rather than consider these dimensions as indicators of *degree* of psychological adjustment, it seems more reasonable to consider them as indicators of *kind* of psychological adjustment. Thus, among conventional people, we could expect to find some for whom unconventionality represented a healthy state of affairs and some for whom it was unhealthy. The same would be true for conventional people, people who are socially outgoing, and people who are socially withdrawn.

The personality differences noted here can all be grouped into two categories. On the other hand there are the differences related to signs of psychological disturbance, unconventionality and awareness of psychological problems. These characteristics, which are hard to tell apart, all seem connected with the person's inner life—with his thoughts, emotions and impulses—and how he deals with them. The fact that choosing a field of study is related to such individual facets indicates what we would of course expect, that a person's intellectual pursuits are integrated in some way with other aspects of his inner life.

The other important category of individual differences includes such things as sociability, confidence in social situations and interest in people. It clearly centers around the person's social life. Since choice of field is also related to these kinds of attributes, we may suppose that the sort of intellectual activities a person pursues implies something about how he relates to other people, and vice versa.

The connection may be only superficial; some pursuits involve more contact with people than others, and a person's choice of field may be influenced by how much social contact he wants. Or the connection may be more profound. It might well be discovered that individuals have basic patterns of relating to things outside themselves, to people as well as to objects and ideas.

A better understanding of the way personality relates to intellectual interest would provide a sounder basis for selecting students. It would also help in counseling the individual student concerning his choice of field. We should remember, however, that guiding a student toward a field that best fits his *present* characteristics tends to preserve the status quo both in the individual and in the field he enters. Ideally, the student ought to pursue the curriculum that would produce in him the most beneficial growth, even if it meant taking a course in which he did badly and had a very trying time; but in the face of academic and social pressure to get good grades, the demands of employers that people study whatever they plan to work at, and the general "materialistic" view of education as preparation rather than as development, it is understandable that students, with the blessings of their counselors, play it safe.

8

The Career
Has Its Shadow

David C. Beardslee
Donald D. O'Dowd

Rapid change, both in higher education and in American occupational structure during the last three-quarters of a century, has greatly affected the relationship between college and career. This is dramatically illustrated by the evolving recruitment patterns of business and industry. Many observers report that until the 1930s it was common for business firms to look with suspicion on the college graduate, preferring to hire and promote people with more limited educational attainments. It is now becoming difficult for a person *without* college training, regardless of his intellectual capacities, to rise in the structure of established business concerns. Similar changes have also taken place in the professions. Engineers without college credentials have all but disappeared.

It is quite clear that college has become the gateway to professional and higher managerial status. This situation is exerting a powerful influence on the orientation of millions of young people approaching college age. Their parents, teachers, guidance counselors and the mass media are constantly impressing upon them that a college education is indispensable for achieving a respectable and satisfying status in American life. Among nonconformist young people, this principle has been called into question in recent years, but the pressure on college-age youth both from adults and from peers, in general emphasizes the vital link between occupation and status, and between occupation and upward mobility—and the simple fact that college training promises a better job. Since each career also implies a certain style of life, desirable or undesirable, it is not surprising that the student feels under considerable pressure to select an occupation early and to cling to it.

This is certainly unfortunate at the college level where many young men and women need to be prepared for generalist roles requiring a maximum of self-confidence, flexibility and originality. Ideally, a liberal arts education would provide a basis on which students whose personal integration is still weak can develop a sense of competence, master and direction that will allow them to choose wisely and not prematurely among occupational alternatives. This process of forming character through higher education is just as vital for women as for men. Women graduates should feel free either to enter careers immediately or to undertake family responsibilities with the confident belief that they can claim a place at a later time in the occupational world because of their personal talents.

The images or stereotypes of occupations that merge in the talk of college students are not always very close to the descriptions of occupations in guidance literature! They frequently do, however, bear definite resemblance to the findings of occupational sociology and psychology. These stereotypes reveal a variety of connotations about careers, each of which is associated with a certain kind of personality, a certain status and a certain style.

Stereotypes of Occupations

Occupational stereotypes provide information about how a

career places a person in the community and what kind of person would commit himself to it. Of particular importance is the marked amount of agreement among students about these nonwork features of several careers. Once a person has expressed preference for some occupation, he is assigned by others the traits—personal and social—associated with that occupation. For college opinion not only governs what one believes of the people out there in the active world, it also affects how one student reacts to another student who is now in the throes of selecting his future personal attributes. Small wonder that choosing a career involves anxiety for college students.

Our own research into these matters was designed to gain more knowledge of the images students attach to the career world. We tried to determine rather precisely how students perceive a number of high-level occupations. The investigation was expected to shed light on the ideal personality traits to which students aspire; and we also wanted to know why liberal arts students overconcentrated their choices on the *professional* occupations.

Questionnaires were administered to a random sample of freshmen and seniors at two universities—one public and one private—and at two highly selective liberal arts colleges.[1] The following vignettes summarize the statistical profiles that emerged from the analysis.

Doctor.   Medicine is rated by students as a calling richly rewarded by high social status, wealth and success. Doctors are favored with high opportunity for advancement, and they derive great personal satisfaction from their work. Male doctors, compared to men in most other occupations, can count on an unusually pretty wife and a happy home life. Doctors are perceived as realists. They approach the world responsibly and with perseverance; they are outstandingly calm, confident, and self-sufficient; and their great stability, caution and rationality are balanced by their adaptability.

---

[1] The original research concerned with stereotypes of men in these occupations. Later studies showed that essentially the same stereotypes apply to women. See O'Dowd, D.D., and Beardslee, D.C. *Development and Consistency of Student Images of Occupation,* Final report, Project 5-0858, U.S. Department of Health, Education and Welfare, ERIC Document ED-028-307.

Unlike some other kinds of practitioners in the world of science, doctors are clearly oriented to people. Although this attitude may be partially a professional concern, still the stereotype image pictures them as thoughtful and unselfish, giving of themselves to others. The doctors' cheerfulness and optimism fit well with their unfailing "human directedness." Their high intelligence appears to be more closely related to their strong, active, masterful qualities than to participation in the highest intellectual culture. No undesirable traits are attributed to doctors; all students recognize the remarkable personal and social attractiveness of their role.

Although the public image of doctors may have been somewhat affected by recent events—malpractice suits and doctor's strikes, for instance—young people may also be aware of the work that recently trained doctors (and some older ones, too) have been doing at free clinics. For these reasons, it is likely that the student stereotype of doctors that has held good for many years still holds for the late 1970's.

Lawyer. The image of the lawyer has many characteristics also attributed to the doctor, but the doctor is usually rated more favorably on traits that they have in common. Lawyers possess high social status, success and wealth. They have considerable opportunity to advance in their work, and they are outstandingly powerful in public affairs.

Lawyers are viewed as outgoing, sociable individuals who like to be with people and are at ease in the company of others. Lawyers share with doctors realistic, persevering, forceful, strong and active qualities.They are effective in the world of objects, events and people.

These characteristics are qualified, however, by a high degree of hardness and self-assertiveness. There is more than a hint of the selfish and manipulative in the lawyer, attributes wholly lacking in the doctor image. The lawyer is perceived as having high intelligence and good taste. Male lawyers are pictures as having pretty wives, but their home life is not seen as particularly happy.

The lawyer image combines most of the rewards promised by the medical profession and possesses many of the same desirable personal properties, while providing somewhat more scope for less service-oriented, less unselfish ambitions Of particular prominence is the stress placed on socialibility and access to public power.

It should be noted that the Watergate scandal, which occurred after these data were collected, might have temporarily altered somewhat the public image of the lawyer, since so many of the officials found to be corrupt were lawyers by training and profession. Nonetheless, it would seem that the long-standing stereotype has remained basically unaltered. Its ambivalent quality has become, if anything, even stronger. For every case of corruption in the legal profession that comes to the attention of today's students, there are many other examples on the other side—the Ralph Nader workers, the American Civil Liberties Union attorneys, and the lawyers working for Common Cause, to name but a few.

College Professors. A dominant feature of this image is the great stress on intellectual competence accompanied by sensitivity to artistic or aesthetic experience. Professors are seen as individuals with colorful, interesting, exciting qualities coupled with a degree of rashness, changeability, emotional difficulties and a lack of adaptability. It is quite likely that they are interesting *because* of their emotional, unpredictable natures.

In spite of these characteristics and a high score on radicalism, they are granted considerable power in public affairs. Students deem the professor a valuable man, and they see in his role a source of great personal satisfaction. On the debit side, the professor is described as not well-to-do and lacking in opportunity for advancement. He does not equal the independent professionals in either social or worldly competence. Whereas the doctor and the lawyer are stable and dependable, he is changeable and unpredictable.

Intellectual qualities are the greatest asset of the college professor. Probably the most striking impression emerging from this profile is its lack of masculinity. It is predominately a volatile picture with the emphasis on intellect, sensitivity and impulsiveness—a combination of characteristics that our culture finds exceedingly non-*macho*.

Scientist. Two strong impressions are conveyed by this profile. First, the scientist is characterized by high intelligence dissociated from artistic concerns and sensitivities. This cool intelligence is linked with strong individualism in personal and political realms. Second, there is a clear lack of interest in people. A good deal of self-control is implied by the description of the scientist as self-sufficient, rational, persevering and emotionally stable. Scientists are seen as having power in public affairs; they are rated only moderately responsible; and they are pictured as quite radical. This suggests that uncertainty about the motives and trustworthiness of the scientist, an uncertainty observed in younger people by other investigators, lingers on in college students.

The personal life of the scientist is thought to be quite shallow. In the student image of the married male scientist, his wife is not perceived as pretty nor is his home life thought to be very happy. But he is rewarded by great personal satisfaction, considerable success, and reasonable opportunity for advancement. Furthermore, he enjoys moderate wealth and social status.

Scientists are cool, self-controlled individuals. They are competent in organizing the world of things, but they are disdainful of the world of people. Materially better rewarded than college professors, scientists contrast strikingly with professors in aesthetic sensibilities and social skills.

Engineer.   Engineering is a less colorful profession for liberal arts students. Engineers are rated generally intelligent but not nearly so strong in this regard as scientists. On the other hand, they are considerably more socially adept than scientists, though no social lions.

Engineers are quite successful and reasonably wealthy, but they gain less satisfaction from their work than scientists derive from pure research. Engineers are also more conservative, and they are more likely to be conformists. Except for these important differences, the stereotype image of the engineer is almost identical with that of the scientist.

School Teacher.   In every classification of careers according to social status, school teachers are located in the second or third tier among the professions. Yet school teaching accounts for the occupational preferences and choices of a substantial percentage of college graduates.

The school-teacher image is dominated by the depressed economic state of the profession. Teachers score conspicuously low in wealth, social status and opportunity for advancement. They are perceived as having little power in public affairs. Male school teachers cannot even command attractive wives although, in the prevailing stereotype they can count on a happy home life—just the opposite of the lawyer's situation.

Teachers are considered intelligent, sensitive, and, like professors, interested in art, although to a lesser degree. Furthermore, they are attentive to people and unselfish in their relations with them. In this regard, they have a dedication to service somewhat like the doctors'. The teacher is rated low in confidence and in hard, assertive properties.

Business Executive.   Business executives are rated extremely high in social status, wealth and success. They have power in public affairs and ample opportunity for advancement. The male executive is pictured as having a very pretty wife. They are judged to be very conservative, but when this conservatism is paired with good taste, a picture of quiet elegance emerges.

They possess the sociability noted in lawyers, accompanied in both men and women executives by a confident, assertive, "masculine" manner. They are also rated strong and active, responsible and persevering. But busines executives, in the student perception, lack both the high intelligence and the hard, rational properties that make lawyers formidable figures. Executives are even less service-oriented than lawyers; they are, in fact, seen as selfish individuals. They are believed to possess a component of excitability and emotional instability—a condition related to the popular belief about executives and ulcers.

Business executives have weaknesses and personal problems that offset to some degree their wealth and status. The road to this role is not as clear or as predictable for most college students as the way to high-status occupations through the professional schools.

Accountant.   This occupation represents a lower-status business activity, perhaps comparable in some ways to the status of school teaching among the professions. The image that surrounds this field is remarkably negative. If doctors are perceived as the heroes, accountants are the antiheroes of the occupational world. They are low in status, not well-to-do and unsuccessful. They have little power in public affairs and not much opportunity for advancement. Their job is rated as the lowest of all the occupations studied in providing personal satisfaction.

Students perceive accountants as conformists, as having minimal social skills and limited intelligence, and as having inadequate personal and aesthetic sensibilities. They are pictured as passive, weak, soft, shallow, cold, submissive, unsure of themselves and evasive in meeting life. Their positive characteristics of caution, stability, conservatism and calmness rest on a shaky emotional interior. This combination is probably linked to the narrowness of their professional specialization, their mastery over such a limited field.

Students have a rather specified model in mind when they produce this wretched portrait. Accountants are apparently seen somewhat as Victorian bookkeepers, chained to their desks and ledgers, from which they have no inclination to depart for traffic with the world or contact with people. Given this description, liberal arts students may even seem to doubt whether the accountant is living flesh and blood.

Artist. On a number of scales artists stand at the end opposite to that of the doctors. The artist's noble sensitivity to matters of aesthetic importance is associated with a variety of traits reflecting violent emotions and impulsive expression. Artists are perceived as intuitive, rash, changeable, excitable, attention demanding, and at the same time, deep, interesting and colorful.

Their outstanding individualism and radicalism accompany a group of traits indicating irresponsibility and unwillingless to contribute to society in a disciplined way. They are uninterested in people and evidently unsuccessful with them. Their moods tends to be dark, depressed and pessimistic.

They only reward that they can expect for their work is a high sense of satisfaction. Neither wealth, nor status, nor any other marks of the rich, full life are associated with artists. Given this description but not told that it applied to "the artist," one might easily connect it with a teenager in the throes of adolescent problems.

Ethical standards among the diverse occupations. Interesting data, collected by George Gallup in 1976, can be added to the foregoing vignettes to complete the picture of student stereotypes of these occupations.[2] In a national survey, college students were presented with this question: "How would you rate the honesty and ethical

---

[2] Gallup, G. "Rating Politicians on Morals, Ethics," *San Francisco Chronicle,* August 23, 1976, p. 8.

standards of the people in these different fields—very high, high, average, low or very low?"

Table 1 shows the percentage of college students who answered "high" or "very high":

TABLE 1
Student Opinion of Ethical Standards
Among Diverse Occupations

Percentage responding
"high" or "very high"

College teachers 70
Medical doctors 66
Engineers 58
Journalists 49
Lawyers 40
Business contractors 21
Business executives 20
Labor union leaders 19
Political officeholders 9
Advertising practitioners 6

Occupational Aspirations and Learning

In their penetrating study of college students' values and beliefs of almost a quarter-century ago, Gillespie and Allport[3] observed that the best way to generalize the American student's goal seemed to be in terms of the search for a rich, full life. They noted further that the college student was not concerned with the political and social problems that surrounded him. He was not even concerned with philosophical or religious issues. Yankelovitch summarized his studies of the values of college youth in the seventies by noting that young people today are trying to synthesize their personal values with traditional career goals. The desire for personal self-fulfillment and the desire for a successful career are not seen as incompatible. "What we see instead is the active pursuit of a career

---

[3] Gillespie, J.M., and Allport, G. W. *Youth's Outlook on the Future*. New York: Doubleday, 1955.

as a means of self-fulfillment, with money, security and possessions included in the overall scheme, partly taken for granted, partly demanded as a matter of right, but subordinate to the main goal of finding the right life-style for expressing their psychological potential".[4]

Almost every academician will agree that this description also fits the student of the 1970s. It is interesting to observe the cycle: after the upheaval of the 1960s, in which social problems took high priority among student concerns, the values of the mid-1950s have reasserted themselves. In a profound sense, the student of today is like the student of two decades ago, involved mainly with himself and his own future.

One of the keys to this future is the occupational role that fulfills the promise of a college education. This place in the occupational system is seen by most students not as a chance to achieve great heights in work, but as an opportunity to find comfort, variety, interesting experiences, and pleasant acquaintances.[5] For students, the occupation even specifies the personal qualities of its present and future members, providing a ready-made personality for those who cannot establish a secure identity from their own experience.

It is likely that widespread agreement among students about the qualities of mind and personality associated with careers limits the *variety* of human types any high-level field can attract. In trying to encourage students to direct their talents toward fields for which they are especially suited, it should be recognized that they often will already be inclining toward other careers. To promote greater freedom of occupational choice and more efficient social utilization of abilities, two things must be done.

First, occupations promising scope to talented people must be presented on more equal terms. In this reeducation process, educators have an important part to play, as have those organizations concerned with maintaining standards in the major occupations.

---

[4] Yankelovitch, D. *The New Morality–A Profile of American Youth in the 70's.* New York: McGraw, 1974, p. 22.

[5] These values are given highest priority in student surveys made in 1975-76 at San Francisco State University and elsewhere. See *Agenda for Tomorrow: Action Today* (the report of the Presidential Long-Range Planning Commission), San Francisco State University, 1976.

Such efforts, however, will probably be limited to their effect, since the image of a career grows out of major cultural trends and receives constant reinforcement from peers, parents, teachers and mass media.

But there is a second way by which the problem may be approached. The interest that students show in careers reflects for many a lack of self-confidence. If therefore, professors can nurture in students those attributes that will strengthen their claim to an independent identity, their dependence on packaged occupational personalities can be lessened. This in turn will increase students' readiness to take a new kind of initiative, to create a place in the world of careers for their own individual talents. In all probability a self-confident youth would stir to the challenges of social and political problems—matters needing dedicated attention—in a way quite beyond the resources of insecure, self-centered young people.

A prime responsibility of education is to see that the *character* of educated individuals enables them to use the fruits of their academic experience. Accepting the concern of students with their own development and their place in the future, it may be possible to use this very concern to engage their energies. Students attach great importance to the growth aspects of their personalities. If their education is organized so as to develop their personal powers, they will grasp its significance and gain a degree of personal autonomy. For example, it is becoming increasingly clear that in every field of endeavor requiring a college education, new skills and concepts must constantly be learned by an alert adult. An education that succeeds in giving adults confidence and flexibility in the face of new learning situations will involve them and equip them for excellence in whatever they are called on to do.

III
Personal Development and the College Experience

How much of what happens to students during the college years—changes in their character, attitudes and values, mental abilities and total personality— are attributable to campus experiences, both curricular and extracurricular? Would the pattern of personal growth have been substantially different if the individual had not attended college? Can the campus factors fostering development in students be identified? If so, are they elements over which faculty members and administrators have control? And if this is so, is it possible to plan these factors—that is, arrange them for maximum effectiveness? Or is the cause-and-effect pattern in the case of each student's development so much a matter of chance and accident that rigorous planning of experiences is a waste of time? Moreover, if changes do take place during the college years, do their effects erode during the immediate postcollege years or are the efforts of the experience more lasting?

Higher education research is not as yet able to answer such questions with any completeness, but scholars in the field have discovered major clues to some of the answers. The four chapters of Part Three show what some of these clues are.

Part Three opens with a personality analysis of the entering freshman, asking what developmental tasks he must learn to perform. It closes with studies of alumni, asking whether the college experience has had any lasting effects.

In Chapter 9, "Freshman Personality: A Stage in Human Development," Nevitt Sanford undertakes to place the entering freshman within a developmental framework. (This freshman is, of course, the college-age student and not the older college entrant.) Assuming that development is progressive and that it may eventuate in such desired states of the person as freedom of impulse, enlightenment of conscience, and differentiation of the ego, Sanford asks what the freshman has already accomplished and what major tasks remain for him to do.

Sanford's main argument is that the freshman is in a distinctive "stage" of development. During this stage, the major problem for him is to tolerate ambiguity and open-endedness in himself while he is preparing for adult roles. Chapter 9 shows how a college with a certain kind of atmosphere and educational program can succeed in helping its freshmen to see themselves as persons-in-transition and to accept what they see.

Reporting on studies that include freshmen as well as alumni, Donald R. Brown, in Chapter 10, "Academic Excellence: Product of Environment and Personality," is concerned with the determinants of achievement in college. Brown shows, with many examples, the way personal traits in a student and the college environment affect each other and together produce academic excellence or the reverse.

In Chapter 11, "Personality Change in Students," Harold Webster, Mervin B. Freedman, and Paul Heist examine various changes that take place during the college years: gains in skill and information, increased mental ability, changed attitudes and values and changes in other personality characteristics. The evidence presented in this essay shows that, in general, students gain in mental ability as well as in skills and information. Indeed, the more able–the "brighter"–young people are to begin with, the longer will their abilities continue to grow. As for attitudes and values, the evidence shows that, between the freshman and senior years in college, there is, in general, change in the direction of greater liberalism and sophistication. Moreover, during the college years, students in general move from an authoritarian position in the direction of greater freedom of impulse and greater complexity in the functioning of the ego.

It is, of course, by no means clear that these changes are due to educational activities deliberately undertaken in the educational programs of the colleges that were studied. The cause-and-effect relationships here are unusually complex, and higher education research has not yet given us a definitive answer. Faculty members, therefore, should not take the evidence presented in Chapter 11 as occasion for general rejoicing; indeed, the strong probability, according to the most recent research available, is that the observed changes in students come about because of experiences that have taken place between classes rather than in them.

Given the evidence of Chapter 11 that seniors are more sophisticated and enlightened in their attitudes and values than are freshmen, it is logical to raise a question about whether such gains are maintained, and for how long, after the graduate returns to the world of business and suburbia. On this point, Mervin B. Freedman, in Chapter 12, "What Happens After College: Studies of Alumni," presents evidence that is at once encouraging and chilling. He comes to the conclusion that the college years are not only crucially formative ones but that they offer what amounts to a "last chance" for enlightenment before entering the expressway of life.

9

Freshman Personality: A Stage in Human Development

Nevitt Sanford

A stage of late adolescence intervenes between adolescence proper and early adulthood which, for convenience, can be labelled "freshman personality." It should be noted immediately, however, that certain high school students and college sophomores as well as freshmen are included in this stage, and it may be that not all juniors and seniors have passed beyond it. But because the phase is often *connected* with age, as it is with going to college, the freshman is more likely to be at this point than are other categories of older or younger people.

For most freshmen the main crisis of adolescence is over, and controlling mechanisms are again in the ascendant. But the controls developed for the purpose of inhibiting impulses are still unseasoned and uncertain; they are likely to operate in a rigid manner, to be overdone, as if the danger of their giving way altogether were still very real. Thus freshmen tend to be like converts to adulthood, enthusiastic supporters and imitators of adult ways, who know what it is to backslide—which they sometimes do.

The achievement of *flexible* control, an arrangement in which there is genuine freedom of impulses because there is little danger of their getting out of hand, still lies ahead. Nevertheless, impulses are now sufficiently inhibited or contained so that young persons can turn their attention to other matters. They are now ready to concentrate on their relations with the world about them—to improve their understanding of that world and to find a place within it.

The Freshman's Authoritarian Propensities

This picture of the psychological situation of freshmen is essentially that of an authoritarian personality. They inhibit impulse by being morally strict, both with themselves and with others. They are ready to meet stiff requirements, to work hard, to conform with what they take to be the prevailing standards of behavior—and they are inclined to be somewhat intolerant of those who do not.

An element of perfectionism, of striving for purity of thought and action is characteristic of freshmen. Needing, and finding, moral heroes, they are apt to demand in them perfection. When, in fact, their idols are shown to have feet of clay, or at least some human weaknesses, freshmen are unprepared for the discovery. Indeed, one of the hardest things about growing up in contemporary America is that at just the time when young people most need models of private and public virtue they are likely to become aware of corruption in high places, organized immorality in some of our major institutions, inconsistencies in our economic system and our sexual mores, and meanness in people close at hand whom they thought they could admire.

If young people are not to remain in an authoritarian stage of development, they must learn to see things as they are, develop an articulate individual power of judgment, and become able to criticize what they judge to be bad. If they do this, however, they court new danger: that they may reject the existing order out of hand and become totally alienated from the society and values represented by their parents and their community. This alienation can, of course, take place while young people are still emotionally—and often economically, as well—dependent on their parents and before they have had time to develop a value system based on their own experience. Young people of this type may constitute a whole subculture. In the last two decades, subcultures of alienated young people have played an influential role in American colleges and in American society. Acute observers of our society have studied these "pockets" within the dominant culture and have labeled them, collectively, "the counterculture." The Beats of the 1950s and the Hippies of the 1960s are representative of such countercultures, and they have, for at least a few years in each decade, dominated the public image of American youth.

The authoritarian propensities of freshmen are closely related to their uncertain self-esteem. They do not know what they can do, how good they are, or what to think of themselves. Just as they look to authority or the social group for guidance in the matter of moral values, so they look to external sources for definition and measurement of themselves—and these sources give conflicting testimony. On the one hand, they are happy to remember their parents' faith in them, the accomplishments of high school and the plaudits received there, and, perhaps particularly, the fact that they were chosen for admission to this or that outstanding institution. On the other hand, they suspect that they are now playing in a different league, and they know that the major tests of life still await them. In this uncertainty, they vacillate between overestimation and underestimation of themselves. Most of them stick to patterns of behavior that have been rewarded in the past and display such confidence as they can muster.

Vulnerability to other people's appraisals makes the average freshman highly susceptible to the influence of his fellow students; their approval or disapproval make or break one's self-conficence. In this situation it is often a good thing that freshmen are given academic grades or —even better—detailed appraisals of strengths and weaknesses, as well as scores on tests of ability and achievement. Bad news may be better than no news—better, that is, than uncertainty or gloomy imaginings. Freshmen flourish best not when they are given no evaluation—that is, when anything and everything is vaguely accepted by teachers and peers—but when they are given searching and hard-hitting analyses of their performances, accompanied by intelligible and realistic pictures of what they can become.

Education and the Developing Person

To understand the developmental stage of freshmen is to know how they might be changed and what the college might do to bring about desirable development. Effective teaching does not deliberately call students' attention to their private motives or mechanisms; instead, it undertakes to show them something of the variety and complexity of the social world of which they are part; it tries to show them the inner feelings and motives and mechanisms of people in general; it seeks to broaden self-awareness by inducing empathy with many kinds of people—real and fictional—and by confronting students with some of the deficiencies of their old, automatically adopted values. The object is to induce in students the experience of conflict and the necessity to make decisions.

The nonacademic college environment may also provide important stimuli to individual development. Students are placed in many situations that require new responses. In the relative anonymity of their college society, they can be free of their home communities' limiting expectations and can play a variety of new social roles. That they may do so at a time when they must seriously consider future roles but do not yet have to commit themselves to any one of them is a great advantage of the college situation.

People can throw themselves into the most challenging and enriching experiences possible when they feel fairly sure of themselves, sure that repressed impulses will not capture them, sure that they will not be made to feel worthless in the eyes of others. To get the most from experiences such as going abroad, getting married, entering into a vocation, and having children—and to do well in such roles—individuals must, in a sense, lose themselves—that is, they must permit themselves to be enveloped by the situation's demands. It is this process that further expands and differentiates the personality. Losing oneself in this way means forgetting to be defensive, doing without external supports for self-esteem, and abandoning behavior that merely served to reassure. Such freedom can exist only where a basic stability underlies the person's self-conception. Individuals who gladly "lose" themselves in new experiences do so only when they feel that their essential identity can survive such experiences—can survive them and assimilate them.

The arch-problem for students is to know how to wait, how to tolerate ambiguity and the open question about themselves while they prepare for the future. The problem is not easy, for they are constantly tempted to take short-cuts to maturity: neglecting the paths to full development by imitating adult behavior and prematurely fitting themsleves into adult roles. It is for the college, therefore, to help them to wait.

To help students wait, however, the college must do more than simply view them as developing persons. It must convince the students to see *themselves* as persons-in-transition and to accept happily what they see. The college must in effect tell them "You are going to change. It is all right, therefore, for you to feel uncertain about your future; what matters is that you enter fully into those activities that can develop you." In other words, what is needed is a stronger definition and greater social acceptance of the role of *student*, so that those who occupy this role may more comforably and easily be what they are—developing persons.

10

Academic Excellence: Product of Environment And Personality

Donald R. Brown

Education is not a disembodied phenomenon. It cannot be applied to an individual the way a bright finish is sprayed on an automobile. Complex and difficult to define, it is, instead, a process which goes on continually as part of each individual's total development. As researchers and teachers have come to realize how interrelated an individual's *intellectual* development and his *total* development are, they have become more interested in the way personal traits and environment affect each other and together produce academic achievement.

In selecting students, some colleges may strive for a combination of high scholastic performance and certain other attributes, such as athletic prowess or leadership qualities. The general aim of the college selection process, however, is to predict academic achievement. Those colleges that do their selecting largely by standardized aptitude and achievement tests have been able, increasingly, to predict, and thus avoid, academic failure. On the other hand, they have also shown a declining ability to predict the *relative* grade performance of those selected. As an example, it is impossible to predict grade performances of students who enter colleges where high College Board requirements restrict the range of talent to only the top-ranking applicants. One of the reasons is that test scores reveal little about motivation. Good grades may be earned by a brilliant, independent, versatile and flexible thinker; equally good grades may be earned by a persistent, well-disciplined, well-organized and obedient student with a good memory.

In a study at Vassar in which the writer was involved some years ago, the investigators asked individual faculty members to name "superior" students in their classes and describe their personal qualities. According to their own statements, the faculty meant by an *ideal* student one who possessed marked intellectual power, who applied that power to intellectual subjects—and did so independently—and whose mind was incisive, analytical and good at synthesis. A student's development, however, according to this ideal image, should not be merely intellectual; other qualities, such as friendliness, helpfulness, cooperativeness and other moral attributes, were also important.

To be named "superior," of course, a student did not need to possess all of these qualities. In the eyes of many teachers, an unusual amount of originality or flexibility or skill at schoolwork often compensated for other lacks. Furthermore, in matters of personality no less than in matters of intellect, the Vassar faculty honored *growth* as well as sheer attainment.

It was concluded that the Vassar faculty admired intellectual ability but preferred to find it housed in a well-integrated, developing, pleasant, purposeful young person. They were not overly influenced by grade performance alone. It must be admitted, however, that the Vassar faculty's values about students were by no means universal. National studies on the undergraduate origins of PhD students indeed supported the notion that scientific and humanistic scholars thrive in different types of college environments. Follow-up studies a decade after these students left the college confirmed the patterns that had been established during their undergraduate careers.They also showed the strong influence that changes in social expectations of women exerted in interacting with these earlier patterns of achievement.

Student Evaluations of College Teachers

What happens when the sides are reversed and the students are asked to evaluate their teachers? It might be expected that students at colleges emphasizing the hard sciences would find their teachers cold and impersonal. But interestingly enough, colleges that produce many natural science PhDs possess faculties that seem warm and informal toward their students. Here, teachers are not embarrassed by open displays of emotion, and they often refer to colleagues by their first names when talking to students. Students do not describe them as "practical" or "efficient" in their dealings, nor do they feel it necessary to address them as "professor" or "doctor."

The faculties in these colleges (as their students see them) demand high academic performance. They see through the pretenses and bluffs of some students, they push them to perform at capacity, and they give challenging exams. They also apply high standards to their faculty colleagues, emphasizing basic research. In their teaching methods, they are relatively nondirective, and they show some tolerance toward student mistakes in social life. A somewhat different picture emerges from student evaluations at colleges that are more productive in the social sciences and humanities. Students identify these institutions with a flexible curriculum and with controversial and energetic teaching.

The data on campus cultures reveal an interesting contrast. Student cultures characterized by humanism, breadth of interests and reflectiveness are conducive to humanistic interests and achievements; both aggression and a high degree of social activity interfere with such achievement. Natural science achievement, however, is typical of student cultures high in "scientism" and aggression; and such achievement is—not suprisingly—inhibited in student cultures that stress social conformity.

Achievement, Personality, and Early Family Life

Further light is shed on the relationships among college achievement, personality and early family life in a study of women who had graduated from Vassar 25 years earlier. From exhaustive research into the lives of these women before, during and after college, five basic patterns of attitudes emerged.

The first group included the *socially active* women. Characteristically, these women led busy social lives as undergraduates and were closely attached to the peer group. Neither notoriously rebellious nor primarily interested in the intellectual aspects of college, they were out for a "good time"—though not at the expense of a college degree. As a rule, they entered college from the better-known private schools where they had undistinguished records academically but gave evidence of "all aroundness, independence, poise and spark."

They very strongly identified with their parents. The fathers, probably Ivy League graduates in law or business, were seen by their daughters as busy, distant figures; their mothers were women of poise, charm, intelligence and great energy, often graduates of the students' Alma Mater. Childhood days were remembered as vague worlds of stability and happiness.

Having left college they occupied themselves with Junior League activities until marriage. After marriage came suburban lives of child-rearing and soul-searching. They became liberal Protestants and left-of-center Republicans. At the time of the study, the data show that the women in this first category, the *socially active* during their college years, were strongly authoritarian as compared with others in their group, and they lacked introspection, complexity and the capacity for further growth. They did not find college intellectually challenging, nor did they gain high academic achievement.

The second group was made up of the *overachievers*. These women had higher college performances than their tested ability would have indicated, yet they were not profession-oriented and showed little evidence of being influenced by faculty values. Family history seemed to be the key to this overachievement—a college-educated mother with high aspirations, a greatly admired father who was a self-made businessman, a vaguely remembered happy home life. Close conformity with strict parental demands led, it seemed, to dutiful college careers where students worked hard, won academic awards, but acquired little serious appreciation of the intellectual life.

Their lives since college followed the conventional suburban form so often caricatured in contemporary writing—routine upper-middle-class or lower-upper-class patterns, narrow in scope and opportunity, lacking much deep meaning, devoid of intellectual pursuits. Socially and politically, they were cautious, conservative. In religion they were traditionalist and Protestant. As a result, these women showed more signs of an approaching crisis related to menopause and aging than did the other groups. All in all, this picture seemed to support the oft-heard observation that excellent grades can be achieved to some extent with only reasonable capacity, little intellectual curiosity, and a good deal of "proper" behavior.

A third group was made up of the *underachievers.* Although their college performances were medium to low, these women often had a high capacity—as shown by their considerable intellectual growth while at college. Analysis of the data indicated that this growth resulted from one or more of these three conditions: either the women came from politically liberal families, or they reacted strongly to the depression of the 1930s during their college years, or their husbands, whom they began dating while in college, were liberal politically.

Although their main interest was marriage (typically to a professional or businessman) and family (three to six children), many became active professionally during the early years of marriage, particularly in sources such as social work or nursery school teaching, where the interest was in people rather than ideas or professional status.

Backgrounds varied in this group. The women went to private but usually progressive and academically sound schools, and they chose their colleges on recommendations from school officials and friends. Family life was happy and secure, with more than the usual amount of freedom and independence and little threat of deprivation for nonconformity. Fathers were competent, "fun" to be with, loving and part of the family picture. Mothers were warm, sociable, happy and accepting; they provided sources of identification.

At the time the study was made of these alumnae, they held

conventional religious beliefs, although they had arrived at these beliefs after much thought. Politically they were moderate, with leanings toward the Democrats or independents, and in spite of family obligations and lack of servants, they were active in the community. Contrary to their earlier dedication of home and family, they were interested in part-time employment and looking forward to it.

A fourth group was made up of the *high achievers*—women of capacity who did very well in college and went on to professional careers. They seldom married and if they did they rarely had children. They went on for advanced degrees and then held responsible professional positions. Problems of identity were solved through their high capacity, strong interests and actual achievements.

Most often their parents were neither socially nor intellectually prominent, they came from public schools (unusual for Vassar students), and they held scholarships. In childhood and adolescence they experienced conflicts arising from domineering and talented mothers, against whom they felt considerable repressed hostility and guilt, yet whose opinions they accepted. In fact, their childhood days, as a group, were not outstandingly happy, nor were they protected from such upsetting events as deaths or economic crises.

The intellectual development of these women may be described as early, intense and continuing. From their earliest days they were decided on an intellectual career, and their colleges were chosen for academic prestige and because scholarship aid was available. These women were oriented toward liberal political and social philosophies, tended to vote Democrat, and were agnostic.

The final group included the *identity seekers*—a miscellany of rather unhappy and confused young people trying to break away from strong, domineering parents or to adjust themselves to the college environment. The backgrounds of the members of this group ranged from extreme upper-class Victorian upbringing to lower-middle-class, small-town girls. And their identity-seeking ranged from open defiance to a maintenance of weak conformity awaiting an opportunity to break.

On the whole, these women were unable to achieve stable lives except after prolonged therapy or drastic changes in environment, or both. They came from unstable or oppressive families, and the sex-role conflict was sometimes so severe that normal heterosexual relations were seriously impaired. These students would have been the ones to profit most from existing therapeutic facilities on campus and from the campus environment in general, but as it was, intellectual interests were largely forsaken in the intensity of the personal struggle. A decade later these same graduates were contacted in late middle life. While a few had taken advantage of changed social circumstances to shift patterns by making drastic changes in their lives, most continued in their well-established life style.

These findings reaffirm the cardinal principle in the selection of students. Every effort ought to be made to channel each student to the type of college that can maximize his or her potential. The experience of the last dozen or more years has shown that it is even necessary to create new types of environments if the society wants to be in a position to serve well as many students as possible.

But another principle lies alongside the first. Although we must appreciate each student's individuality, we must also seek common factors that will allow educational planners to avoid chaos. We must design the fewest possible types of institutional environments for the fullest intellectual development of the most students. Only with a sound knowledge of individual development, a good sense of the society's future needs, and a clear statement of the goals to be achieved can education become less haphazard than it is now.

11

Personality Change In Students

Harold Webster

Mervin B. Freedman

Paul Heist

People change in diverse ways during college. First, a student may simply acquire more information on different topics and become more skilled at performing certain tasks. Secondly, there may be changes in interests and attitudes toward the self and the world. And then, in some cases, there may be fundamental personality changes, accompanied by the emergence of new values.

The change most generally expected of college students is the acquisition of skills and information. It is the educational goal about which there is most agreement among educators. There are two reasons why, among all the kinds of change that occur, this one is more widely sanctioned as a legitimate educational goal. One reason is that the acquisition of skills and information is thought essential for later activities; the second is that it is believed to be achieved individually by hard work. The value of individual effort that produces tangible results is generally acknowledged in our culture; and colleges have been eager to prove themselves by emphasizing the importance of their own tangible rewards, the most immediate of which are grades and diplomas.

Even though grades and diplomas have generally been regarded outside of the educational world as a "sign" of one's education, grades are regarded by many teachers—perhaps a large majority today—as an inadequate measure of educational growth. There are a number of reasons for this belief. First, most instructors directly restrict the meaning of assigned grades by informing students that grades will be based only upon specific kinds of material, usually assigned reading or set problems. Second, when faculty are asked to identify students for whom the college has been most successful in its aims, those named are not always A students. Third, grades achieved in college are usually not closely related to a student's functioning or performance after graduation. Fourth, college grades are only moderately related to recognizable factors in the student's past. Fifth, interviews have shown that the motives impelling students to achieve high grades are often indistinguishable from the desire simply to please and to obey parents or similar authorities who happen to value high grades. Sixth, students and teachers alike often suggest that high grades are only formal requirements—requirements for graduate school, prerequisites for later professional status and the like—and the implication in such suggestions is that grades cannot at the same time be measures of general educational status or development. Seventh, just as the achievement of high grades is insufficient evidence that education is taking place, failure to obtain high grades cannot be taken to show that education has *not* taken place; certainly this is found to be true with persons who later reveal themselves as creative or highly productive. Eighth, other measures of personal growth and development have been established during the last several decades— and these are far more dependable than course grades. Finally, nearly everyone knows a few students in whom the need to achieve high grades seems to interfere with real education.

Nevertheless, despite their obvious limitations, grades are not likely to be abolished. There was a short-lived movement in the mid- and late 1960s to eliminate grades on American campuses, but since the beginning of the present decade, grades have undoubtedly become more, rather than less, difficult to eliminate. Increasing numbers of young people are attending college, and grades based largely on achievement examinations form part of the traditional bureaucratic machinery for "processing" these students. And because of the kind of curriculum in most colleges, grades have to be used as indicators of educational progress, however inadequately they serve that function. Then again, emphasis on formal requirements for admission into various professions, or into graduate school, is increasing rather than decreasing, and the grade-point average during the undergraduate years is still one of the most common yardsticks used to judge applicants—and still one of the best predictors of success in graduate school for students who move directly into graduate programs.

Changes in Mental Ability

There are large differences from one individual to another as to the time of life at which they reach their maximum, or ceiling, of measured mental ability. Some individuals will fail to gain beyond age eighteen, many will continue to gain after age twenty-one.

A number of studies have demonstrated that more intelligent persons not only increase in measured ability at a faster rate than individuals of lesser ability but also stand further from their point of maximum ability—further both in time and in amount of ability. The corollary of this is that at any given age, persons of higher ability in these samples could expect in the future a greater total increase in ability than could persons of lower ability.

The erroneous idea that gifted persons mature early has undoubtedly arisen from comparison of their behavior with others of the same age. Such comparisons provide evidence of superior performance by the gifted, but they cannot give information about the *growth* or maturing of ability within one individual. Historic accounts of youthful, precocious geniuses may seem to contradict our theory, but too often we fail to take into account their later work. The theory is certainly valid for such geniuses as Beethoven, Freud, Virginia Woolf, and Picasso, whose later works reflect increased powers of conception and expression.

It is commonly believed that students' intellects can be trained by the simple expedient of working them very hard. As a result, many of the ablest freshmen enrolled at the "better" colleges today complain that they do not have time to think. And in the more "typical" colleges students assert that a lot of sheer memorizing of minute details is required, that the work is neither new nor challenging. At these colleges the low-ability student has difficulty keeping his head above water. We have interviewed students who spend almost all of their waking moments memorizing material in order to remain—barely—in college. Yet there is little doubt that any student can benefit from education beyond secondary school, providing he is not expected to compete directly with those who far exceed him in ability.

Even though the more intelligent freshman is likely to be less mature than older students, he is well able, because of his high ability, to profit from great freedom in his studies. At the same time, he may need *more* guidance than the student of average ability, guidance tailored to his needs, since the total change in his personality during college is likely to be greater than average. But there is only a very small number of campuses where students receive highly individualized academic advice. Except on the smallest campuses, where all faculty members know every student and participate in joint student evaluations, the amount and kind of guidance students receive from their professors is largely a result of chance factors.

As we come to know more about the educational process it will be found that, owing to the complexity of personality, there are more and more students who are exceptional in some way. Study and appreciation of such diversity among students is more profitable than inventing reasons for ignoring their differences. Faculty members could make a start here by trying to understand both differences in ability and differences in the rate at which abilities mature.

Changes in Values and Attitudes

Research on attitudes and values made during the last three or more decades shows that, generally speaking, college students have changed toward greater liberalism in their political, social and religious outlooks. Moreover, the evidence demonstrates that during the college years students' interests widen. Even the studies made before World War II gave evidence of greater liberalism and greater sophistication among seniors than among freshmen. By the 1960s, data were even sharper and clearer; and now in the 1970s, while there seems to have taken place some reduction of the social idealism exhibited by students during the Johnson and Nixon administrations, the *general* pattern of increased liberalism still prevails.

Religious crises or disillusionments, with consequent shifts in values, are still fairly common among college students today. In most institutions, freshmen are seriously confronted with a wide range of professed religious beliefs and disbeliefs and with a variety of seemingly disparate moral practices. They naturally compare the values of peers and faculty with those of parents, sometimes without much deliberation, but often with some misgivings.

Take religion, for example. In an early study carried out at the Center for Research and Development in Higher Education at the University of California, Berkeley, National Merit scholars attending a wide variety of colleges were asked about their need to believe in a religion. As Table Three shows, the proportions of affirmative replies fell from about ninety percent at the time these students entered college to about fifty percent for men and seventy percent for women at the end of the junior year.

Table 3
National Merit Scholars' Need To Believe In A Religion

	Affirmative Replies	
	Men	Women
At time of college entrance	88%	91%
By end of freshman year	70%	76%
By end of sophomore year	61%	74%
By end of junior year	51%	69%

Thus, in religious attitudes—and in politics and social attitudes, too, as the following data show—the study of National Merit scholars supported the findings of other studies that students become "liberal" during college. When asked how they would vote if they were old enough, thirty percent of these able young scholars checked Republican, about seventeen percent Democrat, and about fifty percent Independent. After two years the humanities majors reduced their Republican vote considerably—for men the change was mostly to Democrat; for women, to Independent. Many mathematics majors who previously had checked Republican also shifted to the Independent category. Subsequent studies also showed that students, during the course of their college experience, become more liberal in the sense of being more sophisticated and independent in their thinking and placing greater value on individual freedom and well-being.

Perhaps the major feature of later studies, as distinguished from the earlier studies discussed previously, is that they have been directed to more generalized tendencies in the personality, tendencies conceived as underlying and integrating particular attitudes and values. In studies of Vassar College students, for example, there were devised measures of the expression of impulses and of certain aspects of ego functioning and development. In this research it was planned to emphasize such personality characteristics as intellectual functioning and achievement, authoritarianism (and its opposites), masculinity-feminity, and psychological health. It was possible to obtain measures of these characteristics—in some cases through carrying out a special program of test development. Brief descriptions of some of the "tests" follow.

Social Maturity.   Low scorers are authoritarian, compulsive, rigid, punitive, submissive to power, conventional, cynical, anti-intellectual and emotionally suppressed. High scorers are relatively free of these characteristics.

Impulse Expression.   High scorers, in contrast to low scorers, have a great readiness to express impulses, or to seek gratification of them, in overt action or in conscious feeling and attitude. High scorers are relatively dominant, aggressive, autonomous, exhibitionistic, and express interests in sex, excitement and change.

Developmental Status.   This scale is made up of attitude items that distinguish younger from older students. In a sense such items reflect development from the freshman to the senior year—hence the name. High scorers (seniors) in comparison with low scorers (freshmen) are flexible and uncompulsive, disinclined to pass judgment on people but critical of the institutional authority of family, state, or religion; high scorers are also nonconforming, free of cynicism, realistic and mature in interests.

Masculine Role. High scorers are active persons with interests and attitudes that have been valued by our culture when they have been exhibited by males and disvalued when they have been exhibited by females; low scorers are, on the contrary, more passive, acquiescent and exhibit interests and attitudes that have been valued by our culture when females have exhibited them but disvalued when exhibited by males.

On all of these measures, seniors have scored higher than freshmen. At the same time some rather striking institutional differences between two leading liberal arts colleges have been observed. Obtained means for Bennington College freshmen on Social Maturity, Developmental Status, and Impulse Expression were greater than the corresponding means for Vassar *seniors*; yet the means at Bennington increased between freshman and senior year. In both schools the older students were more developed, more mature, and more free to express impulses than the younger students; yet the differences between colleges were also impressive. Bennington seniors were the highest of any group on Masculine Role. It seemed reasonable, therefore, to infer that the other high scores of Bennington students were not achieved at the cost of a retrogression to a more conventional or passively feminine role.

These results support the view that differing public images attract different students to the two colleges, and that the differences persist despite developmental processes which lead students in both schools in the same direction—which is one of less conservatism, increased tolerance for individual differences and more freedom to express impulses.

When the same students were examined at different times during their college careers, the results were essentially the same as those just described. Test-retest difference scores were significant, and they increased in magnitude with time spent in college. When plotted, using time as the abscissa, the gains usually formed a convex decelerating curve, showing that greater changes occurred during the earlier part of college careers.

Included in the regular test batteries used at Vassar were the well-known Ethnocentrism (E) scale and the F scale for measuring authoritarianism or antidemocratic trends. Without exception, there were always large decreases in mean scores on these characteristics between freshman and senior years. The personality syndrome now known as authoritarianism constitutes a particular failure of maturity about which a large amount of convincing research of a quantitative type is available. Persons with high F scores have been described as anti-intellectual by a number of investigators. If, as it appears, many college freshmen are anti-intellectual, the study of authoritarianism in college students should be of value in educational research. The fact that many high scorers at Vassar were changeable, to the extent that *large* decreases occurred in their F scores during college whereas others did not change at all, merits further study. It appeared from interviews that in a few authoritarians the earlier fixations were so severe as to prevent a significant decrease in F scores during college.

Vassar students were also studied by means of the Minnesota Multiphasic Personality Inventory, a test designed to measure the type and degree of psychopathology in the personality. Seniors subscribed more frequently than freshmen to statements indicating psychological or physical disturbances and instability. These differences were small, although they were statistically significant for large groups. They were taken as evidence of the seniors' greater openness to experience.

Three of the Vassar scales—Social Maturity, Impulse Expression, and Developmental Status—were also administered at a variety of other women's colleges—for example, a predominantly black college in the South, a Catholic college in Canada, and an Eastern women's college that differed somewhat from Vassar. In all cases the kinds of trends found were similar to those found at Vassar. There were impressive intercollege differences, but whatever the initial freshmen means might have been, the students subsequently gained in scores during college.

The theoretical implication of these findings is that systematic personality changes take place during the college years and that the developmental changes during this period of late adolescence entail certain regularities in the way problems and conflicts are met and resolved.

Limitations on Personality Change

Most new students are enthusiastic about their college experiences, but very few have developed those psychological characteristics that will permit them to become seriously committed to intellectual and aesthetic problems. Only the exceptional student today has the kind of autonomy—or social alienation, perhaps—to defer vocational plans or setting up a household (by oneself or with a marriage partner or lover) in favor of other pursuits. Few, consequently, become interested in learning for its own sake. Despite the tendency to grow more liberal, the vast majority of students today soon forego both experimentation with different roles and the questioning of basic values. They make such sacrifices in order to arrive at a comfortable, fairly definite blueprint of the future as early as they can.

In the 1970s, as in the 1950s, this pervasive caution may be due in part to the absence of conflict during the precollege years. When we studied the background of Vassar students, we found that, contrary to generally accepted theory, adolescence had not been a time of strife or rebelliousness for the majority. In fact, the most common "crises" during secondary school had been worries about acceptance by peers.

In America, college has been regarded as an ally of the parents in the prolongation of adolescence. And the college years are a time in life when there happens to be a maximum concern with—and perhaps in recent years a maximum respect for—problems concerning cultural standards and values. A highly vocal minority notwithstanding, in our affluent society the majority of college students regard social issues or movements as irrelevant to more immediate problems; social reform is considered secondary to such concerns as career, love and marriage, and personal development. The result is the prevalence of an attitude among students of the current generation that appears, to all observers today, to be a good deal more conservative than it has been at any time since 1964.

During late adolescence, as during the college years themselves, student interests normally diversify and intensify. Yet a great many people pass through college without experiencing much change in basic values or without becoming greatly involved in problems that interest professors. The vast enterprise that is American higher education today cherishes traditional values, a premium on vocational training, rewards for hard work and social adjustment. After the flurry of changing values among American students during the last decade, the traditional values have now once again emerged as dominant. As these concerns have moved to the top of the list of priorities, they have exacted their price: the attrition of real interest in intellectual and aesthetic matters.

12

What Happens After College: Studies of Alumni

Mervin B. Freedman

In the long run, the best evaluation of a college education is likely to result from studies of alumni. What are college graduates like five, ten, twenty and thirty years after graduation? How have they been influenced by college experiences?

Few studies have been made in this important area. Most of the empirical studies center on gross sociological factors, such as the income of college graduates, the age at which they marry, or the number of children they have. There are also several studies, chiefly ones utilizing questionnaires, that assess such factors as the aesthetic values of college graduates, their interests and opinions, and their attitudes toward various aspects of their college careers.

Rare indeed are studies of the same people as students in college and again as alumni. In one such study done before World War II, Pace[1] surveyed the men and women who had entered the University of Minnesota in 1924, 1925, 1928, and 1929 by means of a fifty-two page questionnaire. About half the subjects were graduates, the others having withdrawn prior to graduation. Pace's general findings were confirmed fifteen years later by Jacob[2] in a famous study of the late 1950s. These investigators found that the lives of alumni were centered in the "private" sphere, with the family, work and recreation as the predominant interests. The alumni voted, but otherwise tended to be politically passive. Nor did intellectual and aesthetic pursuits loom large in their lives.

The chief differences between graduates and the people who dropped out of college were in the vocational realm: the income of the graduates was somewhat higher and their reported job satisfaction somewhat greater. Otherwise, differences were inconsequential. Such findings led these investigators to suggest that (in Pace's words) "colleges may not be producing the cultural values they so frequently claim."

A second study completed in the 1950s reported on questionnaire returns from more than 9000 respondents representing more than 1000 colleges.[3] According to the findings, satisfaction with a college experience in general was almost universal: ninety-eight percent of the respondents would choose to go to college again, and eighty-four percent would choose the same college.

This satisfaction did not hold, however, for the general type of curriculum or course pursued in college. In fact, this area was the focus of greatest dissatisfaction with the college experience. In the matter of general versus more specific kinds of education, forty-four percent were satisfied with what they had had, thirty-five percent wished they had received a more specific kind of training, and twenty-one percent would have preferred a more general educational experience.

Graduates in the humanities were distinguished by their rela-

---

[1]Pace, C.R. *They Went to College.* Minneapolis: University of Minnesota Press, 1941

[2]Jacob, P.E. *Changing Values in College.* New York: Harper and Brothers, 1957.

[3]Havemann, E., and West, P.S. *They Went to College.* New York: Harcourt, Brace, 1952.

tively low incomes, and the situation was "even worse for social science graduates." In the professions, those who had had a more general type of undergraduate education tended to be "the more active and interested citizens." The college graduates most dissatisfied with general education were those in business.

Students with high grades were more likely to enter professions, and in a given profession to earn more money, than were students with lower grades. Grades tended to be related to financial success in all fields except business. The degree of satisfaction with the college experience, although related to grades, was little related to type and extent of extracurricular activity. Alumni who had obtained higher grades as students were more content than others with their college, their major and their extent of specialization.

Characteristics of College Alumni

Income.   Most studies have demonstrated a direct relationship between amount of schooling and amount of income. College graduates have predominated in the higher-paying occupations and have earned more money job for job than people who have no college or who have left college prior to graduation. As for differences between the sexes, the data show, as might be expected, that when educational level and occupation are equated for the two sexes the incomes of women have been lower than those of men.

In recent years, however, studies have discerned a decline in the purely economic rewards of a college education. As college education becomes accessible to more and more people, its particular value as an avenue to large financial gain diminishes. And as the incomes of groups with less education rise as a result of union activity and social legislation, the gap between college-educated people and others narrows. Some recent studies, analyzing the problem completely in terms of dollars spent on a college education and the additional dollars earned by college graduates, have concluded that—*as a financial investment*—there is some doubt that a college education carries the value it did in the past.

Values, Attitudes, and Opinions.   There is evidence that the values, attitudes and opinions with which one leaves college are likely to persist into later life with but little modification. Consequently the college years take on enormous importance; one cannot think of them as simply one period among others in which substantial modification also takes place. For many students, apparently, any changes that may occur in values, attitudes and opinions end with graduation.

The origins of changes in values, attitudes and opinions during the college years are obscure. It could be that such changes reflect more the social forces impinging on the college and its students than the effect of deliberate educational policy. But even if this be the case, the college years are characterized by a degree of openness to change that is not later duplicated. Research data confirm the observation of William James: "Outside of their own business, the ideas gained by men before they are 25 are practically the only ideas they shall have in their lives."

Studies of Vassar College Alumnae

An extensive study of Vassar College alumnae collected data on ninety women—fifty alumnae of the classes 1929 to 1935 and forty alumnae of the classes 1954, 1955, and 1956. Since these women were volunteers who responded to invitations to be studied and interviewed, they cannot be assumed to be representative of their fellow alumnae in each class. It is likely, however, that the great majority of patterns of life and modes of thought characterizing Vassar College alumnae in general may be found among the women who were interviewed, although we cannot tell exactly how predominant these patterns are.

It appears that many of these alumnae had enjoyed a sense of accomplishment after graduation—either in additional schooling or at work—that they did not experience as undergraduates. To some extent this may have been a function of lessened competition. At Vassar College they were competing academically with many other intelligent and studious women. After graduation, the competition was probably much less keen. Many of the married alumnae reported a similar kind of experience when they took part in community activities such as the League of Women Voters. For the most part, they found themselves able to handle with dispatch the demands made upon them.

We cannot help wondering whether many of these women would not have benefited by experiencing the same sense of accomplishment *during* their undergraduate years rather than afterward. If their college life had been so enriched, their achievements—both before and after graduation—might have been greater. Not that stern competition is solely to blame for the lack of a sense of accomplishment during the school years. Academic procedures themselves may often reinforce feelings of guilt instead of fostering feelings of competence and adequacy in students. This is particularly likely to happen with college *women* who are usually anxious to please and do the right thing.

The Middle-Aged Educated Woman. In an affluent society, housewives in the upper socio-economic half of the population are likely to have some twenty or thirty years of relative freedom after their children have become at least partly self-sufficient. The point at which the housewife rather suddenly acquires this freedom can be a time of emotional stress. Take, for example, the fifty Vassar alumnae who graduated between 1929 and 1935 who were interviewed in depth. The study showed that some women who had previously seemed quite stable emotionally later experienced some kind of personality difficulty. These women had ordered their lives around various forms of external definition: school and college, marriage, then children. These were the things that everyone did, and they kept the young wife very busy—for a while.

Then, quite suddenly, the youngest child entered adolescence, and the housewife no longer felt very much needed—certainly not in the physical or material way that she had been previously. For perhaps the first time in her life, she found herself thrown back on her own resources. Bereft of external guideposts to provide continuity and order she faced a psychological crisis that could better have been dealt with at an earlier age.

At an earlier age, however, few alumnae had thought much about what life would be like in fifteen or twenty years. Of course the situation was somewhat different for those alumnae with major professional or career commitments. These women were ready to remain in the home when the children were small, but they intended to resume their careers as soon as family commitments made this possible. The majority of alumnae, however, who had no strong involvements outside home and family were little concerned for the long-range future. Busy with their daily and monthly rounds of activities, they appeared to feel that the future would take care of itself.

Difference in Educational Patterns between Younger and Older Alumnae.   When Vassar alumnae of 1954 to 1956 are contrasted with those of 1929 to 1935, what seems most striking is the absence of clear-cut educational patterns among the younger group. Among the pre-World War II graduates, a strong commitment on the part of a woman to intellectual pursuits or to a professional career carried with it a more or less explicit assumption that marriage might thereby be precluded. But this was not true of those who graduated in the 1950s. At that time, almost all Vassar students expected to marry. On the other hand, fewer students during those years were preoccupied with social activities to the exclusion of intellectual interests, and a higher proportion of the gifted ones were stimulated to achievements that accorded with their abilities. To this extent, the blurring of the more distinctive patterns that characterized the pre-World War II group may be regarded as an intellectual step forward.

But this clouding of boundaries has another side. In the 1920s and 1930s there was a "high-achievement" group of Vassar students for whom intellectual life was all; during the last quarter-century, such students have been less evident. Gone, or almost gone, is the kind of young lady who skipped lunch so that she could have more time to spend in the library, who went through four years of college without a date and hardly felt that she was missing anything because her studies were so fascinating.

Even the most dedicated of current students are likely to lead balanced lives and to have their share of recreation and social life. Just as the increasing homogeneity of our society has delimited sharp ethnic and regional differences, so it may be observed that the current educational patterns within student society are less sharply distinguished.

The Problem of Continued Growth.   Most of the younger group of alumnae had married and were getting along quite well. They reported few difficulties or strains and their test scores showed that, compared with their state as seniors, they were relatively stable emotionally and free of anxiety. But the picture has one flaw. There is some indication that for many of the students personality growth stops after graduation. During the college years themselves, by contrast, considerable growth takes place. Changes in mental ability and functioning, in attitudes and opinions, and in other qualities of personality—for example, authoritarianism and impulse expression—occur in this period. (See Chapter 11.) Seniors are more developed and more complex than freshmen. They are less bland and more flexible, more aware of themselves and more open to new experiences. In this sense we might say that college seniors are now *ready* to be educated. The resistance to new experiences characteristic of so many freshmen has been dissolved—or at least eroded.

But what happens after graduation? Do we see in the graduates some integration of the personality at a higher level of complexity than we find in seniors? The test findings at Vassar revealed no important changes in personality among the majority of alumnae during three or four years after graduation, except that alumnae are more stable and less neurotic than they were as seniors. In a minority of cases, on the other hand, considerable change in personality does seem to have occurred. Perhaps what stands out more than anything else in these studies of alumnae is the *complex* relationship between college years and later life. By comparison, it is relatively easy to compare graduates of different colleges or different age groups, or to compare graduates as a whole with individuals who never went to college. In such cases, clear differences can be discovered between the groups being compared. This is not so when we try relating college experience to later life however. One student who graduated with honors goes on to do well in graduate school. Her classmate, who also graduated with honors, is a failure academically in graduate school. Family-oriented "underachievers" may be alert and alive intellectually twenty years after graduation, whereas family-oriented "overachievers," the better students in a formal scholastic sense, have stagnated intellectually. And so on for other educational types.

In short, when we consider ends in education, we must go beyond the college years themselves; we must view all of life as potentially a developing process. And so, when we ask about "ideal" student characteristics, and how they can best be fostered, we should also ask this: Will those characteristics *persist* into later years—*can* they persist—*how* can they persist?

IV
Campus Environments and Institutional Settings

In very large measure, what students learn in college is determined by their fellow students or, more precisely, by the norms of behavior, attitudes and values that prevail in the peer groups to which each student must belong. What are these groups that make up campus society, what are their norms, and what are the means by which conformity with these norms is induced?

These are the questions upon which Chapter 13, "Student Peer-Group Influence," by T. M. Newcomb, mainly focuses. In Newcomb's theoretical framework, the conditions of peer-group formation are primarily precollege acquaintance, present propinquity and similarity of the students' attitudes and interests. The main basis for the group's influence upon its members is to be found in the fact that, because human beings need each other, the group acquires power to reward conformity and to punish dissidence. The amount of peer-group influence varies with such conditions as the size and homogeneity of the group, its isolation from groups having divergent norms, and the importance the individual attaches to being accepted by his peers or to fulfilling obligations as interpreted by them. Newcomb argues that peer-group influence and the college's educational objectives are not necessarily antithetical. He points, in fact, to some conditions under which educational purposes may be served through the processes of peer groups. An important part of the professor's task, Newcomb says, is to try to arrange matters so that the peer groups' power to induce change will be most likely to serve the goals that the professor himself holds.

In Chapter 14, "Freedom and Authority on the Campus," Harold Taylor tells what happened at Sarah Lawrence in the 1950s—a story that dramatizes precisely *the dilemma that every innovative campus faces in the 1980s: how to avoid the immense disadvantages of all-out permissiveness— the stance of the progressive-education movement in its earlier stages— without returning to an authoritarian set-up.*

What happened at Sarah Lawrence in the 1950s was that a great many of the students, perhaps a majority, were seeking some kind of escape from freedom—*that is, they desired more structure in the curriculum and more participation by the faculty in matters that had been left to student govern- ment. This is exactly parallel to pressures from students in the 1970s: after freedom was gained in the 1960s, students began to favor change in the direction of the traditional college regimen.*

Taylor's solution to the problem is not simply to say what everyone knows, that neither the authoritatian set-up nor the old laissez-faire policy is the right way. He shows, in some detail, what the liberal or progressive way, brought up-to-date, requires. Students must not be permitted to escape from freedom; but faculty, on the other hand, must not permit themselves to escape from authority. Faculty members must stand for something, and they must enter prominently into the lives of students. "Independence" is not something that they can give to students; it cannot be developed through authoritarian discipline nor through an all-out permissiveness for which students generally are not prepared. It is to be attained through the experience of relationships with adults who are willing to govern events in accordance with knowledge of each student's developmental stage and in the interest of values that the student may learn to appreciate.

Chapter 15, "Environments for Learning," by George G. Stern, is devoted to one specific aspect of the relationship between student and college: the relationships between types of student personalities and types of institutional environments. Using the Activities Index (which measures dispositions of personality) and the College Characteristics Index (which measures the various kinds of pressures that are brought to bear upon students), Stern's research sought to discover how student bodies are composed, how colleges come to exert the pressures that they do, how images of colleges are built up in the minds of the public, and what kinds of colleges exert the most influence upon the attitudes and values of students. Chapter 15 presents Stern's major conclusions. Readers will be particularly interested in Stern's report of an experiment in which a college teacher successfully attempted to change the basic modes of thought in a group of students who had been identified (without the professor's knowledge) as authoritarian.

The chapters of Part Four demonstrate the importance of campus environment and institutional settings to the teaching-learning enterprise on the American campus. Colleges want students to change in certain ways; but if this is to happen, the officers in control of educational programs must first discover what are the conditions and the processes of such change. The three chapters of this section point to complexities that almost all academicians are aware of—but for most professors and administrators, the awareness lacks the precision that is needed if this knowledge is to do any good.

13

Student Peer-Group Influence

T. M. Newcomb

Birds of a feather flock together, and the kind of feathering that seems to be the most essential for the human species is that of interests. People are most likely to interact and in all probability to develop close relationships when a shared interest in some aspect of their common environment brings them together.

Common interests include common problems, although of course only those that are not too private. Many of the problems of the late adolescent in our society are the kind that invite college students to share them with each other. One such problem is frequently the struggle for independence. By its very nature this problem can be shared more with peers than with parents or teachers. In college, moreover, many students for the first time find themselves cut off from intimacies with adults; they probably see little of their parents, and—except in unusual circumstances—their teachers neither invite intimacies nor welcome students into faculty society.

Such a combination of circumstances is hardly calculated to aid students in their search for identity, precisely at the time when they are least certain about it. Small wonder, then, that students tend to be drawn together; their common problems make them ready material for the formation of strong peer groups. Membership in a peer group is likely to influence directly students' attitudes and may also—though this is less likely—influence their general skills, specific capacities, or basic personality traits.

Conditions That Promote Peer-Group Influence

There are at least four fairly well-established conditions that promote student peer groups' influence on their members' attitudes. No one of them is an essential condition; perhaps any single one of the conditions, under exactly the right circumstances, might prove effective in the absence of the others. When marked peer-group effects have been noted, however, it has been most common to find several or all of these conditions obtaining.

Size of Groups.   By itself, membership in very large populations is not likely to bring about the strong interpersonal relationships that are so important an ingredient in peer-group effects on attitudes. In fact, small groups—entities where interpersonal relationships *can* be established—often transmit the attitudes for which a larger population (like "the college") stands. Membership in the college population without the small groups' mediation would probably not mean much.

Homogeneity.   A second condition involves the relative similarity of group members. Homogeneity of age, sex, ethnic background, social class, or religious affiliation contributes to effective peer-group influence, primarily because a homogeneity of *attitudes* tends to go along with such similarities.

The group, in turn, that appears to agree in attitudes is all the more likely to convince the individual that such attitudes are "right." Closely related to this factor is the condition of *isolation*—relative isolation from groups with other norms. Here we mean physical isolation rather than a cutoff in real communication.

When the role of peer groups in education is considered, it should be noted that the condition of isolation produces a wry effect. Faculty members frequently bemoan the directions in which the peer group seems to be taking its members; professors even wonder why student values are not more thoroughly permeated with faculty values. Yet by contributing to students' isolation, professors actually nourish the object of their complaint.

Importance to Individuals of Group-Supported Attitudes. The fourth and final condition of peer-group effectiveness is obvious—the importance to individual members of group-supported attitudes. Other things being equal, the greater the importance attached to attitudes for which the group stands, the greater will be the group's solidarity. Whether the group itself engenders a high premium on group attitudes, or whether the individual valued group attitudes highly even before he became a member, the connection between group solidarity and the importance attached to group attitudes will remain.

The Impact of Peer Groups. Among faculty members there is a strong assumption that the "quality of the college product" is more fully accounted for by characteristics that individual students initially bring to college than in any other single way. A great number of faculty members, furthermore, assume that peer-group influence comes second in importance, leaving professorial tutelage in third-rank place.

When professors assign third place to their own influence, they are not necessarily denigrating their own roles as educators. The characteristics of new students (intelligence level, for example) are indeed important, but not necessarily because they remain unaltered through college. On the contrary, the importance of some initial characteristics lies in their capacity to produce and accommodate *change*. In these instances, professors may provide the necessary mechanism for bringing about change.

And if, as seems to be the case, peer groups are also potent sources of change, the task of the educators may be stated as follows: they must try to ensure that student potential for change and peer groups' power to induce change will be most likely to serve the educational objectives that the professors themselves hold.

As student bodies in most American colleges have become larger and less homogeneous, there has correspondingly arisen a kind of academic anonymity. The majority of students develop friendships with others whom they know as persons but not as students, that is, individuals who are sharing the excitement of academic-intellectual discovery. As academic and nonacademic matters are organized on most campuses, individual students who know each other well, and who are important to each other outside the classroom, are not likely to share excitement *within* the same classroom. There are exceptions, but they are all too infrequent; in general, the domain of peer-group influence overlaps but little with the domain of intellect.

Most college faculty members are no less capable of offering intellectual excitement today than they used to be. They now operate, however, mainly in social systems where whatever excitement they *do* offer is little shared by students outside the classrooms. As a result, their academic impact is not compounded and magnified by student interaction.

Time was when colleges were typically small, their student bodies relatively homogeneous, and their general atmosphere that of a well-knit community. During the past decades, however, many colleges have tended to lose these characteristics. The result has been that peer-group influences are as potent as ever, but increasingly divorced from intellectual concerns. It is no accident that the more conspicuous exceptions to this general trend toward student isolation from intellectual concerns are colleges that remain small, relatively homogeneous, and closely integrated communities. Small colleges can, almost without trying, provide the essential conditions for mobilizing peer-group influence around intellectual concerns. To do the same thing, larger colleges will have to do some hard thinking.

Conditions that Reinforce Faculty Influence

If a teacher's influence is to be effective, it must be caught up in the norms of student groups, and the degree to which this occurs bears no necessary relationship to frequency of direct faculty contact with students. It can even operate at a distance, transmitted by some students to others—provided that colleges are willing to supply the necessary conditions.

What are these conditions? First, the existence of a formal membership group is necessary, both moderate in size and characterized by relative homogeneity of interests—especially interests that are friendly to the educator's objectives. The formal group should be large enough to provide the individual with a range of choice in selecting companions, but not so large that individuals will be unlikely to recognize each other. The implication here is that larger colleges should be composed of smaller units—with 300 to 400 students, perhaps, the optimal size.

Second, in the residential college it is important to use the fact that student living arrangements provide the major single source of daily contact. Peer-group influence is almost certain to be enhanced, for better or for worse, if there is a considerable overlap between membership in formal college units and in living units.

The third condition has to do with instruction and faculty contact. It calls, again, for overlap. This time, the requirement is that academic life overlaps *both* with formal college unit and with living unit. In the typical large university it is hardly more than a chance occurrence if a set of students, whose personal relationships are close, find themselves simultaneously excited by the same lecture, the same book, or the same seminar, with resulting reverberations in their peer-group life so that they reinforce and sustain one another's excitement. To base such an occurrence on *more* than pure chance, the curriculum, the housing of students, and other facets of college life must be suitably arranged. When this is done, the mere frequency of student-faculty contacts will cease to be a matter for concern.

Whether contact occurs in the classroom or in the Student Union—preferably both—there is one central question that must be asked: To what extent are students discovering that ideas suggested by faculty contact are worth further exploration with each other? If the discovery is being made, the teacher's influence can be strengthened and multiplied; if not, the multiple will all too often be zero.

14

Freedom and Authority on the Campus

Harold Taylor

Liberal philosophy is based on the principle that people become better when freed from authority, when they make their own choices and think for themselves, when they act out of personal judgment. The liberal and progressive movements of this century have called for the liberation of the individual from the authority of the state, the church, the family, from moral coercion and cultural orthodoxy. The general theory which holds together these applications of the liberal position is the idea that the true human community is a group of individuals bound together by common interests and an ethic of mutual respect.

As the liberal sees it, therefore, "authority" is a set of general agreements which the members of the community are willing to abide by. These agreements change from time to time as circumstances change, the community develops and different experiences are shared in common.

When these ideas are translated into educational practice, the school and the college are organized as institutional models for a liberal society. The teacher is not an authoritarian leader who tells his students what they should know, what they should think or what they should do. He is a friend and guide who is helping students to become educated by the experiences he is able to bring to them. He does not wish to wield intellectual or personal authority over the minds and attitudes of his students. He does not direct their ideas toward established conclusions but acts in ways designed to help them to form their own judgments. Students in the innovative college may choose the course they will study, take part in forming educational policy, form their own self-government for student and college affairs.

In the same way, the principal of the progressive school or the president of the innovative college is not an administrator running faculty and students, but a chairman of the whole, serving at the will of the governing board, the faculty and the students—a democratic leader who orchestrates the variety of interests, judgments, opinions and decisions of all those connected with the educational institution, including students, faculty, parents, the board of control, members of the community and alumni.

By contrast with the innovative, liberal college model, American colleges have historically taken a great deal of responsibility and authority for students, with explicit rules which must be observed if the students are to remain in college, and with the authority of the dean and the president used to enforce college-made rules. In earlier years the college served in place of the family as the arbiter of conduct. This has been particularly true of the colleges for women, where rules have been strict and rigorously applied.

Over the years, however, the concept of college authority administered by the dean to those in his charge has shifted away from the punitive toward permissive policies. Students now often have a part in forming policy, for it is assumed that learning to handle personal-social problems is one phase of the process of maturing in the young adult.

Student Freedom: An Internal State

Among the experimental colleges that grew out of the new movement in education during the 1920s and 1930s, a new concept of social structure and the relation of freedom to authority was developed. This concept rested on the idea that, by planning a certain kind of social community, educators could create ideal conditions for individual fulfillment. Through planning, the democratic virtues of tolerance, understanding, generosity, cooperation and respect for freedom could be taught as values *implicit in the social structure.*

As an experimental college, Sarah Lawrence has tried in a number of ways since its beginning more than fifty years ago, to build such a community. The principle underlying Sarah Lawrence practice at the founding was that students should be liberated from all restrictions of college authority and should be given powers of self-government for which they took full responsibility. The students were asked to make the rules themselves through a system of representative government and to administer the rules through a student discipline committee without faculty control or supervision. The students were also responsible for making up their own social groups, both in forming student organizations and societies and in choosing friends with whom they wished to live in the dormitories. There were no sororities or honorary societies, and no prizes, awards, grades, or any other symbols of prestige except those won through the respect of others for service to the community.

Throughout the 1930s and 1940s, this degree of freedom was vigorously used, and the student prerogatives were jealously guarded against any suggestion by the faculty or administration that they should be changed or modified. Students expressed their views strongly on most subjects, organized student meetings to take political action, kept their literary magazine, student newspaper, and student organizations almost completely to themselves, and seldom requested help from the faculty or administration in student affairs. The Student Council and the Student Discipline Committee made the rules and dealt with infractions; council and committee members shared actively in making college policy through a Joint Committee of students and faculty and through the Student Curriculum Committee.

Beginning about 1950, however, the older assumptions on which the college system rested were shown to be in need of revision. It could no longer be assumed that liberation into freedom was the exhilarating experience that it had been for earlier generations of Sarah Lawrence students. Whereas in earlier years it had been possible to count on the strong motivation and initiative of students to conduct their own affairs, to form new organizations, to invent new projects either in social welfare or in intellectual fields, it now became clear that for many students, the responsibility for self-government was often a burden to bear rather than a right to be maintained. For others, the Sarah Lawrence system of community government was one to which they had already become accustomed in high school, and it lacked the degree of freshness as far as their experience as students was concerned. Many able students who would have been first-rate student officers refused to accept nomination in student elections. They felt they did not wish to take the time away from their college work. They also felt that they had had all the experience they could profitably absorb in the field of student affairs by their involvement in such matters in high school.

Nor was there a high degree of vitality in the concept of student freedom itself, since it was already theirs and it was not necessary to fight to keep it. From 1950 on, interest in political action declined to the point that even a student meeting on McCarthyism—one of the leading national issues in the early 1950s—could not attract an audience. During those years, students tended to devote themselves to their own studies, to their own friends. They were apathetic about events or occasions planned for the whole college. They made less effort than before to identify themselves with the rest of the student body or with the college as an institution. They preferred to work within a smaller framework in which only the teachers with whom they studied and the small number of friends who meant most to them were significant parts of their college life.

Beginning about the same time, morale in the dormitories also showed evidence of decline. Infractions of student rules were more frequent than before and the mechanisms by which the students could correct the situation were little used. Some house presidents responsible for the conduct of individuals within their houses often failed to report glaring infractions; other who did report them were punitive in their attitude and caused dissension in the houses when they exercised their authority. At the same time, attempts on the part of the college administration to provide more guidance were opposed by the students.

Why did new attitudes come to dominate the student society? Some of the causes no doubt were the pressures against political unorthodoxy that characterized America in the 1950s and the special pressures directed against Sarah Lawrence by congressional committees and patriotic groups. Then there was the helplessness that young people felt when they thought about an international situation dominated by the Cold War. These forces certainly played a part, but there were other factors, too. One of these was the possibility that a system of complete self-determination did not necessarily liberate the student. Undergraduates who were given complete freedom to make their own decisions often did not wish to do so, and not wishing to do so, they did not achieve a real, inner freedom.

Freedom and Authority: Some Ambiguous Areas

The student generation of the 1950s taught American educators that the creation of a campus ethos of freedom was a far more subtle process than they had supposed. A number of factors made that generation of students different from the students of the 1930s and 1940s—and some of these differences can perhaps account for the shift in student attitude toward the external freedoms which they encountered. The generation of students who were in college in the early 1950s was born during the years from 1935 to 1940. During their first six years these students were living in a society recovering from a depression. They then entered the war years with a growing period of prosperity for their families and a postwar period in which the world closed in more and more upon the United States, while the country increased in prosperity and power. The combination of tension from the world situation and the growth in national prosperity produced an attitude of caution and conservatism in the country that was bound to be reflected in the attitude of families and of children to their lives.

At the same time, the growth of a new attitude to child-rearing meant that most parents in bringing up this generation made a genuine effort to understand their children and not to impose parental authority in ways which might inhibit them. As a result, it became extremely difficult for children to rebel, since they were being "understood" rather than repressed. This has its consequences in giving them nothing but feather pillows to fight and in developing an attitude of self-understanding before there is a great deal of self to understand.

The conditions which came to exist in the 1950s persisted into the next decade as well—and the problems they engendered became even more acute in the early 1960s, the era when, to the young, anyone over thirty was suspect. By this time, most sixteen-year-olds were sufficiently sophisticated to know the limits of power possessed by their parents if it were to be put to the test. Moreover, young people were prepared to live an independent emotional life by depriving the parents of a return of affection, by appearing a minimum amount of time at home, by surface conformity to demands, or by simply leaving home altogether. With the removal of the concept of parental authority, the balance of power in family life shifted to the young. Having staked everything on a warm and affectionate relationship with their children, the parents could not resort to older methods of authority with its expectation of respect and obedience.

In this situation, the strongest force that parents could exert for compliance with family wishes was to induce a feeling of guilt on the part of the children for causing distress to parents whose requests were disregarded, a guilt which from time to time has had its own aggressive manifestations in a confused rebellion and a sense of frustration.

A new syndrome thus emerged in which there was no longer a clear-cut authority-freedom issue for the adolescent but, instead, ambivalent feelings of obligation, responsibility and guilt. Whatever satisfaction there may be in *open* rebellion was stifled at the source. The adolescent was unable to rebel, since before overt rebellion could occur, his parents demonstrated their "understanding" of his wish to rebel by assuring him that it is perfectly natural. The tension of opposites, so often a part in the healthy emotional situation of the adolescent, disappeared in a warm bath of parental affection. The parents therefore had no control over their child, whereas the child did not yet have sufficient experience to exert control over himself.

These developments in the late 1950s and early 1960s created a new and different attitude on the part of college students to the authority of their parents. It also created a different attitude to the authority of their college. Such a shift in attitude had been foreshadowed by a change in the social structure of the high school and preparatory school. Much more was being arranged for the students, although at the same time students were given more responsibility in educational and social policy-making. Added to this was the provision of entertainment by football games, television, radio, mass magazines and community projects. The attitude of young people toward entertainment in general became that of spectators, and they no longer took up with same enthusiasm their opportunities for self-expression, either in student planning or in social affairs.

A kind of balance was thus achieved in the 1950s—order within a permissive ethos—until the political and social policies of the nation, in the mid-1960s, pushed the delicate structure into disequilibrium. But at length, with the new decade of the 1970s, a new balance has been achieved and a new period of order within a permissive ethos has begun. In certain basic ways, the decade of the Seventies, on many campuses was very much like the decade of Fifties at Sarah Larence.

Some Research at Sarah Lawrence

During the years from 1948 to 1952, a group of Sarah Lawrence faculty members conducted a research project designed to discover something about the process of change and growth in college students.[1] The social life of the campus, the relationship of students to each other and to the college, their morale, their personal concerns, their attitude to the educational system as it was then operating—these were all part of the research interests of those who carried out the study.

In what follows, some material has been taken from the Sarah Lawrence research which might throw light on the question of how the concept of student freedom worked in practice. The results of this research during those transitional years can provide an object lesson for those administrators, faculty members and students who

---

[1] Murphy, L., and Raushenbush, E. (Eds). *Achievement in the College Years.* New York: Harper & Brothers, 1960.

are trying to find workable models of student freedom today.

During the early 1950s the transfer of responsibility to the students for running their own affairs was producing apathy rather than the creative results that had been customarily expected. If faculty members, on principle, remained aloof from working with the students in organizing student affairs, very little happened. Students were more often than not frustrated and discouraged. They said that they had few ideas of their own and, even if they had them, they would not know how to carry them out in the face of the apathy of other students. They spoke continually of the need for faculty guidance. By taking attitudes which, in educational terms, were intended to make the students independent of adult authority, the faculty seemed in fact to have made them more dependent.

Student Morale.   The factor of student morale is directly related to the question of how students respond to the absence of the satisfaction of working well with a teacher or in a course. This kind of experience was mentioned by forty-three percent of the students. A third of them mentioned the satisfaction of general intellectual achievement, specifically such satisfactions as learning to read well, to take in new ideas, the chance to work independently and in small classes. The investigators had expected to find a fairly large number of answers which would put a high value on the amount of personal freedom granted to the students and on the richness of the cultural life available on the campus. This did not turn out to be the case. Only three percent mentioned as of particular importance the amount of personal freedom granted; seven percent mentioned activities outside their courses as being their most important experiences at the college. Since the degree of personal freedom was as great as is possible, consonant with the ordinary social proprieties, the investigators could only conclude that the students, very shortly after their arrival at the college, took that freedom for granted.

The investigators also asked the students what they worried about when they *were* worried and presented a list of forty-eight "worries" with the request to check "the ones which have been of some concern to you during the past year." The list was fairly comprehensive and was based on knowledge of the students; for example, items had to do with concern about money, conflict with the family, or not being popular.

Without comparable statistics on the responses of students on other campuses, it would not be possible to say whether the social organization of the Sarah Lawrence campus—which tried to eliminate competition, social snobbery, or false prestige values—accomplished more in this direction than the conventional system. But it is significant in a free system that only a very few students in the total number had worries connected with not being popular or not achieving student prestige. Nor did the lack of rules seem to be as important as the investigators had been led to believe by student comment, since only one percent of the students mentioned this in their replies.

The Role of the Faculty.   The normal concerns of the college student—difficulties in concentration, feelings of inadequacy, lack of self-identity, worries about personal relationships—seem not to have developed to extremes of anxiety through the openness of the Sarah Lawrence system. The investigators counted on a direct relationship between students and teachers to meet some of these concerns. Each student had a faculty adviser, known as a Don, with whom she usually conferred once each week and who was responsible for the general welfare of the student.

The investigators were interested in knowing how far the students counted on the advice and help of faculty members and to whom the students went with their personal concerns. In their answers to the questionnaire, nearly four-fifths of the students listed "a friend" as the person to whom they talked. Over half mentioned their mothers, and about two-fifths mentioned their dons. Almost as many mentioned male friends or their fathers.

Counting those who talked with a faculty member other than their don, there were well over half the students who turned to faculty members for guidance; about as many turned to their mothers, while around eighty percent talked to other students. This confirms the notion that most of the talk about personal problems goes on *between* students and that the relationships among students in the residences are the greatest single factor in their general attitude toward the college and toward themselves. (See Chapter 13.)

In further discussions with the students it became clear that they were against the idea of residential counselors or faculty members.

Certainly they wanted the presence of faculty members around the campus, at student meetings, or as informal visitors to the dormitories, but not as representatives of college authority. The student house presidents were, in fact, in the role of residential counselors, and it became clear through further analysis and discussion that the quality of life within a given residence depended most of all on the qualifications of the housing president for holding office. Student suggestions about this problem resulted in marked changes in the nominations and election procedures, and in changes in the methods by which student choices for residence in a given house were screened and allocated.

This was one of the most revealing parts of the study. The combination of the research results and further discussion with a variety of students showed that the big reasons for student apathy or frustration—the world situation, public pressures, McCarthyism and so on—were less important than the spirit and personal relationships of the students among themselves. When it was seen that a group of thirty students who lived together could develop negative, nagging, and emotionally unhealthy attitudes simply from three or four of their number who were working out their problems at the expense of the rest, the need for more organization of residence life became obvious.

It also became obvious that in the selection of a student body to function in a free community it was of first importance to consider the personal attributes of the applicants every bit as seriously as their academic qualifications. Intellectually ambitious students with a drive toward personal gratification could, if present in sufficient numbers in a given residence, produce sufficient tension and difficulty within their own environment to prevent the healthy development of the students around them and to block their own growth. This is true not merely for experimental and innovative colleges, but for those conventional colleges that emphasize what are called high academic standards, by which is usually meant a population of students who get good grades in high school.

The "Social" Life.   At the time of the Sarah Lawrence research, the campus was usually deserted on weekends, and the Student Entertainment Committee found that when it went to the trouble of arranging a party or planning a concert, or in general making the weekend at the college an interesting and stimulating one, very few students stayed. The questionnaires revealed that nearly sixty percent of the student body left the campus on about sixty percent of the weekends. Since the students did this of their own volition and had the means of planning events for themselves if they wished to stay, they were asked whether they were satisfied with this arrangement. The answers indicated that sixty-seven percent thought there was something wrong with the way weekends were arranged at the college. Moreover, thirty-seven percent said that they would have stayed had there been something interesting to do.

The criticism of the college's social life most often heard was that it did not exist on weekends. Yet when given a full opportunity to make it exist, the students were unable to plan anything for themselves that they found interesting enough to engage in. After seeing the results of the study, the college itself took the initiative in planning such events as intercollegiate conferences, tennis tournaments, student concerts and student theater performances on weekends. Following the initiation of the new weekend program, the questionnaire was administered once again. In answer to the same question, only forty-five percent of the students—as against the previous sixty-seven percent—found the social life inadequate.

When these data were being collected, something was discovered about the way in which the students spent the time they had for recreation, social life and entertainment. When presented with a list of eighteen sparetime activities the students put "engage in bull sessions" first (seventy-two percent), followed by "listen to records" (seventy-one percent), "go to concerts, plays, etc." (sixty-six percent), "read newspapers" (sixty-five percent), "read unassigned books" (sixty-four percent), "write letters" (fifty-nine percent), "listen to the radio" (fifty-two percent), "do household chores" (forty-nine percent), and "go to the movies" (forty-five percent). Only nineteen percent indicated that they watched television—but there were only two television sets available to them on the campus at that time and television programs, during those years, were still quite poor.

The preferences for private activities with small groups of friends suggested to the investigators that the regular attitude which college students are assumed to possess—the wish for incessant togetherness, to live the intercollegiate sporting life, to be "social"—did not exist in any degree on the Sarah Lawrence campus. Although the students missed the regulation college events and would have liked more of them, they found substitutes in activities which on the whole seem preferable to the things that might have been substituted. They wanted their social life to take place around common intellectual interests rather than on the basis of conventional dating practices. On the basis of these preferences, this writer concluded that the students had the great advantage of possessing private interests and having occasional periods of loneliness.

The Student and the Curriculum. A phenomenon of the 1950s which concerned the investigators was the amount of criticism by the students of the free curriculum and unconventional methods at Sarah Lawrence, a kind of criticism which had not seemed to exist at the college during the 1930s and 1940s. Students began to ask questions at student meetings about why Sarah Lawrence offered no lecture and survey courses in Western Civilization of the kind that existed at other colleges, why there was not more systematic coverage of departmental subject matter, why there could not be examinations and grades so that a student would know her performance compared with that of others.

Student views of the Sarah Lawrence educational methods were therefore solicited, and it was found that approximately eighty-five percent of the students supported the discussion method, although many of them called for more positive control by the teachers. The most important finding was that fifty-two percent of the freshmen and seventy-six percent of the seniors asked for *more* direction!

Social and Political Attitudes. The fact about the student attitude of the 1950s that has been most noted by historians of education is the students' lack of involvement in social issues or political action. The irony in the Sarah Lawrence situation was that the college had a public image of a place where radical thinking was fostered and where freedom of thought nourished political radicalism—when, in fact, the students were generally conservative in their politics and, as the research showed, were not influenced in a given political direction by their Sarah Lawrence education. A study of political attitudes was made during the height of McCarthyism when the college was attacked over a period of two-and-a-half years by a variety of organizations and individuals. The effect of the complete freedom of political action given to the Sarah Lawrence students was that they favored strongly the defense of academic freedom by the college but did very little on their own initiative either in arranging meetings to discuss political issues or in taking specific action. On the basis of the research findings, it is evident that in the early 1950s Sarah Lawrence students in general (like students in other colleges) were conservative, that they tended to accept their society as they found it, that their college education did not affect their political affiliation in any marked degree.

It is not the function of a college to make an effort to change students' political affiliation. It *is* its function to teach students to become aware of social and political issues, to enable them to reach independent judgments on the merits of such issues and to understand and participate as citizens in the functioning of the American system of government. Enough is known about the way the Sarah Lawrence students conducted their own community affairs to say that the initiative in raising political and social issues did not come from them and that, unless the issues were raised in the context of classroom and course discussions or in student meetings sponsored jointly by faculty and students, it is unlikely that they would have been raised at all.

Conclusion: Transactional Relationships And Intellectual Growth

The findings of this study pointed to only one possible conclusion: If students are given responsibility and authority for an autonomous student community without a direct and working connection with the two other essential community components—the faculty and the administration—the system grinds to a stop and ceases to function as a true community.

These research findings, however, clearly also support the fundamental principle on which experimental colleges like Sarah Lawrence are based: True intellectual growth feeds on environmental factors of all kinds—emotional, social and physical. The growth in ethical sensibility occurs as an effect of the total college atmosphere, but the seed of idealism is sown in the environment by teachers: it is not magically produced by the student community through the operation of a free social system. It is fallacious to assume, as the older theory of progressive education did, that absence of institutional authority and the award of freedom to the young in a radically democratic system will develop an understanding of democracy. On the contrary, in many cases such a process actually tends to foster authoritarian attitudes. The fallacy lies in assuming that because students have student rights and an equal *status* with faculty and administration they should perform the same *role*. If this fallacy is acted upon in educational planning, then what *must* occur is exactly what occurred in the late 1960s— students insist on the right to make decisions on all questions, regardless of competence, experience, or knowledge and regardless of the rights and judgment of faculty and administration. It also results in so much student bickering over legalisms and procedure that no student—except those engaged in the process for the purpose of disrupting it—enjoys or benefits from any part of real self-government.

The teacher does not contribute to student freedom by withdrawal from a going relationship with the student subculture, nor by the older, nondirective, permissive approach to students. On the other hand, the alternative to laissez-faire or permissive attitudes is not a revival of institutional authority to control the students, any more than the answer to student requests for an examination system, grades, survey courses and a conventional academic apparatus is to give it to them.

The faculty-student relationship must be conceived as *transactional* rather than mutually autonomous. The danger to be avoided on the one hand is a kind of orthodox liberal piety which by good fellowship smothers a community with so much tolerance and understanding that everyone becomes a neutered, polite and conformist liberal. The danger on the other hand is that if there are no clear-cut aims, rules and procedures with sanctions and authority of some kind against violations, there is endless discussion, ambiguity, confusion, and emotional fatigue from devoting too much energy to discussion and not enough to getting on with the program.

Students need all the freedom the college can give them. But they need equally to learn by example whom and what they can respect. This double concept lies at the center of the transactional relationship between faculty members and students.

15

Environments For Learning

George C. Stern

The educational psychologist generally studies the influence of the emotions and personality on learning from the point of view of the individual learners—their motives, inhibitions, aspirations and fears—for the ultimate purpose of helping them to become more receptive to education. There are, however, other factors, independent of the learner, that are associated with the emotional atmosphere surrounding the learning experience itself. These are also of considerable significance in the learning process, and they will be given attention here.

In the 1930s experimental comparisons of the effects of democratic and autocratic atmospheres on group performance drew attention for the first time to the sociopsychological aspects of environments in which learning takes place. These studies were the forerunners of nondirective innovations in psychotherapy and of permissiveness in pediatrics. The implications of these new conceptions of personality development seemed clear for the educator: the key to learning must lie in the establishment of more democratic, nondirective and permissive classroom environments. The evidence from subsequent studies of the relative effects of student-centered versus instructor-centered teaching techniques proved ambiguous, however. And the research of the last twenty-five years shows that group atmosphere and individual student growth are interactive; the success of the learning experience depends on the optimal combination of the teacher's artistry in creating a particular group ethos and the needs of the individual student.

The Authoritarian Personality and General Education

The literature on classroom atmosphere emphasizes the ecological relationship between certain kinds of student personalities and certain kinds of academic environments. Researchers have been able to isolate different personality types in student populations and have studied how each type responds in a unique way to what appears on the surface to be a common educational setting. The following paragraphs identify some of the major personality types and summarize the typical responses revealed by the researchers.

Authoritarian Personalities. Authoritarian personality types, identified by their pervasive fundamentalist ideological commitments, tend to underachieve in the social sciences and humanities and to dislike both of these areas strongly. Their occupational choices lie in business, law, medicine and engineering, and they view higher education as having no other purpose than that of specific vocational preparation.

The typical authoritarian student prefers studying alone in the same neat and orderly place throughout the year. He identifies any sort of group study with a bull session in which nothing definite is settled. He rejects theoretical discussions in class for the same reason, and he prefers a straightforward exposition by the instructor to any other classroom activity. The authoritarian has rigid time schedules for studying, reading and review, and he relies heavily on formal study aids and the suggestions of his teacher, on outlining and notetaking, and on rote memorization of significant facts. When the reading materials are difficult, he goes to the instructor or to better students for help.

Students of this type who were enrolled in an outstanding general education program, when questioned about it, expressed dissatisfaction with the program: they complained of the lack of professional courses and the looseness of a pedagogical approach that did not require attendance and that expected students to formulate and answer their own questions. They viewed the program as diffuse and lacking in specificity. Such students made poorer grades and showed more emotional disturbance and a higher frequency of withdrawal than the rest of their classmates.

Anti-Authoritarian Personalities.   The anti-authoritarian personalities were identified on the basis of an ideological orientation stressing internationalism and relativism. They excel in the social sciences and the humanities, and most of them plan professional careers in one or the other of these areas.

Anti-authoritarians say they prefer cooperative study because they like to hear other points of view, enjoy discussions and like being with people. Class discussions of side issues are similarly enjoyed, and these students take notes of stimulating and challenging ideas which they intend to explore later. They do not care where they study as long as it is quiet. Readings challenge them, and they seek out additional materials to improve their understanding. Preparation for final examinations involves an attempt to arrive at some sense of the course as a totality.

Although outstanding as students, with broad cultural and intellectual interests, the anti-authoritarians are likely to be regarded with mixed feelings by instructors as a result of their challenging argumentative manner, marked independence and social and intellectual impulsiveness.

The Authoritarian Personality in a Special Atmosphere.   A social science instructor who had been assigned without his knowledge to sections composed exclusively of each of these types of students observed that the students in one of his sections lacked curiosity and initiative. This turned out to be the class consisting of students of the authoritarian type. The instructor found it very difficult to get them involved in a class discussion, although direct questions indicated that they were well informed on the text. He found that he was constantly tempted to lecture to them. On the other hand, the students in the class consisting of anti-authoritarians impressed him at first with their critical attitude. They asked many questions about his teaching procedures, wanting to know why various things were done. At first cautious, he subsequently decided that their criticism and controversy was friendly, and he came to enjoy the fact that they took nothing for granted.

Authoritarians did not like this particular course and tended to do poorly in it. Anti-authoritarians, on the other hand, enjoyed it and got the highest grades. Investigators had arrived at this generalization by studying students of both types assigned randomly to other instructors in mixed sections. But—and this finding is significant—the authoritarians in the experimental section did just as well on the final common objective examination as did the anti-authoritarians—and better than the authoritarians distributed among nonexperimental discussion groups. (The authoritarians' high level of achievement does not seem attributable to the general superiority of the instructor in the experimental section since his anti-authoritarian section did no better than other anti-authoritarians distributed among nonexperimental discussion groups.)

The instructor of the experimental sections emphasized that this primary objective was to stimulate the free exchange of ideas, superabundant among the anti-authoritarians but initially nonexistent for the authoritarians. His efforts to get the authoritarians to respond included continued pressure in the form of direct questions, a refusal to lecture or to provide direct answers, and encouragement and acceptance of any response for the students. But the instructor's most important—and most successful—techniques consisted of a kind of role-playing where he offered arguments in favor of extreme and unpopular points of view. The following excerpts are from the instructor's journal:

> Week 3: Major discussions were about women in politics. I took the position initally that women were useless except for maternity purposes. I refused to call on any woman, accepted and agreed with all male opinions and added to the slurs on the females until every girl in the class was ready to tear the plaster off the wall. From impasses, we moved on . . . .
> Week 5: I took the position that voting was useless . . . .

> Week 7: I favored "slavery," that is, putting the mob in any civiliza-
> tion into its place—"so you intelligent folks can operate a *good*
> democracy."

The slavery issue marked the turning point. In his journal the
instructor observed that the authoritarians began "to fight back
against the brutally dogmatic totalitarian rantings of the professor.
I tried to seduce them to totalitarianism, and they indignantly, but
politely, told me I was wrong." The following session the authoritarians finally broke down and began asking one interpretive
question after another about the course, behaving for the first time
in a manner similar to that which had characterized the anti-
authoritarians in the opening days of the term.

The findings of this study point not simply to the advantages of
the discussion method but, more significantly, to the techniques the
instructor used to achieve an effective level of discussion among
students who had been unable to participate. For the anti-
authoritarians the special techniques were actually supefluous;
these students showed no gains and succeeded mainly in demonstrating a competence they had already enjoyed prior to taking the
course. The authoritarians, on the other hand, had been both
deficient and resistant, but they proved clearly responsive to the
specialized techniques to which they had been exposed.

Student Ecology

The cases just described, along with other studies, lead to the
conclusion that the same educational ends can be achieved by very
different types of students if the environment is appropriately
modified for each type. An environment must be suited to the
species if optimal growth is to take place.

But what *is* an optimal environment for learning? Pearls come
from aggravated oysters, but milk comes from contented cows.
Which metaphor is appropriate for education? Each seems to have
its place, according to the kind of student and the aims of an
educational program. The answer is that the characteristics of the
student and the objects of the program must both be employed as
guides in the design of the most effective environments for learning.

V
New
Teaching,
New
Learning

The six essays of Part Five explore the teaching-learning process and the classroom settings and curricular structures that surround and often support—but also often impede—teaching and learning in American colleges and universities.

In Chapter 16, "The Teacher as Model," Joseph Adelson shows something of the various ways in which students use the personality of the teacher in the maintenance or development of their own personalities. On the basis of his own theory of "modeling," Adelson distinguishes several major types of positive models among professors—the teacher as "shaman," the teacher as "priest," the teacher as "mystic healer"—and then, in a brief but eye-opening section of the chapter discusses several negative models professors often supply to students.

In Chapter 17, "The Classroom: Personal Development and Interpersonal Relations," Joseph Katz delineates some of the variables of personality that bear on the teacher's work. He then calls attention to a number of personality characteristics of the teacher which underlie the enormous variability in attitudes and behavior that may be observed in practice. And he then goes on to show that these characteristics of personality determine the kinds of goals that the teachers set themselves, the ways in which they view students, singly or in the aggregate, and the means by which they undertake to reach their goals.

Katz takes the position that teachers' modes of thought, their conception of knowledge, and their theory of how it is to be pursued are all integral with their functioning as a personality. Perhaps the most important function of the essay is to show some of the ways in which the different personality dispositions of students are affected by the varying aspects of the teachers' personality and behavior.

Chapter 18, "Curriculum and Personality," by Joseph Katz and Nevitt Sanford, views the curriculum in the light of the personality theory presented in earlier chapters. This theory is used here by Katz and Sanford as the basis for their attempt to formulate a hypothesis about the nature of learning in college, to appraise existing college programs, and to speculate as to what kind of curriculum would have to be designed if faculty members were guided by this theory of personality as they set their goals and as they devise methods for reaching them.

In Chapter 19, "Changing Functions of the Professor," Robert H. Knapp poses a fundamental question. He believes—in company with many educators—that the three major functions of the American professor ought to be combined in a balanced and cohesive unity. The functions he distin-

guishes are: engaging in research, transmitting information and helping students develop as people. A main tendency in American education, he asserts, has been toward a separation of these functions. The increasing emphasis on research has been accompanied by a decreasing accent on personal development, while the research and information-giving functions have tended to grow apart.

Today there is confusion and conflict. Forces at work in the colleges and in society at large pull the professor in different directions, making it increasingly difficult for any one person to perform according to the various role-expectations all at the same time.

W. J. McKeachie suggests, in Chapter 20, "Approaches to Teaching," that the separation of the informational and character-building functions of the professor may not have gone as far as Knapp fears. When, during the past forty years or more, researchers have asked which activities of the teacher—what techniques and procedures—lead to the best results, the best researchers have used as criteria not merely the learning of course material, as measured by grades on examinations, but also desirable changes in attitudes and values. More than this, a major conclusion from numerous experiments on the conditions of learning is that particular arrangements or methods—for example, large or small classes, or lecture versus discussion modes—are not as important as are the various psychological factors operating in the relationship between the teacher and the learner. In a significant section of Chapter 20, McKeachie explains the revolution in thinking about teaching and learning that has taken place during the last decade and presents what he believes are fourteen major tenets of the new approach.

Among the psychological factors in the teaching-learning relationship stressed by McKeachie, one in particular—the conditions that create "active" or "passive" students—is explored by Joseph Axelrod in Chapter 21, "Teaching by Discussion and 'Active' Learning." Axelrod describes four different discussion modes of teaching and shows how each one correlates with a different *student behavior state on the "active-passive" continuum. A major purpose of Chapter 21 is to show the reader how inadequate, in this situation, "either-or" thinking is: the commonplace view that if a class is not a lecture it must be a discussion or that if students are not "passive," they must be "active."*

In most of Part five, the reader will find that the authors offer data and hypotheses rather than fully tested propositions. The reason, as we have earlier stated, is that the scholarly discipline of "higher education" is still so undeveloped. But the hypotheses presented here, we hasten to add, are based on systematic observation and a wide array of data. These chapters are not to be confused with most of the literature that has appeared on college teaching which, as Adelson points out at the very beginning of Part Five, is more often inspiring than enlightening and in which we miss a sense of the complexity and ambiguity that we know characterizes the teacher's work.

16

The Teacher As Model

Joseph Adelson

Discussions of the good teacher are likely to leave us more up-lifted than enlightened. The descriptions we read generally amount to little more than assemblages of virtues; we miss in them a sense of the complexity and ambiguity that we know characterizes the teacher's work.

Here are some paradoxes to help us begin: a teacher may be a good teacher yet not serve as a model to any of his students; he may inspire his students and yet fail to influence them; he may influence them without inspiring them; he may be a model for them and yet not be an effective teacher. These paradoxes make the point—an obvious one but generally overlooked in the more solemn and global discussions of the teacher—that charisma, competence and influence do not necessarily go hand in hand. A great many college teachers, perhaps most of them, are "good" teachers—good in the sense that they are conscientious and devoted, that they are lucid, articulate and fair-minded lecturers, and that more often than not they succeed in illuminating the subject matter. Their students learn from them and often learn very much; yet these teachers do not ultimately make much of a difference in their students' lives beyond the learning they impart.

At another extreme we have those rare teachers who stir and enchant their students, and yet who may be spectacularly inept in teaching subject matter. There is a certain kind of professor in some ways a truly great man, who is so ebullient, erratic, and distractible, so easily carried away by the rocketing course of his thought that his students, even the bright ones, just sit there, benumbed, bewildered and finally enthralled. They know they are close to a presence, and they are willing to suffer incoherence to join vicariously in that demonic enthusiasm.

What we must do, plainly, is to recognize the pluralism in teaching—that is, the many styles of influence and the many modes of connection that bind student and teacher to each other. There are three of these modes which, while very different one from the others, have this in common: the teacher, in addition to imparting conventional knowledge, plays the role of healer. These modes can be labeled the teacher as shaman, the teacher as priest and the teacher as mystic healer.

The Teacher as Shaman

Here the teacher's orientation is narcissistic, although his public manner may not reveal this. He is not necessarily vain or exhibitionistic; he may in fact appear to be withdrawn, diffident, even humble. Primarily, however, he keeps the audience's attention focused on himself. He invites the student to observe the personality in its encounter with the subject matter. He stresses charm, skill and manner in the self's entanglement with ideas.

When the narcissistic orientation is combined with unusual gifts, we have a charismatic teacher, one of those outstanding and memorable personalities who seem more than life-size. The charismatic teacher is marked by power, energy and commitment—power in the sense of sheer intellectual strength or uncommon perceptiveness and originality, energy in the sense of unusual force or vivacity of personality, and commitment in the sense of a deep absorption in the self and its work. Generally, all of these qualities are present to some degree. Energy without power turns out to be mere flamboyance; power without energy or commitment is likely to be bloodless, arid, enervating.

The Teacher as Priest

The priestly healer claims his power not through personal endowment, like the shaman, but through his office. He is the agent of an omnipotent authority. He stresses his membership in a powerful or admirable collectivity—for example, physics, psychoanalysis or classical scholarship. The narcissistic teacher to some degree stands apart from his discipline and seems to say, "I am valuable for myself." The priestly teacher says, "I am valuable for what I belong to. I represent and personify a collective identity."

Collectivities differ in their openness, their degree of organization, their status vis-a-vis other groups. Some are easy to enter, whereas others are closed; some are loose and informal, bound by common interest and camaraderie, and others are stratified and formal; some are marginal in status, whereas others are secure, entrenched elites. Other differences involve the teacher's status in the collectivity: the undergraduate teacher may proselytize, seeking recruits among the promising students; the graduate or professional-school teacher will first indoctrinate, then examine, and finally ordain the recruit.

There is no question of the potency of the priestly mode of teaching. It achieves its effectiveness for a great many different reasons. Teacher and student are generally in a close relationship to each other. Students are encouraged to model their activities after the teacher's, very much as in those charming experiments on imprinting where baby ducks follow the decoy. We also find a good deal of close coaching, both of behavior and of ideology. In most cases, the teaching is both positive and negative—that is, students are not only trained to develop new behaviors but are also required to eliminate competing or discordant responses. Generally, students are given an unambiguous ideal of character and behavior. They may be allowed, as part of the strategy of training, to feel uncertain about whether they are meeting this ideal, but the ideal itself is usually clear-cut enough. In some instances, the collectivity offers an encompassing doctrine, and students are exhorted to reinterpret their experiences in the vocabulary of the doctrine; when this is not the case, the training itself demands so complete a commitment of time and energy that the students' ideational worlds narrow to include only the collectivity and its concerns. The teacher customarily enjoys a great deal of power in relation to the students, and this reinforces the students' dependency. The students' ties to the collectivity are further reinforced by their close association with peers—rivals, fellow-aspirants, fellow-sufferers—who share their trials, sustain them in moments of doubt, restore their flagging spirits, and keep alive their competitive drive.

This mode of teaching is effective because it offers students a stake in a collective, utopian purpose and because it promises such tangible rewards as power, position, money and intellectual exlusiveness. Less obviously, but quite as important, the collectivity makes its appeal to students in helping them to resolve internal confusions. Their participation allows a distinct identity choice; it supports that choice by collective approval; and it reduces intellectual and moral ambiguity.

The dominance of this mode of teaching in the graduate and professional schools, although regrettable, is probably inevitable. It is more disturbing to note its steady encroachment in undergraduate education. For many college teachers the introductory courses have less value for themselves than they have as a net in which to trap the bright undergraduates, and the advanced courses increasingly serve only to screen and socialize students for what most faculty members deem "the great good place"—namely, the graduate school. Furthermore, academic counseling at the freshman and sophomore level frequently produces a guerrilla warfare between disciplines, each seeking to capture the promising talents for itself, without too much regard for students' needs and interests. If matters have not become worse than they already are, it is not because the disciplines have any genuine concern for undergraduates or for liberal ideals of education; it is because the leviathans have managed to neutralize each other's demands. Even so, the pressure of required courses and prerequisites serves to force students into premature career commitments, while the onerous demands on their time (especially in the laboratory courses, but also increasingly in other fields) keep them from trying anything else.

The Teacher as Mystic Healer

The mystic healer finds the source of illness in the patient's personality. He rids his patient of disease by helping him to correct an inner flaw or to realize a hidden strength. The analogy here, and perhaps it is a remote one, is to the teacher I will term altruistic.

He concentrates neither on himself nor on the subject matter nor on the discipline, but on the student. He says, in effect, "I will help you become what you are." We may recall Michelangelo's approach to sculpture; looking at the raw block of marble, he tried to uncover the statue within it. So does the altruistic teacher regard his unformed students. He keeps his own achievement and personality secondary, and he works to help students find what is best and most essential within themselves.

At this point we are uncomfortably close to the rhetoric of the college brochure. This is what colleges tell us they do; and yet we know how very rarely we find altruistic teaching. Why is it so rare? For one thing, it is a model-less approach to teaching; the teacher points neither to himself nor to some immediately visible figure, but chooses to work with his student's potential and toward an intrinisically abstract or remote ideal. Also, this mode of teaching demands great acumen and great sensitivity—that is, the ability to vary one's attack according to the student and to the specific phase of teaching, now lenient, now stern, now encouraging, now critical.

The reason that the altruistic mode of teaching is so rarely *successful* lies deeper, however. The mode is selfless. It demands that the teacher set aside, for the moment at least, his own desires and concerns to devote himself without hidden ambivalence to the needs of another. In short, the teacher's altruism must be genuine; and altruism, as we know, is a fragile and unsteady trait, all too frequently reactive, born out of its opposite. If the teacher's selflessness is false, expedient, or mechanical, if it comes out of a failure in self-esteem, or if it gives way to an underlying envy—and in the nature of things, these are real and everpresent possibilities—the teaching at best will not succeed and at worst may end in damaging the student.

Teachers as Negative Models

This reminds us of what might otherwise escape our attention, that the teacher may sometimes serve as a negative or anti-model. Here the students use the teachers as a lodestar from which they sail away as rapidly as they can, seeming to say, "Whatever he is for, we will be against."

Teachers who exercise this power of revulsion are, in their own way, charismatic types; indeed, the teacher who is charismatically positive for some will be negative for others. He breeds disciples or enemies; few remain unmoved. If we follow a student's development closely enough we generally discover both positive and negative models. The decision to be or become like someone goes hand in hand with a negative choice of identity and ideal.

Value Changes.   An even more important topic on the negative side of modeling concerns the teacher whose value changes—the disappointing model. In the main, students learn to be realistic about their teachers, enough so that they are spared any strong sense of disappointment. Indeed, they manage it so well that we are likely to remain unaware that even the "normal" student undergoes at some time some crisis, however minor, concerning the clay feet of an intellectual idol.

The students' response to disappointment depends not only on their susceptibility but also on the type of flaw they discover in the teacher. It makes a difference whether or not the failing affects the students' image of the teacher as a teacher. Greater strain is put on students when the model's fault involves academic performance than when it is unrelated to how the teacher does his work. When the flaw does not involve the teacher's work, the students can more easily sustain their image of him in the teaching role.

Moral Failures.   Probably the most difficult type of failure for students to accept is a moral one. The word *moral* here is meant to convey such qualities as integrity, fairness, ethical sensitivity and courage. Students are not overly demoralized to discover that their model's personal qualities are not quite what they had thought or hoped, that their teacher is not as intelligent, penetrating, or perceptive as he first appeared to be. It is, in fact, part of the maturation of students that they learn to give up a belief that parents are all-competent. But a moral failure is not so easily accepted, and if it is serious enough in nature it is likely to be disheartening or even a shattering experience for students.

The teacher's life is as filled with moral tension and ambiguity as any other, but the moral dimension is most visibly operative in areas that do not affect students—for example, in departmental politics. Consequently, moral issues do not ordinarily become problematic in the teacher-student relationship. But when they do, everyone involved becomes intensely aware of their tacit importance.

College students have had a unique opportunity, during the loyalty oath troubles of the 1950s and the incidents of unrest on many American campuses in the 1960s, to observe how the moral qualities of their teachers, ordinarily taken for granted and so overlooked, could assume overweening importance in moments of moral crisis. Those were uncanny times for students. With one part of themselves, they lived in the routine of things, concerned with courses, examinations and dissertations; but all the while, their inner, central attention was focused elsewhere, held in a fretful preoccupation with the morality play in which their teachers were involved. They wondered how things would turn out, of course, but beyond and deeper than that, the intimate compelling question was whether their positive models would behave honorably.

They did not, most of them, although for a time students kept themselves from recognizing this, largely by allying themselves psychically with the very few who acted heroically while ignoring the very many who did not. It taught students, on the one hand, that moral courage is possible, and on the other, that it is uncommon. All in all, it was a quick and unpleasant education. Perhaps it is just as well for all of us, teachers and students alike, that serious moral examinations occur rarely.

17

The Classroom: Personality Development And Interpersonal Relations

Joseph Katz

A great many college professors do not have an extended interest in exploring the ultimate effect of college education. This lack of interest is so striking that it cannot be explained simply as neglect. Nor can it be attributed merely to a hesitation to engage in self-study. It stems, rather, from a deep-lying philosophy—from the college teacher's conviction that the subject matter he teaches has absolute worth, quite aside from its effect on his students. Such a conviction is not free from half-conscious doubts, but it has strong roots nonetheless.

Characteristics of the College Teacher

Typical college teachers see themselves as offering knowledge of the world as they have grasped it. In presenting this knowledge, they regard any modification of it a regrettable concession, a dilution which must be kept to the minimum. When these college teachers look at themselves, they see themselves as vendors standing at their stalls in the fair of knowledge, confident in their specialty and hopeful that those who can appreciate it will come and taste. In fact, for the majority of college teachers, their specialty gives them a primary focus with which to organize their life and make it meaningful. They are little trained, and often little disposed, to see the college student—who is not a specialist—in the student's own perspective. They are likewise ill-prepared to make the vital distinction between the process of advancing and preserving knowledge and the process of educating others.

College teachers are highly professionalized in regard to their scholarship, that is, their relationship to the subject matter they teach. As educators, however—that is, in their relationship to their students—they are almost completely amateur. They do not know what the effects of their teaching are, for they lack systematic ways of gauging these effects. It follows that they have no reliable means for improving themselves as teachers, for increasing their effect on students in the specific direction they wish to go. For the most part, they arrive in the classroom unprepared, not in their own knowledge, but for communication. Most college teachers have probably never once analyzed systematically a single classroom hour to find out how effectively they can communicate. Instead, they rely on examinations, comments by students and faculty remarks about what students have said. Some teachers occasionally pass questionnaires around. Above all, there is the behavior of the class itself, quiet or restless, attentive or bored. But the skill and aptitude required to evaluate class reaction, and to differentiate individuals and groups in the class, are frequently lacking. Such clues, even when they are noticed by a scholar who has never been trained to perform the teaching task, cannot be accurately read, for they are filtered through the teacher's anxiety, vanity, obtuseness or optimism; and as a result they tend to confirm initial prejudices.

Everyone in higher education agrees that, given the influence that college teachers have or might have on their students, a professor without some sensitivity to human interactions will probably do a poor teaching job. Two tasks must therefore take priority in the years ahead. The first task is discovering the best means to increase teachers' awareness of these matters and creating in them the desire to become aware of them. The second task is exploring ways of "matching" students with certain needs and preferences to professors who have the capacity, the background and the interest to deal with these particular needs and preferences.

The Process of Becoming Deadwood

It is obvious that the conditions under which many professors in undergraduate colleges work invite stagnation. All but a few of the students are always of the same age group. They arrive in their courses with the same naivete as the students of the year before, and their professors, instead of going on from where they left off the year before, must start all over again. From time to time, a teacher will meet a former student who asks, "Are you still teaching such-and-such course?" The very question seems to imply stagnation: the student, it is implied, has gone on to other things, with or without using what he has learned in the course, but the professor is still there—and will be there for decades to come.

But for all too many college teachers, the classroom seems to offer insufficient challenge and stimulation to keep them intellectually and emotionally alive. What is so frequently talked about as undergraduate apathy has it equivalent in the "deadwood" among the faculty. The "deadwood" process is a special case of demoralization caused by conditions of work. This demoralization stems, in part, from ignorance about what is achieved in the classroom. Without a clear evaluation of the classroom process, almost anything can be justified as beneficial to *someone* in the class, and in the end nothing seems to make much difference.

The absence of any mechanism for assessing the teacher is regarded, in the prevailing ideology, as a condition of freedom and independence in teaching. But it has an unrecognized side effect—it deprives most teachers of a firm sense of accomplishment and a firm sense of mistakes from which to learn. Without self-evaluation, teaching leads inevitably to a cycle of repetition. Only detailed, sophisticated and continuing assessment can make the teaching experience a cumulative thing and thus instruct the instructor.

Strange as it may sound to the outsider, institutional devices for keeping the learning process alive for faculty are extremely under-developed on most campuses. Mainly, whatever learning does occur takes place in isolation. Teachers are separated not only from their professional colleagues nationally but even from departmental colleagues locally. When faculty members in a college department get together in meetings, less time is spent discussing ideas and problems of teaching than is spent discussing administrative questions and college or university politics.

Many faculty members who have been colleagues together for many years find that they can no longer stimulate or learn much from one another—or worse, that they no longer intellectually respect one another. In such cases, seminars attended by invited colleagues from elsewhere and periodic residences of "visiting firemen" might be of some value in counteracting intellectual isolation. Another source of learning may be colleagues in the other departments. Colleges that have no graduate school attached are missing a unique opportunity. Where there are no graduate departments the faculties, because of their much lesser specialization, have an intriguing opportunity for investigating how knowledge and methods from differing fields can best be pooled. Here indeed there is open to the faculty a novel research function, quite beside the effect of interdepartmental learning on teaching and teachers. Moreover, there could be more external devices, beginning with the stipulation that no professor repeat the same course too many times. Teachers might frequently give courses in departments other than their own, and the visiting and exchange system be-tween schools could be organized on a systematic basis, enabling teachers to become acquainted with a variety of institutions and colleges. A system of circulation may work as well for the college as for the carp pond.

In some localities, consortia of neighboring colleges have insti-tuted faculty exchange programs that are minimally disruptive for faculty members because they do not necessitate change of resi-dence. Yet they have the advantage of providing faculty members some new—and potentially exciting—intellectual environments.

The Classroom as the Teacher Sees It

Given the absence of clear-cut goals and measures of progress toward them, college teachers are inclined to resort to magical thinking. Some teachers, for instance, will assert that any student can benefit merely from being in a classroom; if the immediate results are meager, they are glossed over by reference to supposed long-range effects. Many college teachers see the value of higher learning less in the subject matter of courses than in the discipline that students must learn—and even in the self-denial that many working students find necessary—if they are to persist toward academic degrees. Among the more cynical teachers, college is viewed as a convenient episode that delays a student's entrance into the labor market.

It is a chastening experience for a professor to listen to interviews with students while they are in school or even several years after they have left college. There are few references to the classroom. Rare, too, is any mention of the personality characteristics of teachers, but even that appears more often than any attention to the content of courses. This does not imply that the influence of subject matter is negligible in American colleges, but the evidence does show that, both during and after college, most students do not speak at length about their classroom experiences or about any great and exciting ideas to which they may have been introduced in their various courses.

The problem is not fundamentally different from the one the Lynds posed more than a half a century ago regarding high school education, in their study of the small Indiana city they called Middletown. The Lynds wondered why, in a society where going to school was so highly valued, the academic content of education was considered to be the special province of grinds and freaks and why the athlete rather than the scholar was likely to be idolized.

Part of the answer, of course, lies in our popular culture. The American college curriculum—born of and shaped by the needs of a small, European, intellectual and managerial class—rests mainly in the custody of teachers who still identify largely with that class. The courses these teachers design, however, are offered to young people with vastly different interests—jobs, sports, cars, the intricacies of making out sexually and a wide variety of other adolescent pursuits. Moreover, the adult society into which these young people move when they leave college does not generally embrace the values that the college teachers have offered to the students.

The Classroom from the Student's Point of View

Like faculty members, students arrive in the classroom insufficiently prepared. They have first been shuffled through a rather soulless and bureaucratic process of registration that is concerned with credit points, prerequisites, and grade point averages. They find themselves herded into frequently uncomfortable classrooms, facing the backs of other students' heads. Reading assignments are given, as well as frequent quizzes, tests, exams and papers. Written work may be read not by the teachers but by arrogant or timid graduate students. Objective tests may be a further step in making learning impersonal. The whole process is recorded and presided over by the computer, which has now taken the place of the registrar—a college officer who, in the past, was an often friendly human to whom students could turn if problems arose.

The students' individual evaluations of their teachers express a wide range of attitudes—from seeing them as representatives of reality to seeing them as representatives of unreality, with corresponding attitudes toward subject matter and ways of presenting it. The members of the class will have common concerns about a teacher, with obvious variation in intensity. How is he going to grade? Is he going to work the class hard or not? How is he going to present his material, and what learning effect is he going to call forth from his students? The students' evaluation of their teacher is continuous. An initial liking of the teacher's quality as an entertainer may give way to the realization that this goes on at the expense of learning. For some students, a course and its teacher jell only when review is made before the final examination. In retrospect, even years after, a course may be seen as hollow, although at the time it was taken it seemed subtle and profound—an illusion created by the teacher's verbal agility or seemingly meaningful obscurity.

Transference in the Classroom. It is frequently held that a teacher's enthusiasm is *a* major, if not *the* major, factor in arousing the enthusiasm of his students. The students' reaction to the teacher's enthusiasm is only one facet of a more complex and underlying phenomenon—the transference and countertransference relationships between teacher and students.

The term *transference*, borrowed from psychoanalysis, needs to be redefined for the classroom context. The college teacher is a special transference object for his students. He is an "in between" object—he is in between parents and the adult relations the student will establish in and after college. College itself, for large numbers of students, means living away from home for the first time, and thus it is transitional between adolescence and adulthood. Teachers may thus become "associates" in the students' minds as they rebel against the established culture. This is a role to which some faculty members lend themselves readily, being permanent rebels themselves. But teachers often pay insufficient attention to the transitory nature of the students' rebelliousness. When the rebelliousness wanes, it is likely to be replaced with the establishment. Often what the college teacher misses is the opportunity to help the students find secure identities other than the traditional ones when they are seeking a new equilibrium. Other students react to teachers as if they *are* established culture—indeed, many faculty members today represent its values—and then the brunt of rebelliousness may be experienced by the teachers, too. In still other students there is a pre-rebellious attachment or compliance. College teachers tend to take these very varied reactions at their face value—that is, they see them as "objective" responses to themselves and their subject matter, and then they adopt "objective" ways of dealing with them. The intensity of the transference naturally varies with the school and with individual students. Transference may be at a minimum where the classroom is regarded as a nuisance in the pursuit of socioeconomic advancement or of fun, as with the student attending a large university who exclaimed, "I love school, but I hate classes!" But wherever learning takes place, the transference reaction also has a certain intensity and calls forth all the variety of manipulative, erotic, compliant, defiant, passive, aggressive and other reactions. These reactions both facilitate and interfere with learning.

Professors, of course, do not do the only teaching on college campuses or even the main part of it. Students teach themselves and each other, and this teaching goes on in and out of the classroom. Some professors are sensitive to this process and are able to put it to use, make it serve their educational goals. This process has not yet been closely studied, and techniques for capturing this resource need to be systematically described.

The fact that the majority of college students are or recently were adolescents means that their intellectuality and their whole personalities have a transitional character. Parents seem to know this better than teachers. They are apt to think of college as a "phase," whereas professors want to see the college experience as a much more solid, less tentative, part of the students' lives. College teachers, by seeing college as a phase, could help students utilize their rebellions and gropings more effectively, so that the college phase would be more fully a *stage in development* and less of a passing episode in the lives of students.

18

Curriculum and Personality

Joseph Katz

Nevitt Sanford

Despite the central place of the curriculum in college programs, its effects on students have not yet been systematically investigated. There is, of course, a vast literature on the curriculum, but most of it describes existing programs and proposals for reform. Not many researchers in higher education have studied the effects of different curricular structures on the development of students.

It seems to have been almost universally assumed by educators that the college curriculum, as presently constituted, defines the goals of achievement for the students and that the nature of the curriculum is to be largely determined by the present state of the "body of knowledge." Furthermore, most educators identify the "body of knowledge" in a given field with what is covered in a typical graduate school program—a very debatable identification. In planning curricula, educators pay only limited attention to the role such knowledge may play in the whole *development* of the student. It is usually glibly assumed that the better the mental capacities of the students, the more they will assimilate of the "body of knowledge"—and the more they absorb, the better it will be for them.

Practical and Imaginative Functions of Knowledge

Knowledge performs two main functions for humans—the practical and the imaginative. In its practical function, knowledge acts in the service of survival by contributing to man's mastery of the forces within and around him: the outer world, comprising both nature and human society, and the inner world of impulses. The attempt to understand, predict and control these inner and outer forces has always characterized the pursuit of knowledge.

The other side of the intellectual pursuit has been an imaginative extension of the real world. This imaginative extension of reality has really served two quite different purposes: enriching reality by lifting the person beyond sensuous and practical immediacy; and providing a vehicle for withdrawing from reality. The fundamental difference between the two purposes is that the second may be served at the expense of the individual's vital and essential relations with reality, whereas the first strengthens these relations.

Since imagination is necessary to master the real world, there is actually no sharp distinction between the practical and the imaginative dimensions of knowledge. The phantasies of an Ezekiel or the architectural plans of a Solari—even when they seem to defy gravity—may become tomorrow's reality. Thus imagination seems to be both a dependent and an independent entity in the make-up of human personality. In its dependent function it serves the purposes of mastering reality. In its independent function it is close to being, and perhaps is, a primary need. Even the most prosaic task can scarcely be performed without some admixture of imagination.

If we are interested in freeing the imagination—opening the individual to experience and encouraging creativity and spontaneity—we have no recourse but to free the individual's impulse life. And here lies a central problem for the educator, because modern schools, and perhaps even colleges, are largely concerned with suppressing a student's impulses, while building up to the highest degree possible his self-control. Much of this is necessary, but the fact is that unless a person's impulses are freed in certain directions—including the direction of phantasy—he will lack the spontaneity with which creative imagination is intimately linked. The educator's job, therefore, should be to show the student that his childhood impulses can indeed find gratification in the world of literature and music and art, and in creative activity in science.

At the same time we must recognize that knowledge of facts may be acquired now and stored, only to bear fruit later in some fresh insight or some creative achievement of the individual. Much college education, indeed, is based on the assumption that such acquisition of knowledge may eventually serve the individual. Surely this does happen, but it is easy to overestimate the frequency of such occurrences.

Classroom Presentation

In discussing the effects of curriculum, it is necessary to distinguish between content and mode of presentation. Although mode of presentation is related to subject matter, quite different subjects may have similar modes—an English literature and a chemistry professor, for example, may both use a lecture method that stresses the mastery of facts and principles. Conversely, two literature professors or two science colleagues might teach the same novelists or the same theories explaining certain biochemical phenomena by using entirely different teaching styles. Although clear correlations have not yet been definitely established, it is nonetheless clear to researchers in the field of college teaching that certain teaching modes favor the development of student personality while others have the opposite effect.

Modes that Hinder Development.   Many of the modes that hinder development serve a common ideal of discipline and hard work. To enforce *external* discipline, the grading system can be used as a stick. Likewise, the "weekly quiz," demanding the regular collection of tidbits of knowledge, ensures that work (of some kind) goes on unabated. Idleness is the archenemy of any compulsive system, and the students are kept so busy on some campuses today that it is harder to make an appointment with a student than with a professor.

A further common characteristic of teaching methods hostile to development is the emphasis on "right" answers. The student gets the notion that there is only one answer or at best a very limited set of right answers to any one question, that the teacher is in possession of these answers, and that he expects the student to master lecture notes or textbooks in order to be able to produce the answers, ones that appropriately match a given question. This process does not require—in fact, discourages—inquiry or reflection.

Impersonality is a third factor hindering development. In interviews with students it has been found that they very often link their most significant educational experiences to teachers with whom they have had some personal relation in and out of the classroom. Even in a class of 100 or more students, learning seems to be aided a great deal if the student can establish some sort of personal relationship with the professor. This is easier to do when the teacher's own personality is very vivid. And if a student plans to enter the professor's field of specialization, anticipation of a professional bond with the teacher may well make the student feel a personal relationship, even though, from the professor's standpoint, no such relationship exists.

Development is also hampered by a purely abstract approach to the subject matter. Many teachers and programs, in their attempt to avoid this approach, have tried strenuously to tie subject matter to concrete events, particularly events which may crop up in the students' own future experiences. When this is done, however, it often means that the teacher implants a stereotype of what the student's futures will be, rather than drawing on their very real, *present* experiences and their current interests.

Excessive emphasis on method of inquiry per se and excessive pigeonholing of subjects represent two other enemies of development. The importance attached to method becomes excessive when students are taught more details of method than they need for their level of inquiry. Such excess is due both to the sophistication that procedures have achieved in all fields of learning and to the purism of many teachers, particularly teachers who are at the same time researchers. It is likely to leave the students at first frustrated and then either indifferent or intransigent. Very often, a whole "beginning" course will be devoted to teaching the students the tools and vocabulary they will need if they continue to work in the field—an inappropriate experience for the students for whom the beginning course is the only one they will take in that field.

Pigeonholing springs in part from the fact that universities have departments, and departments govern curriculum. Only occasionally will teachers report, with agreeable surprise, that a student has related something to another course. Apparently students tend first to segment information from the rest of their personalities, and then to segment departments of information from each other. The knowledge taught students by outside agents—course lectures and required reading—is seldom really connected with their own spontaneous thoughts. As a result, they feel that they can remember "course material" more easily if they leave it in the compartmentalized form in which they received it. Pigeonholed and temporarily forgotten, it is only to be drawn upon when the schoolroom bell rings for it again.

Modes that Assist Personality Development.   The pursuit of objectivity is a major factor in developing personality. Yet perceptions of reality that are undistorted by wishes and anxieties are one of the hardest things for the human organism to acquire. The emphasis on objective evidence that pervades much of college teaching is an important antidote to distortion. Intellectual mastery—particularly when college students discover abilities in a subject hitherto unknown to them—may become a basis for revision of their self-image and of much of their inner and outer life. Furthermore, by broadening their knowledge of what human experiences are possible, individuals can be stimulated to fresh experiences of their own.

The pursuit of objectivity requires joint attention to the students' impulses and to their thoughts. Otherwise the two will neither combine nor balance, and the individual will be in effect two people—an emotional person dominated by impulse and an intellectual person dominated by thought.

The pursuit of objectivity and logic need not be only an individual experience; it can also be a social experience—learning with and in view of others. The present school setup tends to make classroom learning competitive, thus putting it into contrast with many extracurricular activities which are cooperative. Under certain circumstances, classroom learning can impress upon the students *both* the fundamental otherness of their fellows and the communication that is possible with them. We do not mean a superficial otherdirectedness, but that community which thrives best when its members have achieved their own distinctively separate identities. In contrast, present classrooms are characterized by a high degree of isolation of students from each other, an ironic corollary of students' failure to develop individually.

Another ally of the developing personality is learning to think by hypothesis. Hypotheses begin in hunches and require free association of ideas as a necessary condition. Individuals can produce hypotheses only if they are willing to relate subjects that superficially may seem quite *un*related. Some teachers maintain that it is precisely this profusion of phantasy that needs to be disciplined. And it takes extraordinary skill and sensitivity on the part of the professor to distinguish between a student's genuinely creative activity and a woolly, vacuous abstraction that has lost any clear and logical connection with the impulsive hunch that prompted it. The ability to distinguish between these often spells the difference between poor teachers—however well-intentioned they might be—and excellent ones.

The Curriculum

Content: The Freshman Curriculum.   It is in the freshman year that the failures of the curricula at conventional colleges—that is, at the vast majority of American colleges—are most glaring. Typically, freshmen arrive on the campus filled with enthusiasm, in eager anticipation of the intellectual experiences they are about to have. By the end of the year, not a few have dropped out and a large proportion of the remainder are ready for what in some colleges is known as the "sophomore slump." On some campuses, indeed, the "sophomore slump" occurs in the spring of the freshman year. This is often a period of considerably reduced academic interest and efforts, accompanied by a dawning awareness that college is not coming up to advanced billing. What remains is the hope that exciting experiences will come in the upper division, where a student can focus on a specialized field.

But many entering college students today have smaller expectations and fewer illusions. They are prepared to play the game of getting good grades, and they enter into gamesmanship with the same coolness year in and year out. Here is a sample of some freshman conversation on a large research-oriented campus:

> I wanted to take 210 this fall so I could get into 316 next year, but the only section I could fit into my schedule was filled. So I'm going to take 140 and get that out of the way. Did you know that you could substitute 185 for 180 and count it toward your natural science requirement? Freshmen can take it with permission of the instructor.

These comments pertain, of course, to the traditional type of curriculum, drawn up with a minimum of attention to how students learn, but with a maximum of concern with how knowledge may be organized on paper and how the departments' privileges may be represented. There are many "breadth" (or "distribution") requirements and many prerequisites for courses that the student will need to take later. Thus, for many students, the whole freshman year is taken up with "necessary evils," and for most there are few courses that can be regarded as ends in themselves. A significant learning experience is not likely to take place where there is a wide discrepancy between the student's purpose in taking a course and the goals the instructor sets for the course participants.

The point is sometimes made that existing arrangements serve well to "weed out" inferior students. But studies show that many potential learners go out along with the unable and the indifferent. In many cases, moreover, remaining in college is less a matter of scholastic ability than of gamesmanship or the capacity to adapt oneself to conventional pressures.

Existing programs are easy to criticize. But what is to be done? One suggestion is that, where the foremost concern is with the development of personality, the major aim of the freshman year should be to *win* students to the intellectual enterprise. With full recognition of the fact that for many it is now or never, every effort should be made to capture the imagination of students, to give them a sense of what it means to become deeply involved in a discipline or subject. They should be helped to learn things that make a difference in themselves and to become members of a community that is devoted to the pursuit of truth.

Most essentially, students must be shown that college education is a means for the expression of their impulse lives and an opportunity for gratifying their natural curiosity. Colleges should ignore conceptions of what freshmen "ought to know," whether the concern be with their preparation for more advanced courses or with a suitable sampling of organized knowledge. Colleges should concentrate on giving these students experiences that set in motion the development that is wanted.

Each course should be conceived as an end in itself. It should be designed first and foremost to develop the complete personality, and to do this the freshman course must be geared to the freshman's stage of development. Subject matter has a crucial role to play, but the results will have little to do with how much is "covered." It is ironic that elementary courses are taught with an eye toward advanced courses and the information that is likely to be required for students to succeed in *those* courses. Yet in the advanced courses teachers frequently assume—or discover—that very little has been learned in the elementary courses; and so, to make sure of "proper coverage," the teacher proceeds to teach what all of the students have presumably had before.

The relation of high school courses to college courses, and college courses to graduate courses, is much the same. Little is known about what undergraduate courses make the best preparation for graduate work in, for example, psychology or philosophy. There is nothing, in fact, to suggest that the undergraduate psychology major or the undergraduate philosophy major is best; indeed, some psychologists and philosophers prefer graduate students who have had little formal study in psychology or philosophy, but much literature and the fine arts, mathematics and science.

The Curriculum and the Liberation of Students.   In considering the effect of courses on student development, it must be remembered that the official titles of college courses give only the crudest idea of what particular teachers actually *do* in any particular class. If we take typical instances, however, it can be said that literature courses hold more appeal for the impulse life than does, for instance, chemistry. It goes without saying that chemistry can, and should, involve highly creative work, but for this to happen in chemistry courses—as they are typically presented in the American college—extra effort must be made to encourage spontaneous impulse.

Considering, then, the typical ways in which the various subject matters are treated in conventional programs, these subjects can be ranged by their proximity to the life of the imagination. Such a list would proceed from subjects like English to sociology and to physics. This is not an evaluative ranking; it is simply an indication of proximity to direct appeal to impulse and feelings. Typically, students broaden their impulse lives through subjects that evoke impulse—namely, the humanities. At the same time, students turn analytic and become more aware of their hold on reality by contact with the applied sciences.

Taking literature as an illustration, it can be assumed that novels and stories or plays will be taught in such a way that the students will understand the characters before judging them. The students' natural inclination may be to judge characters in literature—as well as real people elsewhere—by the values that they bring to college. If their anxiety is so great that they cannot tolerate any change in these values, they will probably not do well in the literature course. But if, on the other hand, they discover that *anything* can be done in the imagination, that everything that they have so far imagined has been done by somebody, and that those who did these things *can* be understood, they are bound to admit into their own schemes of things a broader range of human potentialities. These potentialities, they can see, are present in themselves as well as in others.

The point about literature is not simply that it releases fundamental impulses to be expressed in their original fundamental form—this could hardly be called freedom. Instead, it gives the individual some of the very things that made the creation of that literature possible. It supplies a vehicle for transforming the impulse life in such a way that it meets the requirements of reality and of conscience, *but meets them just barely.* If such transformation occurs through the study of literature, it will affect the individual's performance in other courses and in life generally. In other words, change wrought by education in one discipline ramifies throughout the personality and affects ways of responding to any discipline.

The literature illustration shows not only how the study of literature can transform the impulse life of the students so that growth takes place, but it also illustrates an even more fundamental principle: Once the teacher of *any* subject grasps the theory of personality development, new ways can be devised of using course material to enhance the student's growth. Courses in a variety of subject matters, for example, can serve to challenge the cognitive structures, the concepts of world and self, and the like, that students bring with them when they enter college. These structures undoubtedly derive mainly from family and community. For the most part, they have been taken over automatically and have not been the product of the student's own thoughts and experiences. Here the study of philosophy, the history of ideas, the comparative study of religion, and similar subject matters, could provide the necessary challenge if the material is taught in certain ways. One of the philosophy's principal aims is to instill the notion that all systems of beliefs and concepts are tentative and flexible, that at various points they have their equivalents in other systems. In the same manner, by studying comparative religion the great variety of beliefs which have called forth people's emotion can be examined. Such study can bring about understanding where the students might have felt strangeness or even repugnance before.

Studies of freshman and senior student groups show that the values and beliefs with which students leave college are often not very different from the values and beliefs with which they enter college. There is, however, the possibility that these values and beliefs are now held in a different way, that they have a firmer basis in the subject's own experience and thought, and hence a different relation to other processes of the personality. It might also be expected that, regardless of what the values and beliefs at the moment actually are, the student has the means for improving decisions in this area as time goes on.

But what about mathematics and natural science? As these subjects are so often taught today they help to maintain within the individual a defense mechanism, playing into the hands of the conventional, the restrictive, the suppressive functions of a personality. Study in mathematics and science can all too easily help turn out a well-disciplined, well-controlled, well-behaved young lady or young man who grimly accepts the formulas, memorizes a mass of factual material, and hands in meticulous lab reports. But things do not have to be this way. The teaching of science can convey a spirit rather than simply facts or precise techniques; it can lead the student along side avenues of curiosity as well as immerse him in one discipline. Science, after all, is out to upset the existing order of things. It is essentially daring and unconventional. Its rules and discipline derive out of its own processes and needs and have nothing to do with conventional morality. Many young people who choose science, however, hope thereby to capitalize on their prematurely organized consciences. When science is chosen for this reason, when its discipline is used to support the suppressing and controlling functions of the personality, it is not likely to free the individual later on. Would it not be better, both for science and for society, to recruit those students who demand freedom, who are passionate and curious and out to discover and to change the world? Only then, such students having been found, should the necessary disciplines be taught.

Conditions of Curriculum Reform. In any revision of the curriculum, at least four conditions must obtain: (1) clearer articulation of different approaches to teaching than now exists; (2) the development of a *curricular science,* a continuing process of experimentation guided by theory (the prescriptions pointed to by such experiments would be less useful if they were not constantly injected into the curriculum); (3) self-examination of teachers; and (4) recognition that any curriculum will have a different impact on different students.

The curriculum *can* be potent in developing personality. The modern curriculum's failure to realize this potential stems from the fact that its present guardians make no sophisticated attempt to contact the student's impulse life.

19

Changing Functions of the College Professor

Robert H. Knapp

The several hundred thousand Americans today who are engaged in college and university teaching constitute a professional class that is impressive both in numbers and in its potential influence on the shaping of American civilization. The rise of this profession in recent years has been sensationally rapid. At the turn of the century the country had about 20,000 college teachers; forty years later Charles Beard could observe that college professors "represented a larger proportion of the population set aside for scholarly pursuits than had been the case since the dissolution of monasteries and convents." In short, a vast and historically unique professional class had emerged in American society.

The college professor in America has been asked to perform

three quite disparate functions: first, original research; second, the imparting of knowledge; and third, the inculcation of values and the development of character. According to time and circumstances, the relative weight of these functions has varied, but even so, most of the paradoxes and vicissitudes of the profession have resulted from the inherent difficulty in mixing all three. In the long run, the character-developing function of American professors has declined, whereas their research and teaching functions have grown apart to form two quite distinct callings.

A View of the Past

During the seventeenth and eighteenth centuries and the first half of the nineteenth, the central focus of the American university remained relatively unchanged. It maintained a clear commitment to "classical" education, placing heavy emphasis on Greek, Latin, history, theology, and other subjects particularly germaine to the clerical calling. The professor in this phase of development was, by all modern standards, an intellectual generalist who might at once profess natural history, ethics and theology while remaining a Latin or Greek scholar.

In the latter half of the nineteenth century, however, several new factors appeared that had profound effects on the professor's role. The first of these was the rise of state-supported institutions, stimulated particularly by the Morrill Land-Grant College Act of 1862. This development can be seen as a sort of secularization process; higher education now became deeply concerned with technology, science, and other practical affairs, while the older clerical and classical emphasis was largely superseded. Closely related with this change was the rise of natural science, in itself a major trend. Finally, there was the emergence of the elective curriculum whereby students gained some freedom to choose courses. Originating at Harvard and quickly spreading elsewhere, the elective system went hand in hand with the rise of science, the crumbling of the old classical domination, and the growth of departmentalism.

These, then, were the main developments affecting American higher education during the late nineteenth century. Although they did not strike every institution equally, their impact on the college teaching profession was to be immense.

And what after the turn of the century? First, as already noted, there was a clear decline in the character-developing function so vital to American colleges and universities during the period of close religious control. The causes of this decline were several. One was the diffuse secularization which gradually and progressively took hold of American higher education. A second cause was the increasing emphasis on the practical problems facing the society; as the college professor increasingly concentrated on imparting technical and compartmentalized information, the supervision of character development passed through a period of neglect. Presently, however, the development of student character found new custodians—the counselor, the campus psychiatrist, the specialist in guidance. In some institutions, to be sure, the professor is still held responsible for inculcating morals and even religious convictions, but for the most part his character-developing function has become purely passive—the setting of a good example.

A second major trend since 1900 has been the rise of the doctrine of academic freedom. Younger members of the profession frequently assume that in appealing to this principle they are invoking an ancient and honored tradition in American higher education. Such is clearly not the case. Prior to the First World War the idea had little currency, and surely little force. The rise of the doctrine of academic freedom has done much to bolster a sense of security and dignity among college professors at times when their freedom was restricted by forces like McCarthyism in the 1950s and the establishment pressures toward "law and order" on the campus in the 1960s.

A third significant development since the opening of the twentieth century has been the sprouting of professional societies. As early as 1883, faculty members teaching the modern languages banded together in an attempt to achieve academic respectability in a world that accorded them only second-class citizenship. The growth of such associations was both a consequence of and a cause for the tendency of professors to identify with their disciplines rather than their colleges. In this regard, as in other university developments since World War I, science has been in the vanguard.

Another trend, in somewhat similar spirit, has been the rising importance of research and publication as marks of professional success and as the avenue to promotion and advancement. This is often the sole criterion on which employment in colleges and universities is granted or withheld—though in recent years, as a result of the student rebellions of the 1960s, lip service is given on most campuses to the criterion labeled "teaching effectiveness." One finds, particularly among younger members of the profession, an almost obsessive concern with early and persistent publication. This concern is supported by the entire pattern of doctorate training which is now the major pathway to admission into the profession of college teaching. The PhD has been aptly named the "union card" of the professor.

A fifth trend is the cyclical nature of the college professor's influence in public affairs. The political allegiance of college professors has been, for a group of their education and class origins, far to the left of other professions. Over the past four decades, college professors generally have been Democrats rather than Republicans, and in both parties they have supported the liberal wing. The influence of professors in national policy, as might be expected, has been stronger during liberal administrations and has declined when conservative presidents, legislators and judges have come to power. The public image of the professor was at the ebb of the cycle in the early 1950s (when he was required to deny any disloyalty to his country) and again under the Nixon presidency when he was under pressure to deny any sympathy with the youthful counterculture. But in recent years it is clear that the cycle is taking a more favorable turn.

A View of the Future

It is becoming increasingly difficult for the typical teacher at the large college or university—including faculty at the community colleges—to carry out the three historic functions of college teachers: character development, academic instruction and research. The pastoral or character-developing function which dominated the sectarian institutions of this country in the eighteenth and nineteenth centuries will be increasingly delegated to specialists, and the professor, even now, is being called on less and less to concern himself with the individual character development of his students. At the same time, a segment of the college teaching profession has cut itself off from the main body of the profession and has become a class dedicated principally to research and only incidentally to instruction.

Thus, for most college professors, the teaching of cognitive knowledge has become the prime function. Ever more devoted to the work of instruction, and ever more bureaucratized in that work, they have steadily relinquished all responsibility in either creative and original scholarship or character building. Only rare individuals, placed in fortunate circumstances, are able, today, to achieve the ideal unity that combines character development, academic instruction, and research. Unless present conditions change radically, it is not likely that these three functions will be reunited for the vast majority of college teachers.

20

Approaches
to Teaching

W.J. McKeachie

Teaching is the heart of higher education. The main standard for judging the effectiveness of administrative organization or of curricular planning is whether it facilitates good teaching. In turn, the ultimate criteria of effective teaching are desired changes in students, changes toward whatever higher education is expected to produce.

Student Motivation

All learning is closely tied to motivation. People learn what they want to learn; they have great difficulty in learning material which does not interest them. The college teacher should recognize that this is a principle resting at the very center of the teaching-learning process. Although professors would like to teach only students who are eager to learn, most of them need to recognize that not all students will be deeply interested in everything the professors would like to teach.

One of the primary problems, therefore, is how to motivate students. Among the motivations that already exist in campus culture, some conflict with others. For example, most students want to do well in school, and there will thus be some motivation for achievement. At the same time, most students want to be liked. In some colleges, students who want acceptance by their classmates find that they must avoid any conspicuous display of academic achievement. As a consequence, many students on those campuses suffer from a real conflict between the need to get good grades and the need to be well liked. One way for a student to resolve this conflict is to work hard enough to get good grades—but without commitment to the life of the mind. Apathy, in one sense, is a face-saving device for students in a campus culture which does not value commitment to education. Another way to resolve the conflict is to work hard only in courses that "turn one on," neglecting the courses that do not. Students who follow this pattern are thus able to prove to their fellow students (and to themselves) that they have not given in to institutional pressures.

Thus, many students have conflicting motivations. One common conflict is between independence and dependence. This means that students are likely to resent the teacher who directs their activities too closely, but they are also likely to feel anxiety when given independence. As a result of this conflict, some students voice disagreements with the teacher, not from any rational grounds but simply as a way of expressing anxiety.

The most potent motivational device is grades. Grades have traditionally been the symbol of achievement—the Dean's List, the honor roll and all the rest. When a student has really been interested in learning, grades have represented an expert's appraisal of his success; when he has been interested in getting into professional school, good grades have been the key that will unlock graduate school doors; when he has wanted to play football, grades have been necessary for maintaining eligibility. Grade point averages were scrutinized by draft boards during the Vietnam war and they are scrutinized by insurance companies when they write automobile policies for college students. The majority of students have been motivated to get passing grades if only to remain in college.

Most professors are a little embarrassed by this state of affairs. After some experimentation with loosening up the grading system, professors have returned to their belief that grades are one of the necessary evils of teaching. They try to discount grades when they discuss the organization of courses, and they try to arrive at grades in such a way that they can avoid trouble with disappointed students. *But they frequently fail to use grades to bring about the sort of learning that is desired.*

Because grades have again become important to the students of the 1980s, the average student will learn whatever is necessary to get a satisfactory grade. If grades are based on the memorization of details, students will memorize the text. If students believe that grades are based on their ability to integrate and apply principles, they will attempt to do this, too. In short, motivation depends a great deal on how each course is evaluated and what the professor's expectations of students are. A teacher's job is not done when he interests his class. The amount students learn depends on the amount the professor teaches, but the relation between the two is not simple. At a certain point, it may well be that the more professors teach, the less students learn.

Some years ago, some teaching fellows in psychology were arguing about how to present the nervous system. One group argued that since students would not remember all the details the teachers should omit them and teach only the basic essentials everyone ought to know. Another group agreed that students would forget much of what they learned but drew different conclusions: "If they are going to forget a large percentage, we need to teach much more detail than we expect them to remember." The combatants agreed that they would try their ideas in their own classes and compare the results on the final exam. The outcome was clear. The students whose instructors had omitted details were clearly superior to those whose instructors had given them the whole story.

Fortunately, it is possible to teach more and to have it remembered better. The magic formula really is *organization*. People can learn and remember much more when the details they learn interrelate and fit into a larger framework. Good teaching, therefore, helps the learner find the framework within which to fit new facts. The poor teacher is the one who simply communicates masses of material in which the student can see no organization. The ideal learning experience begins with a problem that is so meaningful that the students are always just a step *ahead* of the teacher in approaching a solution.

It is a common belief that a student's motives are fixed, but this notion is false. Students naturally enjoy learning for its own sake, and nurturing the intrinsic motivation for education is one of the most important aims of education.

Feedback and Active Learning

If students are expected to learn skills—including the whole range of intellectual skills that colleges place at the base of their training in all fields—then they have to practice. But practice does not necessarily make perfect. Practice works only when the learner learns the *results* of his practice—that is, when he receives feedback. A number of experiments have demonstrated that *active* learning—learning which demands student initiative—is generally more effective than passive learning. One reason for encouraging activity is that it provides opportunities for feedback. For example, certain discussion techniques help develop intellectual skills because students actively do the thinking and there is an opportunity to check their thinking against the thinking of others. Of course, not all feedback has to come from the instructor, but students, in order to learn, need to test out their ideas in a situation in which the results are evident.

Teaching Methods

Large Lectures versus Small Discussions.   One attractive solution to the problem of teaching more students is to replace some of the small discussion classes with larger lecture classes. This practice is often justified by a number of studies that have found no significant difference in effectiveness between lectures and discussions. But the data must not be read simple-mindedly. Those studies that have found no differences used tests asking students to show knowledge of subject matter. A number of other experiments have found significant differences favoring discussions over lectures. They have used measures other than the mastery of subject-matter knowledge. An experiment on class size carried out at Miami University showed that large classes were virtually as effective as small classes in transmitting information, but small classes were more effective in producing changes in psychological misconceptions, problem-solving in marketing and attitudes toward the courses.

Here, as elsewhere, there is no simple answer to the question "What teaching method is best?" As this research indicates, the question must be countered with "Best for what?" If the most important objective is transmitting information, lectures (or reading assignments) should probably be used instead of discussions. If, on the other hand, the primary concern is with teaching critical thinking, a change in attitudes, or other complex objectives, certain types of discussion appear to be the method of choice.

Types of Discussions. One of the difficulties in evaluating comparisons of teaching methods is that a wide variety of kinds of teaching may be included under single labels of "lecture" or "discussion." The term "discussion" covers every kind of class session in which students and professors exchange words—including, for example, everything from bull sessions to highly organized question-answer sessions. Fortunately, there are a number of experiments comparing different styles of discussion. These, too, tend to come out with negative results, but once again there are occasional, significant differences, and these are consistent.

In a large number of studies, marked differences in attitudes, in ability to apply concepts, or in group membership skills have been found between discussion techniques emphasizing freer student participation and those with stricter control by the instructor. In these studies, the difference favored the more student-centered discussion.

This consideration of lecture and discussion methods may be summed up by the phrase "Examine your goals." College catalogs speak in glowing generalities about skill in the use of the intellect and preparation for personal responsibility. Knowledge is an important ingredient for achieving these goals, but to promote the fullest intellectual development, methods must be used which give students an opportunity to practice thinking for themselves.Before educators commit themselves to one pattern of instruction, they need to analyze the specific aims of each course and the way in which various teaching techniques and aids can best achieve each objective.

Independent Study.   One of the central aims of any educational program is to render the teacher dispensable and enable the student to become a self-learner. Independent study courses, coming at the right time in a student's program are one way of accomplishing this goal. Unfortunately, the potential advantages of giving students independent study do not seem to have been achieved in most experiments. Not only do students not learn any more; they also fail to develop independence.

Encouraging results, however, were obtained in experiments on independent study at a number of campuses. At the University of Colorado, for instance, students continued to meet their instructors in weekly classes and were free to consult them whenever they desired. Actual reduction of contact hours was only about ten percent. With this fairly high degree of instructor supervision, students discussing problems in student-led discussion groups were superior to their conventional classmates on three measures: in making difficult applications, in learning new materials and in curiosity.

Independent study thus holds promise, but it is still no panacea. What is more, there is another factor which complicates the simple decision to inaugurate independent study programs on a large scale. Evidence from studies at Michigan, Antioch and Oberlin suggests that some students are better able to profit from independent study than others. Unfortunately, there are no reliable ways of identifying these students in advance. Moreover, even if these students could be picked out, there are as yet no well-tested methods of training them to do independent work.

Programmed Learning.   The great hoped-for revolution in learning, predicted a quarter-century ago by educational media specialists, has not yet taken place. Programmed learning is still very much a fringe activity on most campuses. The computerized "hardware" is sophisticated, but the teaching materials—the programs—are generally still primitive.

When the presentation by programmed learning is compared with the usual textbook approach, the programmed material tends to be superior for retention but inferior in speed of learning. Programs which provide special review or "skip" sequences for the poorer or better students tend to improve learning as compared with rigid "linear" programs.

Effective Teaching Styles: New Approaches in Research and Theory

In the last decade, psychology has witnessed a revolution in thinking about learning and thinking. The older associationist-behaviorist approaches have been superseded by and incorporated into newer information-processing approaches that are derived in part from computer analogies and in part from a long tradition of cognitive theories. These approaches—identified by the label of cognitive psychology—seek to explain behavior in terms of mental processes.

In the light of these new approaches, as well as the research to date in higher education, I have arrived at a number of tenets. They are put forward, not as final answers, but as statements that may be helpful in analyzing problems and suggesting possible solutions.

1. Human beings are learning organisms: they seek, organize, code, store and retrieve information all of their lives. They build on cognitive structures to continue learning throughout life, and they are continually seeking meaning.

2. Human beings can remember images. They can remember transcriptions of the exact words that are used in a lecture or in a textbook. They can also remember meanings, depending upon the demands of a given situation.

3. There is a strong tendency, in our society at least, to store and retrieve *meanings* rather than exact reproductions of what is experienced. What meaning a student gets depends not only upon the student's past experience and expectancies, but also on the stu-

dent's learning strategy or style.[1]

4. Professors teach students not only the *knowledge* of specific disciplines (history, biology, or psychology, for example), but also modes of thought and strategies for learning.[2] Indeed, form is more crucial in the teaching process than content. Two professors using different means may be equally successful in transmitting the same information, but when it comes to broader understandings the two professors may have quite different effects on different learners. Comparisons of different methods of college teaching show no significant differences when students are tested for informational knowledge, but there are differences among teaching methods in retention, application, transfer and other outcomes.[3] At the very least, the approach of cognitive psychology stresses the need to be aware of several kinds of outcomes—not just *how much* is learned, but also *what kinds of learning* take place.

5. When students learn something in the classroom, the consequences may not be the same as when they acquire the same item of knowledge under other conditions—for example, from peers, from books or from direct experience. There is no reason to believe, however, that one of these modes is always superior to the others. Not all learning—to give one example—should be experiential. Written language is a powerful and efficient tool.

6. Not only are different teaching methods differentially effective for different learning outcomes, but teaching methods are also differentially effective for different learners.[4]

----

[1]Marton, F., and Saljo, R. "On Qualitative Differences in Learning: I—Outcome and Process." *British Journal of Educational Psychology*, 46, 1976, pp. 4-11.

[2]Olson, D. "Toward a Theory of Instructional Means." *Educational Psychologist*, 12, 1976, pp. 14-35.

[3]McKeachie, W. J., and Kulik, J. A. "The Effectiveness of Instruction in Higher Education." In F. N. Kerlinger (Ed.), *Review of Research in Education*. Vol. 3 (Itasca, Illinois: Peacock, 1975); Mayer R. E. "Acquisition Processes and Resilience Under Varying Testing Conditions for Structurally Different Problem-Solving Procedures." *Journal of Educational Psychology*, 66, 1974, pp. 644-656.

[4]Egan, D. E., and Greeno, J. G. "Acquiring Cognitive Structure by Discovery and Rule Learning." *Journal of Educational Psychology*, 64 (1), 1973, pp. 85-97; Greeno, J. G. "Process of Understanding in Studying from Text," paper prepared for the symposium "Information Processing Analyses of Instruction," American

7. The outcome of teaching depends upon student characteristics, teacher characteristics, goals, subject matter and methods.[5] Hence, the flexibility and variability of approaches on the part of the professor are likely to be more effective than any single method.

8. Since students are not able to identify their own most effective learning strategies, it appears desirable to teach them how to do it. But the best means for achieving this goal in the college classroom are yet to be discovered. The question should also be asked: Could students be taught to develop a larger repertoire of learning strategies? Professors should be able to adapt their teaching methods to the learning strategies of students, and students should be able to adopt the learning strategy most effective for whatever teaching method they encounter.

9. The teacher's testing practices may influence a student's learning strategies. Essay tests are likely to produce deeper and better learning than objective tests. The classic study in this area antedates information-processing approaches by three decades,[6] but these early findings have been confirmed by more recent studies.[7] The comments a professor makes on a student's paper may also be influential, especially when they go beyond pointing to errors or inadequacies and pose questions and make suggestions that steer a student to more sophisticated, deeper levels.[8]

10. Teachers are important as models for students.[9]

Educational Research Association, San Francisco, April 1976; Leith, G. O. M. "Conflict and Interference: Studies of the Facilitating Effects of Reviews in Learning Sequences." *Programmed Learning and Educational Technology*, 8, 1971, pp. 41-50.

[5]Cronbach, L. J., and Snow, R. E. *Aptitudes and Instructional Methods: A Handbook for Research on Interaction*, New York: Iwington, 1977.

[6]McCluskey, H. Y. "An Experimental Comparison of Two Methods of Correcting the Outcomes of Examinations." *School and Society*, 40, 1934, pp. 566-568.

[7]Marton, F., and Saljo, R. "On Qualitative Differences in Learning: I—Outcome and Process." *British Journal of Educational Psychology*, 46, 1976, pp. 4-11.

[8]Johnson, D. M. "Increasing Originality on Essay Examinations in Psychology." *Teaching of Psychology*, 2, 1975, pp. 99-102.

[9]Bandura, A. *Social Learning Theory* (Englewood Cliffs, New Jersey: Prentice Hall, 1976); Eelen, P., and D'Ydewalle, G. "Producing or Observing Response-

11. In every classroom, interaction is taking place simultaneously at three levels: (a) a subject matter is being transmitted while (b) a cognitive structure or framework of thought is supplied (for it is through that framework that the content or subject matter is perceived), and at the same time (c) a complex set of emotional relationships is being acted out by the professors and the students as they make contact with one another. So far, researchers have been able to tell professors little about how to integrate these three levels in such ways as to optimize education.

12. A teacher may teach a student not only a given subject matter but also two other things: how best to learn that subject matter and how best to learn from that particular teacher.

13. A professor may increase his effectiveness in the classroom as much—or more—by helping students understand their own learning processes as by applying varying teaching strategies.[10]

14. A neat paradox: The teacher can be effective in helping students learn only if he or she first makes the effort to learn from the students the structures through which they perceive the problems the teacher places before them. In order for this mutual teaching and learning to take place successfully, the teacher and the students need to carry on discussion in which the students have the opportunity to externalize their problems and their progress. As class size increases, such interaction becomes difficult. Nonetheless, it is imperative to provide opportunities for small-group dialogue and writing.[11]

Satisfactions in Teaching

What are the satisfactions in teaching? Certainly one is the pleasure of seeing a student develop. Another is the pleasure of intellectual interchange with young people possessing questioning minds and fresh ideas. A third satisfaction is the acquisition of

Outcome Contingencies in a Two Response Alternative Task." Psychologica Belgica, 1976, pp. 61-71.

[10] Norman, D. "Teaching Learning Strategies." Mimeographed, April 11,

[11] Leith, G. O. M. "Individual Differences in Learning: Interactions of Personality and Teaching Methods." In Association of Educational Psychologists, *Personality and Academic Progress*, London, 1974.

disciples who respect and admire their teachers.

These satisfactions are difficult to secure without close and sustained personal contact with students. For teachers to know their students well enough to see their progress, it is necessary to have small classes—not only because small classes permit more individual interaction with students, but also because they let teachers use written assignments, essay tests and other evaluation methods that give the teachers greater understanding of what the students are thinking.

Moreover, if the satisfaction of *seeing* students develop is important to the teacher, opportunities must be created for contact between instructor and student over a period longer that a one-semester course. One advantage of a small college over a large university—whether the small college exists independently or whether it is situated, as a semi-autonomous unit with its own students and faculty, on a large university campus—is that the student in a small college not only is more likely to come into contact with his instructor outside the classroom but is also more likely to elect later courses from the same instructor. And in a community where professors know most of the students, professors are more likely to discuss students with other professors. In a large university, by contrast, the professor may teach a student for one semester and never see him again. He is very unlikely to discuss the student with other professors because he does not know which of his colleagues know the student.

If the size of a college is important to faculty-student relationships, it is also important to the quality of education students receive from each other. On the one hand, the large university with a diverse student population offers its members the chance to gain breadth, tolerance and new perspectives from their contacts with one another. On the other hand, large size is likely to reduce intellectual exchange between students. Granted, there is nothing to prevent students at a large college from discussing with friends interesting problems raised by their professors. But students are probably more likely to do so if they live near others who are concerned about the same things; and in a large college the statistical chances that another in the same class will be in the same living group are smaller than in a small college. Students in a large college with many courses, even those students in different sections of the same course, have few common intellectual experiences. As a result, it is difficult for them to communicate about intellectual problems outside class, and the common concerns which become the basis of social communication are football, the student newspaper, dating and dormitory food.

With such barriers to inter-student education, the professor misses the good feeling a teacher experiences when he finds that teaching has provided an intellectual stimulus reaching far beyond the classroom. Of course there are also satisfactions in teaching a large class, as there are in teaching by television. A teacher can gain a very satisfying sense of power from knowing that he is communicating ideas to a large number of students. Where the lecture is televised, the "master teacher" can get satisfaction from carrying through a well-planned lesson without interruption. And where "live" audiences are concerned, the roar of laughter to a joke well-told can be music to a lecturer's ear.

All are real satisfactions, but they seem less directly related to the goals of education than the satisfactions that come from observing student development. What *would* a college be like if the pleasure its faculty got from teaching was mainly that of the good performer?

As colleges increase in size to cope with a growing student population, there is a natural tendency to automate educational processes for the sake of increased efficiency. In industry, assembly-line methods have long been effective. Yet in recent years, firms in the automotive industry and elsewhere have found that workers are even more efficient if instead of performing one specific, repetitive task their jobs are enlarged enough to provide variety and interest. Although there is little likelihood that college administrators will intentionally insist on uniform teaching methods, increasing class size indirectly limits the professor's choice of teaching methods, reducing his ability to select the methods best suited for his objectives and reducing his satisfaction in teaching.

That teachers should enjoy their teaching is doubly important—important not only because their enthusiasm may spread to their students, but important also because their interest will inspire them to keep on improving their teaching strategies. These important effects are quickly lost when teaching becomes so routine and impersonal that it is no longer fun. By contrast, motivated teachers, responding to feedback from students and discussion with colleagues, can develop their teaching styles continually and gain the kind of control that a great teacher must surely possess.

21

Teaching By Discussion and "Active" Learning

Joseph Axelrod

Many faculty members and students still think about college teaching in "either-or" terms: they assume that if the class is not a lecture it must be a discussion, that if the students are not passive they must be active. Systematic observation of scores of college classes by a group of University of California investigators has shown that simple distinctions of this sort are totally inadequate for any detailed analysis of the complex professor-student relationship in the college classroom.[1] What the investigators found, in fact, was

---

[1] More than a hundred visits were made to college classrooms during the period when this writer directed a research project on college teaching at the Center for

that there are four quite different teaching modes that are conventionally called "discussion" and that there are many behavior states lying between fully "active" and fully "passive" that are exhibited by students in a classroom.

Of the four modes of teaching by discussion, two encourage relatively greater "passivity" on the part of the students, while the other two modes set conditions that encourage students to be relatively "active." The first two are more common, and they will be described first. In classes where they are practiced, the major activity is a set of "exercises"—very often difficult and complex—set by the instructor and performed by the students. Usually the student response is immediately approved or corrected by the instructor.

In the first of these—labelled Mode 1 here—the class activity consists of *drill* exercises of one kind or another, sometimes involving motor-kinetic features, that help students master a skill in such areas of knowledge as, for example, language, mathematics, logic, computer science, the helping services and the communication arts. In the second category—Mode 2—the major class activity consists of exercises of the question-recitation variety, intended primarily to help students acquire informational knowledge—that is, a knowledge of facts and principles pertaining to a given subject.

Modes 1 and 2 differ in outward appearance: Mode 2 often deals explicitly with concepts and principles, cause-and-effect relationships, and other "intellectual" topics, while the subject matters of courses that tend to follow Mode 1 are nonintellectual in nature. But in both Modes 1 and 2, the basic processes that characterize the student-professor relationship in the classroom are similar. In both, the instructor is the authority figure who knows the answers and corrects the students. While the students are more "active" than in a standard lecture class, they are more "passive" than in classes that follow one of the other two discussion modes—Modes 3 and 4.

Modes 3 and 4 are less common than Modes 1 and 2, but they can

Research and Development in Higher Education at the University of California, Berkeley, and during the years following. See Axelrod, J. *The University Teacher as Artist*, San Francisco: Jossey-Bass, 1973.

easily be observed in many classrooms on every campus. They are characterized by a professor-student interchange that is in the nature of a dialogue (rather than a drill or recitation response as in Modes 1 and 2), but there is a crucial difference between them: a class session in Mode 4 is a *structured inquiry through dialogue*, while a class session in Mode 3 consists primarily of a *loose flow of conversation* between professor and students.

All four discussion modes have two features in common which distinguish them from the standard lecture mode of teaching. The first is an obvious feature: overt student participation that is not merely incidental. The second is an effect of the first feature: there always appear during the class session important instructor behaviors that cannot be structured or planned (in anything more than a general way) in advance of the session. The reason is that the instructors' behavior at any given moment in discussion classes will depend on the kind of student response they receive. All bona-fide discussion classes are, to a greater or lesser degree, *improvisational* in nature, even where general planning is done in advance.

Modes 1 and 2: Teaching Through Drills and Recitations

A class session in Mode 1 is dominated by class exercises of the drill variety. The most obvious examples are to be found in courses devoted to helping students master some motor-kinetic skill. In the Berkeley research project, the investigators witnessed teaching of high excellence by athletic coaches, typing and shorthand teachers, foreign language drillmasters, and other instructors whose goal it was to develop in students whole new habit patterns involving the motor-kinetic apparatus and the mind. Investigators were especially impressed by two features of this type of teaching: they noticed, first, an unusual sensitivity to the particular needs of individual students and, second, an infallible sense of timing. These accomplishments result from techniques that must appear effortless and are often mistakenly regarded as easy to control.

In Mode 2 classes, the mastery of informational knowledge is the primary objective, and question-and-answer recitations constitute the dominant class activity. Class discussions of the highest excellence (in the opinion of the Berkeley investigators) were observed in courses in English literature, Asian history, psychology, zoology,

and several other disciplines, where student recitation predominated.

Teaching in Modes 1 and 2 is designed to achieve goals that are
generally clear and relatively easy to formulate: the students are
expected to acquire a definite body of information or master
specific motor-kinetic skills or specific mathematical or verbal
skills. Mode 2 teaching stresses the kind of cognitive knowledge
that is acquired primarily by memorization, while Mode 1 teaching
stresses the mastery of skills that are acquired primarily by repetition and practice.

Teaching in these modes is clearly appropriate at certain stages
in a number of disciplines where a skill or a body of information is
to be learned that does not depend on the reasoning process and
where the teacher's objective is to develop in the student an automatic or semi-automatic response to specific cues. The aim of the
teacher is to induce in the students an ability to respond immediately, without reflection. Teachers would be teaching *against*
that aim if they encouraged their students to reason out responses
for each exercise.

The acquisition of a skill (in Mode 1 classes) or a body of information (in Mode 2 classes) is thus attained by repetition and practice,
not by problem-solving that involves a process of inquiry and
discovery. Once the students in these class discussions have agreed
to participate—and it is obvious that they face penalties if they
decide not to participate—they learn that there is almost always a
"best" way to respond to each cue that is given in the sessions. The
cue may ask for recall of a fact or a principle, for a motor-kinetic
response, or for a group or individual verbal response in a drill-
type exercise. For each cue there is usually only *one* response (or, if
the student does not yet have control, a response in only *one*
direction) that the instructor regards as best. No lengthy discussion
of student views is necessary, for this is not an arena in which
opinion is significant. Where student opinion is occasionally elicited, its purpose is merely to provide feedback to the instructor—
that is, to give insight into where the student has gone wrong—or to
serve as a psychological device to put the student or the class at ease.
Thus, a professor who follows the teaching patterns characteristic
of Modes 1 and 2 is regarded by all participants as the ultimate
authority who will give the right response if an error is made. In

short, students are never presented with a problem that has genuine alternative solutions, and the emphasis is never placed on the examination of problems but on satisfactory responses that demonstrate either the mastery of informational knowledge or the control of skills.

Effective teachers in Modes 1 and 2 almost always, to a greater or lesser degree, work improvisationally. They cannot predict exactly how a class session will go. Even though they may plan a class session before it begins, they cannot plan in detail because what they will do or say at any point during the session will depend on the response of the individual student (or of the entire class) to the preceding step in the process. It takes great teaching skill to make all of these on-the-floor decisions wisely and also preserve the flow and rhythm that will elicit and sustain interest and motivate undivided attention.

The conscientious teachers who follow either Mode 1 or Mode 2, however, are not satisfied if the students are merely paying attention to what is occurring in the class session. They want to see their students *involved* in what is occurring, and they do not consider themselves effective teachers unless they can create this involvement. The same intention, of course, is shared by conscientious teachers who follow the standard lecture mode, but there is a difference in the processes that result. In the standard lecture session, the involvement of the students expresses itself only through internal processes and experiences. These students are thus relatively less "active"—which is to say, relatively more "passive"—than the students in Modes 1 and 2 sessions, where student involvement is manifested through external behaviors as well as through internal processes.

As we shall see, students in a Mode 3 class session are encouraged to move even further toward the "active" side of the "passive-active" continuum by another factor that will be noted in the following discussion.

Mode 3: The Professor as Discussion Moderator

Although the "rap session" is now less common as a teaching style than it was a decade ago, it has by no means vanished from the American academic scene. Typically, in a Mode 3 class session, a subject is set in advance, and students prepare for it by doing some assigned reading or by participating in some activity. The class discussion follows no plan: it is structured neither in advance of the class nor as it moves along. Points about the subject under discussion are offered at random by the instructor or by any member of the group who feels impelled to say something. In short, the subject set for the session is not treated systematically or exhaustively. But while the order of topics is haphazard, observers found that when more mature students deal with value dilemmas or experiences in the arts or contemporary social problems, the class discussion is frequently on a high level of intelligence, just as a discussion might be during an evening's social conversation among faculty members.

In such an unstructured context, can a professor accomplish any truly educational goals? It is clear that many conventional educational goals in the cognitive domain of knowledge cannot be attained in such a learning environment, but there are certain goals in the "affective" domain for which a conscientious teacher might expressly select the "rap session" mode. At the time of the Berkeley project, several professors using this teaching mode were interviewed. One of them was in charge of a freshman general education course designed to teach communication skills, and he asserted that his course was responsible for far more than eradicating comma faults and dangling modifiers. "We go way beyond the teaching of written English," he said. "We try to teach our students *that* and a whole range of other things: openness, ease in relating to other people, and other kinds of personal-development goals that we define as part of the communication skills."

This professor believes that the teaching style that affords him the best opportunity to fulfill these goals is what is called here Mode 3. As he moderates a group's conversation and participates in it, his major task—as he sees it—is not to cover a given subject matter but to promote the learning of the habits and attitudes that constitute the course objectives. He does this in two ways: first through a system of approvals and disapprovals of the way in which students "communicate" with one another during these class conversations, and second by demonstrating himself, in his contributions to the conversations, his own ease in relating to people, his own ability to keep distortion of the ideas of other people at a minimum, and his own facility in making other personal responses. He thus serves as an adult model for his young students to imitate.

A More "Active" Behavior State.   In a Mode 3 discussion session— if it is successful—the student's external behaviors are different in one essential way from those of students in Modes 1 and 2 classes. In Modes 1 and 2 classes, students are personally involved but take their cues, at all times, from their professors—they have neither the power nor the desire to change what is occurring during the class session. In a Mode 3 session, by contrast, the professor explicitly delegates to the students the power to change what is happening, along with the *responsibility* to use that power when it will benefit themselves or their classmates. This is a new level of "active" behavior which is not present in classes following Modes 1 and 2.

   This level of student behavior is also present in Mode 4 class sessions where another, even more important, new element is added as well.

Mode 4: The Professor as Socrates Figure

   A professor who follows Discussion Mode 4 has a prototype in his mind that is close to that of the Socratic dialogue: the class session, when it is successful, displays a tight design illustrating the process of joint inquiry and discovery in which the professor and the students engage as partners. They are unequal partners, to be sure, but they are partners, nonetheless.

   The design of the session is not structured in advance but is created as the discussion moves along. This improvisational quality of a Socratic discussion is essential. While all of the discussion modes involve improvisational teaching, this element is especially crucial in a Mode 4 session. If the session is to be a genuine inquiry (rather than a question-answer recitation session like Mode 2), then the discussion leader cannot know when the session starts where or how it will go. This feature is characteristic of the dialogues in which Socrates engaged—as reported, at any rate, in the works of Plato. Neither Socrates nor those with whom he carried on inquiry could predict what they would discover as they engaged in dialogue, or how and when the discoveries would appear. No doubt they anticipated certain possibilities, and such anticipations account, in part, for the pleasure derived from improvisation. But they derived even greater pleasure from perceiving in retrospect that certain developments in the discussions were inevitable, even though the developments came as total surprises.

It has already been noted that the student-professor relationship is different in Modes 1 and 2 (teaching by drill and recitation) from what it is in Modes 3 and 4. In Modes 1 and 2, the professor is an authority figure who gives students their cues or questions and corrects their responses. In Mode 3, students are encouaged to express themselves; and if they feel trust, then no one hesitates to criticize the views of anyone else in the group. But normally, in the "rap session" that constitutes the Mode 3 class, the members of the group do not feel that they are working together to create an entity that comes to have its own existence outside of them. This is precisely what does happen in a Mode 4 session when the discussion is successful. The dialogue takes on a life of its own. It is a very short life, it should be noted: the products of the professor and his students working in Mode 4 are as evanescent as were those created by Socrates and his colleagues. Indeed, in Socrates's own conception of the art of teaching, it is not enough to say that the product is evanescent—it must always *necessarily* be so.

It is important to state explicitly that the dialogue in a Platonic work is never created by Socrates alone, although he is certainly the leader of the participating group. The dialogue is created jointly by him and every member of the group who enters into a relationship with him during the discussion. It is just this relationship that is crucial. More than any other factor, it determines the kind and quality of the product.

A New Level of "Activeness".   The level of student "activeness" present in a successful Mode 4 class session goes one step beyond the level attained in Mode 3. In Mode 3, the professor delegates to the students the power to change what is happening during the class session, and in a successful Mode 3 session students will in fact use that power to benefit themselves and their classmates. But in Mode 4, concerned as the session is with the structure and design of the product its members are jointly creating, student "activeness" is vastly increased. The students in a Mode 4 class are sensitive to the structure and design of the discussion, they feel a responsibility for contributing to the realization of that design, and they use their power (that is, the power to change what is happening, delegated to them by the professor) as a means of meeting that responsibility. In this sense, students in Mode 4 class are more "active" than those in a Mode 3 class.

As already noted, students in classes following Modes 1 and 2 are more "passive" than students in Mode 3 classes. And in turn, students in standard lecture sessions are more "passive" than students in classes following Modes 1 and 2. (It is assumed, for the purposes of these comparisons, that all sessions are about equally successful and that students are encouraged to be as "active" as the mode permits.) But these observations should not lead to the conclusion that students are wholly "passive" in standard lecture sessions. On the contrary, the Berkeley investigators discovered through post-lecture interviews with students that many of them were very much involved with the material being presented by the lecturers and that this involvement, though not manifested through external behaviors (that is, overt participation), did express itself through innumerable internal processes and experiences.

Chart 2 summarizes what the Berkeley investigators discovered to be the correlation between five teaching modes (the four discussion modes plus the standard lecture) and various student "behavior states" on the "active-passive" continuum. Chart 1 offers definitions of these "behavior states."

Which of the Four Modes Is Best?

All four discussion modes are important patterns of teaching in colleges and universities today—as is also, it goes without saying, the standard lecture mode. The Berkeley investigation showed that each of these patterns has its own excellence: within each mode it is possible to do a poor or a superb job. Since practitioners *within* each mode can vary greatly in the quality of their performances, it is legitimate to compare the practitioners with one another, evaluating and attempting to decide whether one is "better" than another. Given the nature of each style, standards can be set and appraisals can be made by qualified judges. This is not to say that the task of appraisal is easy but merely that it is possible and appropriate.

The Berkeley study demonstrated, however, that there is no justification for believing that any one of the teaching modes is intrinsically superior to the others. The conclusion of the investigators, in fact, was this: For every teaching situation, one of these patterns is probably more appropriate than the others. *Which* it is will depend on many factors—the instructor's objectives, the student's goals, the physical setting, the number and kind of students, the specific qualities of the instructor and the teaching styles with which that instructor is most comfortable, the rewards for particular behaviors given to faculty members and to students by the campus society at large, and so on. Above all, the goals of the professor for the students constitutes the most important element in determining which mode is best. It is obvious, for example, that the standard elementary language course would not do well following Modes 3 or 4.

The best teacher, clearly, is the one who has mastered the strategies required in all four modes. But such professors are rare. It was observed in the Berkeley study that faculty members who prefer Modes 1 or 2 tend to be uncomfortable with Modes 3 and 4. Inevitably, such professors attempt to avoid conditions in which they would be expected to use those teaching styles. If they succeed in avoiding these modes, the result is that they deny themselves opportunities to learn to master them.

All four varieties of teaching by discussion described here—as well as the standard lecture mode—are important today, and it is unlikely that the importance of any of them will decrease during the years immediately ahead. It is possible, however, that about the year 2000 there will be developed adequate programs ("software," as they are technically called) for the immensely sophisticated "hardware" that is already available but at present of little use to educators at the university level. For example, computer-assisted instruction shows enormous promise, although programs written for the computer are, by and large, still primitive. If and when the writing of programs for this medium reaches a level of complexity adequate for the tasks now carried out by instructors who follow Modes 1 and 2, then Modes 1 and 2 will become obsolete. But it may take half a century from the time they become obsolete for them actually to disappear from the higher education scene. Con-

Chart 1
Definitions of Six Student Behavior States on the Active-Passive Continuum

	Behavior State	Definition
Passive	A	The student is present in the classroom.
	B	In addition to A, the student is paying attention to what is occurring during the class session.
	C	In addition to B, the student is involved in what is occurring during the class session. The behavior is internal, and the involvement expresses itself through internal processes and experiences.
	D	In addition to C, the involvement is externalized and is manifested through overt behaviors in the classroom.
	E	In addition to D, where the student's external behaviors derive from personal involvement with what is occurring in the class session, there is also a desire to influence (or change altogether) what is occurring. Aware that the professor has delegated that power to students (i.e., the power to change what is occurring), students use it when it will benefit themselves or their classmates.
Active	F	In addition to E, students are sensitive to the design of the class session as an "inquiry" and feel a responsibility for contributing to the realization of that design. They use their power (i.e., the power to change what is occurring in the session, described under E) as a means of meeting that responsibility.

Chart 2

Correlation Between Teaching Modes And Student Behavior States of Activeness-Passiveness

Teaching Modes	Behavior States (as defined in Chart 1)					
	A	B	C	D	E	F
The standard lecture	□	□	◆	○	○	○
Discussion Mode 1 (Drill-type exercise)	□	□	□	◆	○	○
Discussion Mode 2 (Question-answer recitation)	□	□	□	◆	○	○
Discussion Mode 3 (Unstructured conversation)	□	□	□	□	◆	○
Discussion Mode 4 (Structured inquiry through dialogue)	□	□	□	□	□	◆

Key to Symbols:

◆ = The behavior state which the teaching mode, by its very nature, hopes to bring into existence for each student in the class.

○ = Behavior which the teaching mode, by its very nature, discourages in the student (or actually forbids).

□ = Behavior states which are encouraged by the teaching mode as steps necessary to achieve the state marked ◆.

sequently, change is not imminent, and teaching in Modes 1 and 2 will still be in use for decades to come.

As for the future of the standard lecture, the likelihood is that—on the undergraduate level—the profession will come to depend more on a *small number* of superb lecturers of national reputation whose work can be prepared for television showings on various campuses, either in or out of the classroom. This design is already being adopted at some colleges, where the "telelecture" given by a Kenneth Clark or a Jacob Bronowski is followed by small-group meetings using one of the discussion modes. It is very likely that sometime after the year 2000 the standard classroom lecture will gradually disappear—in undergraduate programs—as an activity performed by local professors on their own campuses.

It is quite possible, then, that sometime in the twenty-first century all teaching styles other than Modes 3 or 4, as local activities performed by ordinary faculty members, will cease to exist in bachelor's degree programs.

It does not appear possible, however, that even drastically changing conditions will ever render Mode 3 or Mode 4 class sessions obsolete. Whatever programs are written for the computer to replace the professors who now follow Mode 1 and Mode 2 patterns and whatever new media are developed to reduce the number of professors who present standard classroom lectures, it is extremely unlikely that professors who follow the Mode 3 and Mode 4 patterns will ever be replaced by non-human teaching instruments like books, films, or computers. These teaching modes will continue, even in the next century, to be performed by human beings, working with fairly small groups of students, in a wide number of locations that will continue to be known as centers of learning.

VI
The
Future
of the
American
College

The final section of the volume brings us back to the subject of research and self-study and then looks cautiously into the future of higher education in the United States. These two major topics are of course closely related: if our colleges and universities are not to become the playthings of forces external to the world of learning, then educators themselves will have to acquire as good a knowledge as they possibly can of the phenomena over which they wish to exercise control.

This knowledge cannot come without the research and self-study efforts that are outlined in Chapter 22. In "Directions for Research and Self-Study in Higher Education," Nevitt Sanford presents an analytic scheme that serves as a map of the entire field—the territory that must increasingly become the object of research and study.

There are two major conceptions here: first, the college as a complex organization, in varying degrees separated from the larger society with which it interacts; second, students, of great diversity and complexity as individuals, entering this organization to be developed in such a way that they will possess the qualities desired by those who "operate" (a purposely loaded term) the institution. The essay moves from a discussion of objectives to students and their culture, to student interaction in the learning process, and to the effects of the college experience.

Chapter 23, "Student Development and the American College," also written by Nevitt Sanford, brings together all of the major themes of the book. The section on the education of the intellect and the emotions ties together what many of the authors of previous chapters have had to say about the development in students of rationality, as well as how this development must involve the whole personality. Sanford then goes on to discuss changes in college processes and structures that will promote the individual development of students: changes in curriculum and instruction, in social organization, and in the role of administration.

This final chapter begins by stating a theme that pervades the entire book: all of society's resources should be utilized for the development of children and youth—for that, after all, is mainly what a society is for. The kind of institution that can best carry on such a function is a learning center, Sanford points out, that would be very much like a kind of college. Once such an institution has been created, it in turn owes something to the society which has brought it into being. Its ultimate function is to help that society improve itself. But how can it succeed in this task unless it helps the members of that society—as many as it can reach—develop into the best individuals they are capable of becoming? Higher education does not exist to supply skilled hands or clever administrators to industry, to the state, or even to the universities themselves. Higher education is for teaching people how to live responsibly and how to develop and enjoy a sense of beauty.

22

Directions for Research and Self-Study in Higher Education

Nevitt Sanford

In the 16 years that have elapsed since the appearance of *The American College*, the higher education establishment has begun to emphasize the importance of research in higher education. Almost every college feels strong pressures to engage in "self-study," a process that can be successful only if it involves a structure that is newly built into the daily operation of the college, such as an office of institutional research or a college-wide committee on self-study. The accreditation process, in recent years, has come to require an intensive self-study period preceding an accrediting committee's visit, culminating in a self-study report that analyzes the institution's strengths and weaknesses. In short, higher education research enabling each institution to do an adequate job of self-appraisal is now, finally, becoming a routine operation on the majority of American campuses.

Research and the Ends of Education

Research in higher education, if it is directed to fundamental problems, soon becomes involved with questions of ends. The ends of American higher education have their roots, of course, in the American ethos, and they show a tendency to change with the social scene. It is characteristically American that our institutions of higher learning should be as diversified as they are. They differ in every feature and dimension that marks a college—in size, standards and curriculum; in student quality and faculty quality; in teaching methods, social organization, climate of culture and a host of other ways. But most important, they differ in what they try to do.

A basic feature of American higher education has been its decentralization, for groups of people have always been free to start schools and colleges, in accordance with their needs and with their ideas about salvation. Consequently, virtually every conceivable objective is somewhere represented, although certain pressures toward conformity seem to build as our society becomes increasingly organized.

Education that tries to inculcate skills and knowledge, even for a social or cultural purpose, may be distinguished from education that has as its aim the fullest possible development of the individual. The former begins by asking "What do people need to know? What do they need to know if they are to live in our world and help maintain it?" The tendency of this sort of education is to instruct, to train, to mold individuals according to the requirements of our civilization, society and culture. To the extent that such training succeeds in its purpose, it makes people alike in various respects.

The latter kind of education does not ask what individuals should *know* or *do*, but what qualities they should *achieve*. It makes assumptions about what the individual is, with open-ended visions of what he or she can become, and it measures educational progress in terms of personality change—from prejudiced to broadminded attitudes, say, or from laxness to rigor in thinking. It does not deny that the individual must be *socialized* and must be able to support and adapt to civilization. But it assumes that well-developed individuals can do these things in their own unique ways; that as they expand and become more complex they become increasingly unlike other persons; that only parts of themselves—and often superficial parts—are taken up with the mere *requirements* of life in the modern world. According to this view, the very development of individuals adapts them to their environment and makes them able to use culture in the service of their basic needs. What is more, they can criticize and help to improve society, and through creative activity they can advance civilization.

Students may learn a great deal without changing their personalities in any important way. Much knowledge is quickly forgotten, and people do not change from the forgetting any more than they change from the learning. Even when activities that demand knowledge persist, they may be superficial in the sense that they are not used for a person's inner needs. It is here that graduate education, education in the European universities, and much instruction in our liberal arts colleges fail. They pay no attention to the student's development as a personality. Implicitly or explicitly, educators in these programs commonly assume either that students are already sufficiently developed or that the level of their development does not matter.

Official statements in college documents—materials prepared for accrediting agencies as well as for the potential student—invariably refer to human qualities and human development. In some of these statements, educators responsible for writing them present a reasonable and fairly explicit theory that the educational program will itself actually induce desired changes in the individual. In other instances, the educational theory is less explicit and less reasonable, as when it is supposed that the mere transmission of information will, somehow, automatically lead to development. Even when the program of a college is heavily preprofessional, its defenders are likely to claim that it will have a generally liberalizing effect on "those who are able to benefit from it."

In fact, just the contrary could occur: education of certain kinds could bring about changes in the person that are *not* conducive to personality development. Professional or vocational education often makes the individual identify with one particular occupation, so that his or her behavior is determined by external factors rather than by genuine needs. When this happens, when self-conception is largely dominated by professional membership (as is so often the case in this country), people are likely to restrict their social behavior to the seeming requirements of that membership. Vocational choice that comes too early in the individual's life may induce a kind of premature closure of the personality, an integration or "adjustment" that, being supported by external agencies, may effectively prevent further expansion and differentiation.

These examples show how important it is for educators to understand the relationship between personality development in the individual and his or her ability to acquire various sorts of knowledge. We have just seen how acquisition of certain kinds of knowledge early in a person's life may prevent further development of personality. The reverse is also true. Development in the personality is very likely to favor the processes of education. The stronger and better conceived the individual's motives, the more firmly they are based on inner needs, and the better they are adapted to real possibilities, the more readily will the individual learn the facts and principles that he sets out to learn. The better his judgment, the greater his critical faculties, and the better integrated the diverse parts of himself, the more quickly will he assimilate knowledge and skills that can be shown to have relevance to his purposes.

Fundamental to all such considerations—the relationship between students' academic lives and the development of their personalities—is this basic truth: A person is all of a piece. A student's intellect cannot be disembodied from the rest of his personality, from his "extracurricular self." If teaching effects any changes in intellectual functioning these will ramify throughout his personality, just as, conversely, processes already at work in his personality will help determine what happens in the classroom.

In a sense, therefore, changes in intellectual functioning beyond the mere acquisition of facts—changes that might occur through learning within an academic discipline—are instrumental in other, more general developments in the person. At the same time, there is evidence that certain kinds of personality development have to happen before the individual can be expected to exhibit a genuine love of learning or taste for intellectual activity. Where the educational aim is the development of the individual, it is extremely difficult to separate means from ends or to know what subgoals are necessary to attain more ultimate goals.

Because the distinction between means and ends is not clear— and cannot, by the very nature of the process, be made clear—it is not very easy to know what we mean when we ask how successful a college is in achieving its objectives. The question, of course, is further complicated not only because the word *objectives* is not clear but also because *successful* is not defined in the same way by various educators. Clearly the answer will depend on how we measure "success."

Success in college is usually measured by grades. This, from the college's point of view, represents success. But it may not be success from the point of view of the student or of other interested people. A girl may go to college with the objective, which she shares with her parents, of finding a husband in a higher social class than her own. If she accomplishes this, she is a success from her point of view and from the point of view of her parents and her husband. Her performance in later life may well be such as to win her approval of society at large.

Success in this latter sense is not very highly valued by educators, however. They prefer other performances although even these, from a broader point of view, may not be marks of success in attaining educational objectives. For example, educators may approve mere conformity to a cultural outlook and facility with its symbols, mistaking this for genuine internalization of intellectual values.

We must also distinguish between success in college, as appraised at the time of finishing college, and success in later life. The two may or may not be positively associated. The distinction here is between immediate and ultimate success; it holds for different phases of the student's passage through college as well as for the college-later life relationship. The prediction of long-range success requires follow-up studies; we must confront the very difficult problem of determining whether a later performance was due to the educational experience or whether it sprang from subsequent events.

In selecting applicants, it is one thing to choose students who are likely to graduate and quite another to identify students who show promise of extraordinary accomplishments in life. Minimal objectives such as graduating from college are relatively easy to define and predict; whereas extraordinary performances, in the realm of creative work for example, are difficult to study. But any college that wishes to research its own structures and processes in order to improve them must be prepared to venture into these more difficult realms.

The Entering Student

The student at the end of his undergraduate experience is the product of two complex series of factors: the first constitutes the influences during the college years, and the second consists of all of the student's qualities and characteristics when he or she entered college. The admissions structures and processes have the job of focusing on the second set of factors while the faculty responsible for the curriculum and the personnel responsible for the extracurriculum focus on the first set.

Colleges have long stressed ability and preparation and, to a lesser extent, motivation as the most important aspects of readiness for college. It is here that the mental testing movement in psychology and education has played a highly significant and influential role. Because of their success in prediction, tests of verbal and mathematical ability have for years been widely used in American colleges and universities. As a result, much is known about the verbal and mathematical ability of students entering various institutions and about the differences between young people who go to college and those who do not.

Colleges have widely different standards of work and, accordingly, different levels of entrance requirements. Yet even colleges that, from the nature of their main clientele, might well be designed for low-ability students seldom turn away people of high quality. On the contrary, they will seek such students so as to resemble the institutions of high prestige. Such emulation counts more highly than doing something for average or below-average students. Success seems to depend mainly on the absolute value of the final product, rather than on how much change has been induced; and in turn, the entire admissions process throughout the country is built on the view that the value of the product will depend most heavily on the value of the entering material.

Partly as a result of this view of what constitutes sound admissions policy, the colleges have had to face special problems caused by recent developments in higher education. One such development is the adoption, as federal policy, of the principle of "equalization of educational opportunity," announced to the nation by Richard Nixon in the early 1970s. One result of this policy has been the expansion of community colleges while the range and variety of talent entering the freshman year at the four-year colleges has become progressively narrower.

Another *narrowing* factor, ironically enough, lies in the *expanding* volume of applicants which admissions offices at all the prestigious four-year schools have to handle. Operating in a "seller's market," the dean of admissions at such a school is tempted to select only what he thinks is the "cream"—the same "cream" every other admissions officer is after. At the same time, the cost of a college education, reflecting the enormous inflation that has characterized our economy for some years, has again—as in the period before World War II—come to favor families in the socio-economic top third of the population. "Promising" students who come from lower-income families are being admitted, in token numbers, at the prestigious schools and are being given financial aid. But by and large, members of the college-age population from the lower socio-economic levels are encouraged to enter programs that stress "career education"—a new term that makes vocational education more palatable to educators and the general public.

Admissions officers now basically rely on selection devices that have worked in the past. The challenge to the educational researcher is to discover new tests to determine which students will perform satisfactorily. It is crucial that much more attention be given in the future to personality factors other than verbal and mathematical ability as well as incentives and obstacles in the college situation itself.

The Academic Environment

Fundamental to the analysis of an educational institution is the distinction between its *formal* and *informal* processes. The formal processes consist, most essentially, of all those policies and practices—and the structures that the institution builds to implement the policies and execute the practices—deliberately adopted with a view to influencing students: the curriculum, the departmental structure, the responsibilities of the faculty, methods of teaching, enrollment, attendance, examinations, grading, degrees, counseling, advising, planned extracurricular activities. In studying these aspects of a college, the most important questions a researcher would ask, from the point of view of this book, have to do with whether and in what degree these various features of the students' environment contribute to their development.

The researcher might then study informal processes in the same way that he would study social processes in any collectivity of people. He might, for example, be interested in friendship groups or in the ways in which prestige is conceived and sought. The educational researcher is particularly interested in how processes in the sphere of informal organization help or hamper the attainment of educational goals. Cases where informal processes interfere with planned activity have been the subject of much entertaining, although not always constructive, literature. In a typical study, some issue is debated as if all that is involved is purely rational considerations of how best to achieve some agreed objective, while everybody except those actually taking part understands that the conflict really has arisen out of the status aspirations of two groups of the faculty. Perhaps, as often, it is the other way around: the informal organization contributes in unsuspected ways to the achievement of educational objectives. And this may occur in spite of formal arrangements. For example, there might be an ill-conceived curriculum and a network of repressive requirements and regulations, and yet there may be groups of students whose members stimulate one another intellectually and succeed in reaching a high level of performance.

The influences that affect a student during his or her college years need not—it goes without saying—have *any* relationship with the college at all. Clearly the environment of the developing student is not limited to the college itself; even in a highly organized and relatively isolated residential institution the students are still responsive to diverse aspects of the surrounding social and cultural matrix. For example, the climate of opinion in the community where the college is located: if the community distrusts the college and looks upon it with hostility or contempt, it may help to unify the college society. On the other hand, college officials may be highly sensitive to town opinion. To placate powerful outsiders they might impose such unreasonable restrictions that the students feel victimized by hypocrisy.

Further, there is the effect of the larger society on student expectations about their future. For example, where the society does not offer attractive roles for the highly educated woman, we cannot expect college girls to exert themselves to obtain advanced education. We may expect students to be closer than faculty members to the climate of American culture as a whole; not only have they just left the larger society, but they expect to return to it shortly and, unlike the faculty, they are quite certain about what they are going to do or be. Thus, for instance, at the beginning of the decade of so-called "unrest" in the 1960s, it was the student groups and not the faculty which raised the first strong voices against national policy in Southeast Asia.

The teacher's environment, like that of the student, includes outside social and cultural factors as well as a complexity of forces from within the college system. Outside the college there is the general cultural climate of the day and the situation of the society. These determine the degree of mass pressure toward orthodoxy, toward conformity with popular conceptions of the teacher's role, and toward certain accents in the curriculum (such as a bias toward science and mathematics). Within the college the teacher is subjected to other forces—employment and promotion policies; demands, formal or informal, that a teacher *fit in* to a certain professional role; chauvinism on the part of his department or subdepartment. About him there exists competition of other groups; a faculty society with its rules and regulations, its channels of communication, its system for awarding status; and there is also a faculty culture which demands his allegiance. Even the physical arrangements for living and the commuting habits of the faculty are a molding force: they affect the teacher's social life generally as well as his relationship with the outside world.

Student Society and Student Culture

The faculty's opportunity to influence students depends on many factors, among them: the faculty-student ratio, together with the importance that college authorities and the faculty ethos actually attach to good teaching; the size of the institution or community in which the student is supposed to find an intellectual home; the amount of official or traditional sanction for sports and other cocurricular activities. It may also depend on the physical plant and facilities, with their capacity to suggest the dignity or quality of the educational enterprise; on the living arrangements for students, whether they live so far from the centers of academic activities that a sharp division is encouraged between living and studying; and on the amount of time students spend on campus.

The faculty's influence depends as well on the social organization of the college—the college society—and on the culture of the college. College society as a whole consists of the faculty, the administration, the students, and on many campuses the nonstudent college-age population—that is, the group referred to in the 1960s as the "street people"—which mingles with the students, lives in the campus community, and often even uses campus facilities. At certain very unusual colleges, in addition, members of the governing boards are also members of the college society and know students and faculty on a first-name basis. In each college society, there is always a variety of subsocieties to be observed. Although the members of these subsocieties usually belong exclusively to one or another of the three major population groups—faculty, administration, students, there may be some overlapping. For most students, the most important subsociety is that to which only students belong. This society embraces formal structures, such as the student government and cocurricular activities, and various informal friendship or living or interest groups. Student society may promote the individual's development through offering students opportunities to become familiar with a variety of social roles and by confronting them with situations to which they must learn to adapt themselves.

Researchers in this field study college society and college culture independently, for they are separate phenomena. Each society or subsociety has its own culture—its shared values and beliefs and prescribed ways of behaving. Thus there is an overall college culture in which faculty, administration, and students participate, and there are a number of subcultures. The overall culture will embrace, to some extent at least, the avowed aims and educational philosophy of the college and its ideas and standards respecting levels, styles, and directions of work; and not unrelated to these, there may be values, beliefs, and ways in the realms of religion, politics, economics, arts, and social relations.

Society and culture vary independently. Societies of different colleges, or subsocieties of the same college, may be essentially alike in their structure but yet very different in their values and beliefs. For example, two liberal arts colleges, A and B, are organized in the traditional way, but A stands for preciousness in literature and the arts and extreme conservatism in respect to political and social questions, while B stands for stern Protestant virtues and political and social liberalism. Or to take a second example: of two fraternities having essentially the same social structure, one might go in for athletics and "partying" and the other for campus politics and the values of business.

Similar cultures may be found in social organizations of different types. For example, an approach to contemporary life marked by studied disenchantment and sensation-seeking might be represented in an Eastern private college by a tightly cohering clique living in a luxurious coeducational dormitory, whereas in a large state university the same approach might prevail in a loosely organized group of young men and women, some of whom are married to each other, living "commune" style in a run-down house in the town.

Colleges aim, of course, to transmit culture, to bring about changes in the values and beliefs with which students arrive. But students do not change automatically as soon as new cultural stimuli are presented. A large factor of receptivity is involved, and this seems to be largely a matter of motivation. Perhaps the strongest force behind the adolescents' acceptance of cultural or subcultural norms is their need to belong to some group or to feel that they are supported by other like-minded individuals. Thus it is that the kind of culture that the college student assimilates, given some choice, depends heavily on the social organization of that college; there will be a strong tendency to take over values and beliefs from the group that has the strongest social appeal, and this will usually be a student group.

Although student culture and society are important parts of all students' environments, already in existence at the time they arrive, the researcher must also analyze the ways in which such elements in the environment are shaped by student responses—ways in which students in the mass adapt themselves to the college situation. The researcher has to inquire whether, and to what extent, a separate student society and a separate student culture are necessary, whether they are inevitable concomitants of the students' common age and role or results of failure in adult leadership or of particular ways in which the larger college community is organized. Student cultures may be largely understood in terms of collective responses to problems commonly encountered. But if students are to be educated, such problems must be put in their way, and the crucial question becomes whether the responses elicited are consistent with educational goals. Here, at least, students learn rapidly, and what they learn is expressed in changed attitudes and values. Are these attitudes and values desired ones, from the point of view of the educator? Observation of some existing student cultures indicates that they may or may not be so, and that they may be so in some but not in other of their features. The faculty which engages in a thorough self-study will, then, wish to investigate all of these questions.

Cycles of Interaction

Much of a college community's life involves interaction among faculty and administration and the students. We know well enough that students respond to their college environments, but we should also remember that faculties and administrations react, in turn, to what *students* do. This reaction then creates new (and often important) stimuli to student behavior, and thus there is a fresh circle of interaction.

Let us consider an example. In College Z, a traditional college of high quality, a majority of the faculty agree that they note a serious decline in the general level of the students' effort and performance. As the faculty of College Z discusses this phenomenon in sessions both formal and informal, a sense of outrage builds up, and the general feeling is that there must be a tightening all along the line. Heavier work assignments, more frequent examinations, longer papers, and more required reading are thrown at the student, and classes are conducted in an atmosphere of increased grimness.

Now, for the individual College Z student, this discipline comes not from a particular teacher who knows him but from an impersonal "they." It is plain, furthermore, that some of the faculty members' stake in the new policy stems from vanity rather than devotion to intellectual aims. As a result, the students generally see the tightening up as arbitrary punishment. With a nice appreciation of their situation, they do not rebel openly. That is not the style of the American college student in the 1970s; moreover, College Z, representing the genteel tradition was a "quiet" campus even at the height of the student "unrest" of a decade ago. Instead, College Z students give a sort of passive resistance, although not necessarily with any conscious deliberation. In other words, they do precisely what their professors require but no more; they invent and share among themselves numerous devices for judging the exact nature of the requirements and for carrying them out with a minimum of effort; they establish a kind of "norm" for amount of work and make life difficult for the individual who threatens to exceed it. Particularly do they look askance at any student who "gets too close" to any of the faculty, for this tends to break up the general strategy of doing what is required by the faculty without being influenced by them in any positive way.

Since this response is very similar to the state of affairs which upset the faculty in the first place, it is now met with even stricter requirements. The vicious circle becomes increasingly taut. Now the students seek ways to hold the faculty strictly to their obligations and, if possible, to embarrass them by requesting more office appointments, expecting papers to be corrected on time, asking about books they suspect the instructor has not read, remaining silent and unresponsive in class.

Some College Z faculty members do not go along with the majority; they seek to break what has become the common pattern, to "reach" the students. The students will have none of this. They have developed an effective system for handling their situation, and they do not intend to be put off by any new or different methods of teaching or any appeals to their curiosity or creative impulses. They hold the deviating or innovating teacher to the pattern that has become common.

Students have the power to do this, for there are channels through which their complaints can reach the department chairman or the administration, and by now faculty morale has so deteriorated that the enterprising teacher has no assurance that his colleagues will back him up. Happily, the term now ends; the student leaders graduate, the faculty leaders take a much-needed vacation, and there is a chance for a fresh start.

Cycles of interaction like the one just described or one moving in the opposite direction—for the interaction build-up can of course be constructive—are normal processes in the American college. It is just such interaction cycles that affect the general "atmosphere" or "climate" of a college, which in turn leave a strong imprint on a student who remains there for four years. Any faculty group doing a self-study or any institutional research officer analyzing the campus ethos should look for signs of such cycles. Obviously, the sound researcher will not only seek data that enable him to describe the campus ethos (or whatever aspect is under study) at a particular time, but he will also measure the *direction* in which the cycle is moving. Only with such knowledge can sound recommendations for action be formulated.

The Effects of College Education

Quantitative studies of change in college have been fairly numerous. Most have compared groups of entering freshmen with groups of graduating seniors; some of these have examined the same students (with the same instruments) once at the beginning and once near the end of their college careers. In a few studies the students have been examined at several intervals during college life—a system which gives more precise information about when change actually occurs.

By contrast with the amount of research done on student change, there has been relatively little inquiry into the lasting after-effects of college. Questions which have been asked along this line have largely concentrated on (1) what in college makes people scientists or scholars and (2) what are the economic benefits of a college education. Such research has little bearing on the aims of liberal learning, however much it may decide the prestige of institutions. Much more relevant are the numerous surveys where graduates are asked to say what they derived from college or what college has meant to them. Unfortunately, these last have little scientific foundation.

Since the most fundamental questions in higher education can be answered only by considering the *durable* effects of different systems, we are forced to ask why this area of research has been so sadly neglected. Here we may recall that for the consumer of higher education its general value is not in question. Going to college is the road to membership in a profession and to all the benefits of improved economic and social status. Whenever college graduates are asked in later life what they got out of college they have no difficulty in describing several kinds of important benefits. But the discrepancy between the things that head their lists of benefits and the stated purposes of the colleges is usually glaring.

There is some evidence, however, that college does make a difference. Granted, the impact of higher education on most people is limited by the fact that their life-patterns are pretty well determined before they reach college. For many people, however, the experience may precipitate crucial changes of direction. The fact that scholars who study personality are more inclined than formerly to attach importance to the college years augurs well for future research in this field. Just as the typical Navajo family is now said to comprise a father, a mother, two children, and a Harvard anthropologist, so the time may come when the typical college will be made up of the faculty, administration, students, and educational researchers!

Research and Practice in Higher Education

By and large, the colleges of today seem to welcome the study of their students by psychologists and social scientists, and it has become standard practice to appoint an institutional research officer on a fractional or full-time basis. This is very good; it promises that our fund of knowledge about student development in college will be vastly expanded. Yet at the same time, there is cause for uneasiness. It may be that college faculties have simply become convinced not only that this research will not harm the students but also that it involves no serious threat to the college's time-honored way of doing things. But whatever their hospitality to student studies, most colleges are resistant to change, and since their members suspect that research is an instrument for inducing change, the colleges are resistant to research into their *essential* structure and functioning.

The interrelatedness of research and action is particularly clear in the case of educational experiments. Experimentation does not mean merely innovation but the designing of new programs in accordance with hypotheses and the use of experimental controls to determine the effects of those programs. Such proposals or practices, however, are usually the very ones that encounter opposition from college faculties and administrators. There seem to be two main objections: (1) that it is not possible to perform a truly scientific experiment in education because it is not possible to establish and to maintain the necessary controls, and (2) that if a proper experiment is carried out it may harm the subjects.

The problems of research design involved in educationl experiments of this kind are serious, but not too serious. It would not take too much ingenuity to arrange things in such a way that sound knowledge could be derived from new programs. If students are affected by the knowledge that they are taking part in an experiment, there would be a control group of students who also felt that they were taking part in an experiment. If experimental programs tend to attract the ablest students and teachers, arrangements would be made in advance for the equal distribution of talent among experimental and control groups, and so on for other "variables" that seemed likely to affect results.

The objection that experiments might harm students has more far-reaching implications. Admittedly, passage through an experimental program—say, an experimental college within a college or university—might indeed have some temporarily upsetting or painful effects on students; they might be regarded by other students as unusual, and they might suffer disadvantage in getting a job or applying for graduate school. One answer is that *any* educational program may have harmful effects—and that many of them commonly do. At present all education is experimental, for all education is guided by some kind of theory, however implicit, and the effects of particular policies and practices are largely unknown.

The main point, however, is that where education is concerned social science and social practice cannot really be separated. It is unfortunate that the word "science" so often makes people think of gadgets and guinea pigs rather than of a great humanistic enterprise than can help to free those who practice it as well as those upon whom it is practiced. In social science means and ends are inseparable. When students volunteer for studies of themselves or for experimental educational programs, they are already doing what the advancement of knowledge will permit them and others to do more often—that is, participating as free individuals in activities that can broaden experience and enrich the personality.

Expanding Knowledge and the Aims of Education

A curriculum that has become traditional, a way of organizing teaching that is taken for granted, a type of research that has become fashionable—these things should draw our constant critical attention. This is not because change is likely to be called for, or because change is valuable in itself, but because it is in our defense of the conventional that we are particularly likely to stray from rationality.

The rationality that we demand of ourselves is the same rationality we seek to develop in our students. Rationality is a crowning feature of the developed individual. It is the basic source of his freedom—his degree of freedom from his own unrecognized tendencies, from the pressures of the immediate social group, from the confines of a traditional or parochial outlook, and from some of the limitations of ignorance and incompetence. It is a source not only of *freedom from* but of *freedom to,* for rationality increases the individual's freedom of *choice*, and where there is rationality there is fine awareness of the world and knowledge of how to think and how to feel about its manifold aspects. As a consequence, the rational individual is able to conceive and to pursue his purposes with intelligence and sensibility.

We can best guide the student's development by the force of example. Let the college demonstrate its own efforts to find the truth, especially the hard truth about itself, and we may be sure that many students will find in these a model, an inspiration to use their intelligence in trying to solve their own problems. By the same token, a college that does not strive for rationality fails its students. If a college blindly defends its institutional features, or adheres rigidly to an "educational policy" whose theoretical underpinnings remain unexamined, if it makes and enforces demands whose purpose cannot be made clear to students or which cannot be justified as conducive to ultimate democratic goals, if it permits its officials to do or say, in the interest of public relations, what is not consistent with what students have been told, if it betrays the essential idea of a college or university by accepting external restraints on its freedom of inquiry, its students will become either passive or cynical and alienated from the major society and from themselves.

The highest function of social science is to be an instrument for the development of full rationality. The task of understanding the practices and potentialities of higher education does not belong only to social scientists, however; it is the charge of all those responsible for higher education. Our colleges and universities today are highly diversified, and the present trend is toward more and more specialization. Such differentiation, far from being an evil, is an essential feature of development in a college or an individual, but it increases the necessity of integration, which must keep pace if fragmentation is not to be the final outcome.

One basis for unity in the college could be its concerted attempt to find rational solutions to its educational problems. Here at least is something that all teachers can discuss together; here is an intellectual inquiry in which all can take part. The more the college becomes diversified and yet at the same time comes together in this kind of intellectual cooperation, the more it will do to make its students both as complex and as whole as they are capable of being.

23

Student Development and the American College

Nevitt Sanford

All of the resources of society should be utilized for the development of children and youth. This, after all, is mainly what a society is for. If suitable agencies and institutions do not exist, they will have to be created. The kind of institution that is needed will have to be very much like a kind of college. Even if we were to set up youth reservations, or work camps, or overseas projects, or kinds of facilities or organizations for which no models yet exist, if would be necessary to offer instruction and exercises of a more or less intellectual nature. If colleges did not exist, they would have to be invented.

Development after the age of about two, after the acquisition of language skills, is in considerable part a cognitive—even an "intellectual"—matter. This involves, in a crucial way, the use of symbols whether they may be words or images or thoughts. Development is largely a matter of expanding the range of things that can be appreciated—images, concepts, ideas—and the range of responses, largely involving the use of symbols, that can be made. Books, with their gift of boundless vicariousness, are a great benefit to parents or teachers who would help young people develop themselves. It is through using the symbols of his culture, in the life of the imagination, that the individual may most appropriately, and most joyfully, express his deepest impusles and feelings. It is through solving problems with the use of his intelligence— typically in the manipulation of symbols, and through being held to the requirement of seeking and being guided by the truth—that the individual develops, through exercise, the abilities that enable him to control himself and relate to the demands of reality. And it is largely through confrontation by a wide range of value systems and ethical dilemmas that conscience becomes enlightened and therefore stabilized.

The human individual functions as a unit, and his diverse features develop in interaction one with another. Intelligence, feeling, emotion, and action are inseparable aspects, not separate parts, of behavior. Mature adults know this from their own experience. Their productive work is a very passionate affair; creative endeavor leaves them limp with emotional exhaustion, and the hot pursuit of truth keeps them jumping with excitement. And for them to learn anything new, to have their minds changed, they have first to be practically shattered as personalities and then put together again. Why then should students be regarded as cool and well-oiled machines for storing and retrieving information? There is something to be said for *teaching* machines, for they may spare the teacher some machine-like work, but there is nothing to be said for a *learning* machine.

The Education of the Intellect and the Emotions

It is frequently said that the proper concern of higher education is with the intellect only. But the notion that the intellect is somehow disembodied, separated from the rest of the personality is not only unintelligent, in that it favors no legitimate educational aim, but it is actually perverse in its implications, in that it encourages the assumption that if one takes it upon himself to be a student he cannot at the same time be a human being. Genuine education of the intellect, in fact, must involve the rest of the personality.

An intellectual change can ramify throughout the whole personality and initiate changes in fundamental structures. For example: In Professor X's course in natural science, a student with an authoritarian personality structure has had difficulty in learning certain aspects of mathematics and science. If Professor X can succeed in teaching this student mathematics and science, he could thereby change an authoritarian structure in the personality. Let those teachers who want to influence their students through the presentation of subject matter take heart, and let those teachers who do not want to upset their students but only to train them in some specialty be aware of the fact that they are living dangerously; for ideas implanted at times when there is special readiness for them can have far-reaching effects.

Just as nothing is truly learned until it has been integrated with the purposes of the individual, so no facts and principles that have been learned can serve any worthy human purpose unless they are restrained and guided by character. Intellect without humane feeling can be monstrous, whereas feeling without intelligence is childish. Intelligence and feeling are at their highest and in the best relation one to the other where there is a taste for art and beauty as well as an appreciation of logic and of knowledge.

We may wonder where some educators and educational spokesmen got the idea of the disembodied intellect that is to be developed through the intake, storing, and reproduction of data. Certainly not from the observation of what happens when learning occurs in college. In all probability, they got it from psychology. Psychologists not only abstract such processes as cognition and learning from their context, but they commonly seek to isolate these processes experimentally in the hope of obtaining precise information and demonstrating general laws. In consequence, there is a vast literature—and even a vast, indigestible undergraduate curriculum—in which perception is treated independently of the perceiver and learning independently of the learner. Apparently this kind of psychology still has influence on education. The abstractions of the psychological experimenter have been reified and are used to rationalize current practices. It is ironic that the vaunted general laws derived from laboratory experiments are not really general. They break down as soon as a new variable is introduced into the situation, and since in real life—in the classroom, for example—numerous additional variables are at work, it is impossible to go directly from the laboratory to applications in school. We should not blame the psychological experimenters too much, however. They were probably taught by college professors who thought they could train the intellect without touching the rest of the personality. Such professors likely were under the influence of behaviorism, itself an outgrowth of a long tradition in which the narrowly cognitive has dominated in Western approaches to knowledge.

We do not want to suggest, of course, that there is no psychology applicable to learning in college; there is a fair amount. Of particular relevance are studies of the modification of belief systems, of attitude change, of development over time of social perception. Indeed, we rely on such studies for the argument being made here.

Lifelong Learning

Individual studies of young college graduates show that some have leaped forward, exhibiting more development during the four or five years after college than most students show during their college careers. If some seniors look back with a certain shame upon what they were like as freshmen, we may be sure that some graduates of four years look with amused tolerance upon their senior selves.

It is clear, then, that not everything depends on college. There are educational stimuli in the larger world. What we see in any alumnus depends in part on what has intervened since graduation. All will agree that education should be lifelong. There must be a psychology of this education, a developmental psychology that is concerned with the total life span. Anyone who plans, or offers, or takes part in such education should be guided in part by the facts and theories of individual development.

When we think of development—before, during, or after college—it is important to consider what might be called its progressive nature. There is some order to the succession of developmental changes. The essential idea is that certain things must happen before other events become possible. The child must walk before he can run. The earlier happening contributes to a state of readiness for change, but it does not make the later happening inevitable; an outside stimulus of the right kind is still necessary.

It is a natural consequence of the progressive nature of development that much education has to be *remedial*. Such is the continuity of events that failures at early stages lead to distortions in all later ones. If a boy has not learned to read and write by the time he enters college, there is nothing for it but to go back and straighten him out. By the same token, a college freshman who did not have in high school the experience of totally merging himself with a group of his peers, of uncritically accepting the group's goals, and throwing himself into the effort toward their achievement, should be permitted to have the experience now—so that he can get it out of his system and move on to a more reasoned and independent participation in organized activities. A graduating senior who has not been through a phase of ethical relativism must sooner or later have this educational experience, for otherwise it is hard to see how his values can be genuinely his own. A graduating senior who is still caught in authoritarianism and ethnic or racial prejudice has hardly begun to attain a liberal education; he will be handicapped in all future activities requiring a rational approach to human problems; he must start now to achieve the kind of self-understanding without which he cannot become a whole person.

The Relationship of Individual Development to Other Goals

Higher education has other goals besides individual development, and it is possible to debate the relative importance of these goals. The philosophy that this book reflects puts individual development first because it is the most important goal in its own right. If one were to argue that it is more important for the individual to be adjusted to his society, we would reply: It is more important that he be able to transcend and help to transform society. But the basic argument supporting the view that individual development should have first priority is that it is basic to achievement of all other legitimate goals. Is it our aim to preserve culture? This can best be done by individuals who have been developed to a point where they can appreciate it. Do we wish to create culture? Again, this is mainly done by highly developed individuals, although there are some important exceptions. Is it our desire to train people for vocations that require technical skills? If we have in mind the total job future of the student and not merely his *first* job after completing a postsecondary program, we would insist on developing qualities that are valuable in a great variety of jobs. Preparation for a high-level profession? Good performance in any profession depends heavily on qualities found only in highly developed individuals. Ask professors of engineering to characterize a good engineer, and they will list such qualities as leadership, capacity to make wise decisions, flexibility of thinking, and so on. And the best professors of engineering will try to incorporate into their programs exercises and experiences that will develop these qualities—insofar as their present knowledge about student development enables them to do so.

Given the entering college student as he is, a relatively undeveloped human specimen, nearly everything that happens to him in college is relevant to his development, either favoring or hampering it. Deciding on a career or choosing a major field of study may be favorable to the development of a stable personal identity. On the other hand, early specialization can close off sources of developmentally potent stimuli. Losing oneself in the exploration of an academic discipline can be highly favorable to the development of an autonomous self. But note: it is one thing to argue for encouraging this kind of absorption with problems on the ground that it is good for the discipline or academic subject; it is something else to say that it develops the individual. If the latter is being argued, it is necessary to say how the experience does its work, at what stage of development it is most to be desired, and why it is to be preferred to other developmentally potent experiences.

In sum, the scientific study of education means the continuing examination of innumerable means-ends relationships, and of the origins and consequences of ends, so that our means may become increasingly effective and our ends ever more intelligently chosen.

The Promotion of Individual Development in College

Once we have decided on individual development as a major

goal, we have to think of how all the conditions and processes of the college may be brought into its service. The curriculum, modes of teaching, the social organization of the college community, the faculty and student cultures, the relationship of the college and its larger community—all must be considered as means for the attainment of this goal, and this without neglecting the ways in which these things may promote the achievement of other goals.

Curriculum and instruction.   With respect to curriculum, let it be stressed that there is nothing in the present approach to suggest that subject matter does not count. On the contrary, students who are to develop need culture in almost the same way that they need food. We should, if necessary, ram it down their throats or feed it to them in the form of sugar-coated pills. But let us continuously ask ourselves why we use the ingredients we do.

All the major subjects usually taught in colleges can be taught in developmental ways. These include vocational subjects. Not that any vocation, at the technical level, can be prepared for in college, but vocational courses might provide the means for introducing students to valuable developmental experiences. The great liberal arts subjects are the easiest to support on the ground of developmental theory. History is a great instrument for showing students, quickly and inexpensively, the joys of more or less independent inquiry; philosophy, and especially ethics, is probably still the standby for challenging unexamined belief systems and for giving the student his necessary introduction to relativity of values; and literature is the great means for acquainting the student with his own feelings—by showing him something of the variety and depth of what is humanly possible; and so on. It is an interesting exercise for any teacher to ask himself just how his subject, as he teaches it, contributes to the development of the individual.

Nearly everybody agrees that the teacher is the heart and soul of the educational process. But it is not always agreed why this is so, or what the teacher actually does to influence the student, or what are the processes by which students develop under the teacher's guidance. What is it that teachers do which cannot be done by the computer or by libraries or by television? The whole phonomenon of the teacher-student relationship needs further study and analysis, with attention to both developmental and antidevelopmental modes of teaching.

Let it be said at once that there is nothing in the general theory of personality development in college to suggest that all teachers should be interested in students as persons, or have any special knowledge of them as developing individuals. Indeed, teachers—or administrators—who try to be "one of the boys," try to participate vicariously in the student's adolescent trials and errors, can be positively harmful. No teacher is called upon to do more than teach his subject and to convey his enthusiasm for it. But if a teacher wished to do something more, something that would be very likely to contribute to the students' development, the most fruitful thing would be to exhibit for students how one seeks to discover truth. Teachers must create situations in which their own learning may be observed. One way to do this might be to let the student in on their own research or scholarly activities. Another way to show how they learn would be simply to teach a subject that they know little about—perhaps in cooperation with a colleague who knows more about it. The other way, of course, is to become intellectually interested in students as developing individuals. Why not? Students are so sadly in need of development and, at the same time, in most cases show so much potential for development, that it is hard to understand how so many teachers can remain essentially indifferent on this score.

Social Organization of the College.   When we come to the general social organization of the college community, our main concern—from the developmental point of view—should be to arrange things so that teachers can get at the students and vice versa. College graduates a few years out of college tend to remember very little of what was offered in their courses, but they do remember a few of their teachers. In many, perhaps most, of these cases of the remembered teachers, not a great deal of any one teacher's time was involved. Quite likely he is remembered for some brief encounter, in which something he said or did struck something that was in a special state of readiness in the student. The point is that, in planning campus arrangements to bring faculty and students together in ways that are favorable to the student's development, it is not necessary to assume that a great deal of the teacher's time will be involved. The thing is to have the right kinds of encounters.

With respect to the organization of student life, it should be our aim to bring about a maximal integration of living and learning. Students learn from each other, like lightning it seems, and where they live apart, geographically or psychologically, from the academic centers of the college they may actually acquire a culture that is in many respects in opposition to the intellectual culture to which the faculty would like to introduce them. We must find ways to bring the intellectual life of the college into the establishments where students live. For the commuter college, and especially for the typical community college, this task appears insuperable. But the fact is that, though difficult, the problem *is* solvable. All that it needs is a high priority in the eyes of the faculty and the administration. We must create campuswide, student-faculty or faculty-student communities in which the social needs of students, far from being suppressed, are brought into the service of the intellectual aims of the college.

A true community is one where the more advanced people feel some responsibility for helping other people. And a good way for students to learn something of the social and human purposes of intelligence is to create situations in which they can be helpful to others.

It is proposed, for example, that seniors do a certain amount of teaching of freshmen. Seniors have always become expert in the sociology and social psychology of their own colleges, and they have always passed this knowledge along to entering freshmen. But the process has taken place through underground channels. It is too valuable to be relegated to the realm of the accidental. Let it become part of "the system." Let seniors, working with faculty and others, become familiar with all the new literature on college peer groups, student culture, student-faculty relations, what the administration is up against or up to, how the curriculum is made, and so on. Let them be wise men in the eyes of the freshmen, but let this be based in knowledge that comes from systematic study of the college community and from efforts to understand the processes of their own education. If we move far enough in this direction, everything about the college can become the object of intellectual analysis; and the usual barriers between the academic and the other activities of the college can thus be reduced.

Again, we should explore the possibilities of having seniors do some teaching or help with the teaching of academic subjects. Seniors may tutor freshmen, serve as teaching assistants, or participate in seminars or discussions, showing freshmen how educated men and women conduct themselves in these settings.

This proposal is not primarily for the purpose of helping freshmen nor of helping faculty with their enormous teaching burden; we are thinking, rather, of helping seniors. If we invite seniors to worry about freshmen, they gain a new awareness of themselves. Like the mother who relives her adolescence through that of her daughter, the senior who works closely with freshmen will recall his own freshman self; he will see it in a new light, and he will incorporate this new conception into his personality. But probably most important would be a change in the senior's relationships with faculty members. It has often been said that students never understand their teachers until they become teachers themselves. Let us speed the process of understanding. Let us give seniors a taste of colleagueship, a sense of what it might mean to participate as equals in the activities of the faculty. When seniors are taken on as teaching assistants, they immediatly begin to behave as adults. But a word of caution: when this happens with just a handful of students at one institution, they are put under something of a strain. The movement into adulthood may be too abrupt and may bring alienation from fellow students. It would be better if their teaching activities were institutionalized and performed on a large scale. This would create a student-faculty community in which no student had adulthood too suddenly thrust upon them.

If we could arrange things so that the intellectual activities of students really contribute something to the community in which they live—rather than stand as the means by which they advance themselves at the expense of their friends and neighbors—we would at once promote the intellectual life and the values of decency and social responsibility. The intellectual in our society is much too alienated from his community and consequently much too defensive. Feeling that he is not understood or appreciated, he mutters contemptuously about "togetherness" and sinks more deeply into isolation and meanness. This is most likely to happen to a person who has never had an experience in which his best intellectual endeavor became a part of a group enterprise, so that its social meaning and relevance became apparent to him.

It is an odd thing that it is very hard for us to contrive arrangements in which intellectual endeavors are carried out by teams or accompanied by a team spirit. Research work does, of course, often have this aspect—though the competition among researchers, especially in the hard sciences, is legend. But we are speaking here, of course, of a kind of team project in which cooperation rather than competition is the motive force. It is rare that undergraduates take part in activity of this sort. Perhaps those who work on school newspapers learn something of intellectual cooperation but, by and large, in hard academic work it is every person for himself. This encouragement of the student learning alone—in isolation— ought to be replaced by a concept of a learning *community* in which older and more experienced learners help in the education of the younger members and in the turning of the existing social organization into a community of teachers and learners, or teacher-learners.

The Role of Administrators. The administration, and particularly the top administration, must not be left out. It has a critical role in the development of the student's personality. As leaders of the whole enterprise, top administrators must embody its aims and ideals; they cannot be merely the engineers who keep the machinery running. Robert M. Hutchins was for almost a half century a eloquent spokesman for the great traditional values of liberal education. Other administrators have praised the same goals; but rarely has there been a word about how we might achieve these fine things. Hutchins of Chicago did have his method, however, and there are many men and women who feel eternally in his debt. His method was to show in his behavior that he stood for something, that he knew how to make value judgements, and that he had the courage to follow through in action.

Presidents may overlook their role as models for students, and it may appear at times when things are running smoothly that the students are overlooking it, too. But let the presidents make a mistake, act in violation of some ethical norm, compromise once too often with the forces that oppose the true aims of the college, or display some measure of hypocrisy or "phoniness," and the effect on students is immediate and profound. We need only look back to the 1960s to see scores of examples of such reactions.

It would be a fine thing if college presidents could be heroes. If they cannot be, what with all the shopping, housekeeping, and trouble-shooting they have to do, they must at least behave so consistently with our basic values that they can be ignored or taken for granted by students on the assumption that all is well. College presidents have to be wise and just and good men without expecting, or getting, any credit for it.

The Need for College Self-Study

If colleges are to promote individual development, and if this should be their major aim, it follows that they must change many of their practices—perhaps in radical ways. But how do colleges change? How do they change in desired ways and according to plan?

There is hope in some of the new and differently conceived institutions that have recently been founded and will be founded in the years immediately ahead. We know more about education for individual development than is being applied, and innovation is far easier when we start from the beginning than it is within an existing system.

There is hope of progress in the professional schools—hope that the scientific study of education in these settings will greatly expand our knowledge of means-ends relationships in higher education. These schools are accustomed to applying science to practical problems and, as compared with the liberal arts colleges, they are clear about what they want to do, for their purposes are explicitly occupational.

The liberal arts colleges have unstated, even unrecognized aims, and hence the scientific study of their workings could be quite upsetting, for it could lead to painful revelations. Where the existing liberal arts colleges are concerned, we have to put our faith in the further advancement of educational knowledge. The inarticulateness of these colleges about their aims is often baffling, and so is their failure to understand the real sources of their difficulties. In many of these colleges this failure is revealed in the "grave concern" faculty express about such problems as raising standards and getting students to work harder. Generally speaking, the liberal arts colleges are certainly trying to do *something*. It is remarkable, as Santayana noted, how we redouble our efforts as we lose sight of our goals.

What the colleges need most of all, it would seem, is knowledge of themselves, of what they do, and of what they should do. They should acquire this knowledge for themselves with help from psychology and the other social sciences. They should study themselves, focusing on goals of individual student development and asking with respect to each practice how it favors or hampers progress toward these goals. Each teacher should ask this question about his own work. There should be continuing and genuine experimentation with new programs, including colleges within colleges, with careful appraisals of results. This can make knowledge of higher education cumulative at last; and the inquiry itself will serve students directly, by displaying for them, and involving them in, the excitement of the quest.

If our colleges would do all these things they would provide inspiration for us all, for they would be acting to further major ideals of the American tradition—the value of individuals as ends in themselves and the belief in the power of intelligent experimentation to improve both the individual and the total society.

Acknowledgements

Many people helped to prepare this book. Thanks go particularly to Robert Byers, Rupert Wilkerson, and Mary Pullman for their competent and devoted editorial work, and to Christian Bay, Howard Becker, Mervin Freedman and Joseph Katz—all contributing authors of The American College—for participating in our problems and helping with their solution.

We also wish to thank John Warner, Jennifer Grimes, Abraham Nievod and the people at Montaigne for their generous assistance with this revised edition of College and Character.

Index